Cherishing and the Good Life of Learning

Bloomsbury Philosophy of Education

Series editor: Michael Hand
Bloomsbury Philosophy of Education is an international research series
dedicated to the examination of conceptual and normative questions raised by
the practice of education.

Also available in the series
A Critique of Pure Teaching Methods and the Case of Synthetic Phonics,
Andrew Davis
Philosophical Reflections on Neuroscience and Education, William Kitchen

Also available from Bloomsbury
Learning to Flourish, Daniel R. DeNicola
Teaching Virtue, edited by Marius Felderhof and Penny Thompson

Cherishing and the Good Life of Learning

Ethics, Education, Upbringing

Ruth Cigman

BLOOMSBURY ACADEMIC
LONDON • NEW YORK • OXFORD • NEW DELHI • SYDNEY

BLOOMSBURY ACADEMIC
Bloomsbury Publishing Plc
50 Bedford Square, London, WC1B 3DP, UK
1385 Broadway, New York, NY 10018, USA

BLOOMSBURY, BLOOMSBURY ACADEMIC and the Diana logo are trademarks of
Bloomsbury Publishing Plc

First published in Great Britain 2018

Cover design by Clare Turner

A catalogue record for this book is available from the British Library.

A catalog record for this book is available from the Library of Congress.

ISBN: HB: 978-1-4742-7885-0
ePDF: 978-1-4742-7884-3
eBook: 978-1-4742-7883-6

Series: Bloomsbury Philosophy of Education

Typeset by Newgen KnowledgeWorks Pvt. Ltd., Chennai, India
Printed and bound in Great Britain

To find out more about our authors and books visit www.bloomsbury.com
and sign up for our newsletters.

For Adam

Contents

Series Editor's Foreword

Bloomsbury Philosophy of Education is an international research series dedicated to the examination of conceptual and normative questions raised by the practice of education.

Philosophy of education is a branch of philosophy rooted in and attentive to the practical business of educating people. Those working in the field are often based in departments of education rather than departments of philosophy, many have experience of teaching in primary or secondary schools, and all seek to contribute in some way to the improvement of educational interactions, institutions or ideals. Like philosophers of other stripes, philosophers of education are prone to speculative flight, and the altitudes they reach are occasionally dizzying, but their inquiries begin and end on the ground of educational practice, with matters of immediate concern to teachers, parents, administrators and policy-makers.

Two kinds of questions are central to the discipline. *Conceptual* questions have to do with the language we use to formulate educational aims and describe educational processes. At least some of the problems we encounter in our efforts to educate arise from conceptual confusion or corruption – from what Wittgenstein called 'the bewitchment of our intelligence by means of language'. (1953, para. 109) Disciplined attention is needed to such specifically educational concepts as learning and teaching, schooling and socializing, training and indoctrinating, but also to the wider conceptual terrain in which educational discourse sits: what is it to be a person, or to have a mind, or to know or think or flourish, or to be rational, intelligent, autonomous or virtuous? *Normative* questions have to do with the justification of educational norms, aims and policies. What educators do is guided and constrained by principles, goals, imperatives and protocols that may or may not be ethically defensible or appropriate to the task in hand. Philosophers of education interrogate the normative infrastructure of educational practice, with a view to exposing its deficiencies and infirmities and drawing up blueprints for its repair or reconstruction. Frequently, of course, the two kinds of questions overlap: inappropriate aims sometimes rest on conceptual muddles, and our understanding of educational concepts is liable to distortion by ill-founded pedagogical norms.

In terms of scholarly output, philosophy of education is in rude health. The field supports half a dozen major international journals, numerous learned societies and a busy annual calendar of national and international conferences. At present, however, too little of this scholarly output finds a wide audience, and too few of the important ideas introduced in journal articles are expanded into fully developed theories. The aim of this book series is to identify the best new work in the field and encourage its authors to develop, defend and work out the implications of their ideas, in a way that is accessible to a broad readership.

It is hoped that volumes in the series will be of interest not only to scholars and students of philosophy of education and neighbouring branches of philosophy, but also to the wider community of educational researchers, practitioners and policy-makers. All volumes are written for an international audience: while some authors begin with the way an educational problem has been framed in a particular national context, it is the problem itself, not the local framing of it, on which the ensuing arguments bear.

Michael Hand

Acknowledgements

Many people inspired me to think about cherishing by exemplifying it. My father was one of these, and he was blessed by the entry into his life of Norhan Macawaris, who was the immediate stimulus for this book. Huge gratitude is due to her, as well as my brother Daniel.

For their inspiration, encouragement and practical support, I owe thanks to many people – in particular, to Margit Veje, Maureen Kendal, Luciana Meazza, Jan Abram, Chandra Masoliver and Jeff Probst; to the Cotton Tree team, especially Michael Mugishangyezi and Arnold Christo-Leigh, who have been remarkable teachers for us all; to Kiki Betts-Dean, for holding us together and helping with this book's bibliography; to Orlando for his passion and inspiration; and to the cherished children in my life, Anna and Leo Mark.

Amongst academic colleagues, special thanks are due to Joseph Dunne, for feedback, conversations and wise asides that have influenced me more than he knows. I would also like to thank Mary Warnock, from whom I learned much about educational policy and its frequent disjunct with ordinary lives. For encouragement and comments on earlier drafts of chapters, I have benefited from discussions with Martyn Keys, Jan Derry, Judith Suissa and John Vorhaus.

I also want to thank Michael Hand and Kristján Kristjánsson for their helpful and generous reviews. Needless to say, any flaws in this book are mine alone.

The Speech Centre at Crowborough saved me during technical meltdowns; I couldn't have written this book without them.

Last, but by no means least, I owe a special debt of gratitude to my husband Michael.

Part One

We Need to Talk About Children

A Sense of Moral Crisis

This book is about a drama of ideas. Its theme is children, the futures they represent and the adults who guide them, prepare them for those futures. It is about our hopes and anxieties concerning the young, and our efforts, as I shall say, to resolve them. It is natural, perhaps, to seek to resolve anxiety with hope, but this is not easy when the forward-looking energy of hope is threatened by a sense of hopelessness. This difficult dynamic and our efforts to speak honestly about it permeate our thoughts about education and upbringing. They have created a drama that, according to the argument of this book, needs to be explored.

The terms 'teaching' and 'learning' are key players in this drama, but the story I shall tell in this book questions their partnership. That children must learn is undeniable; that much learning is brought about by teaching is equally so. Also undeniable is the fact that human beings, like non-human animals, learn a great deal that they have never been taught. This book airs the thought that the imperative to bring about *learning through teaching* has become too dogmatic, too insistent. It exposes an undercurrent of doubt: that *learning from guided and unguided experience* may be a neglected form of learning, lurking in the wings.

At the heart of this drama, like any other, are some imperatives. These are ideas about what is necessary, what is needed, what is important and *must be done*. (We may also call these principles or ideals.) I talk about drama because powerful ideas, like powerful people or nations, are consequential. They set up tensions, provoke resistance. This is no less true in the arena of ideas than in those of human and non-human relations. A drama is a story that embodies conflict: if it is an interesting drama there will be multiple, interweaving conflicts. I believe we see this at the heart of contemporary thinking about the raising and educating of children.

I want to introduce the drama through some stories.

1957

An old redbrick building, set in a concrete playground with some temporary huts along the side. No play area, no vegetation apart from an ancient tree that offers limited opportunities for play. (You can hide behind it, turn it into the Wizard of Oz, but you cannot climb or swing on it.) Class IIA is learning history in one of the huts. The room is crammed with those wooden post-war desks, with opening lids, built-in seats and the engravings of disaffected and amorous children. One desk per child, forty or so ethnically homogeneous children facing the surly teacher at the front. She is Mrs Wymark, thirty something, overweight and bored. She paces, staring at the splayed book in her hand.

The children have been instructed to open their desks and take out the faded hardback primer that has been passed from child to child for well over a decade: *Celtic Britain* is its title. The cover shows a thing the teacher calls a *chariot*, pulled by a team of horses. Mrs Wymark has told the children not to ask too many questions, because they need to move on to the next book in November. So Stephanie, in the third row, bites her lip and wonders: were the girls allowed to ride in *chariots*, as well as the boys? The people inside them look like boys, well, men. Stephanie has studied all the pictures in the book – there aren't many, unfortunately – and has noticed that most of the girls and women stir pots and carry babies.

'Dorothy, will you please read from where we left off on Tuesday. Chapter 2', says Mrs Wymark to the book in her palm. Mrs Wymark doesn't make eye contact with the children unless it is necessary. You have to look into the face of a disobedient child, but for most children instructions released into the air are perfectly adequate.

Dorothy is not a good reader, and as she stumbles through the text, Stephanie gets bored and surreptitiously flicks some pages. On page 17 is a picture of a castle; the book calls it a *hill-fort*. There are some men and horses standing around; most of the horses are chewing grass, the men (wearing skirts!) are doing nothing in particular. In a few minutes Stephanie knows the class will be asked to copy this picture, and she looks forward to this moment because she is trying to understand the shape of a horse – how to capture its curves, its distinctive facial features, the swish of the tail.

Stephanie enjoys art; she likes taking a pencil in her hand and crafting an image, thinking about form and movement, the details of a face or a jacket. History bores her; she wonders what it was like in Celtic Britain (especially for the girls), but there seems no prospect of finding out. All she gets from history lessons are some simple facts: 'people travelled by boat on rivers'. In modern idiom, she feels *disengaged* from history lessons, until she takes a pencil in her hand. There are so many children in the class – she doesn't even know all their names – and the teacher never talks to them, doesn't *really* talk; she does this thing called 'teaching'. Stephanie has never even glimpsed a connection between history and the telling of a story.

After stumbling endlessly through the text, Dorothy reaches page 17. Mrs Wymark then instructs the class to copy the picture, and Stephanie enjoys getting down to work. The next day she will find a gold star in her exercise book, next to the picture of the hill-fort.

After history comes English. The children are instructed to open their desks and take out the exercise book on which they have inscribed in large loopy characters 'Writing'. While Mrs Wymark marks the history books they have just handed in, the children must write a story entitled 'The Tree'. If they like, they can write about the tree in the playground. Or they can choose another tree and make up a story about it.

Stephanie is feeling glum. A few days ago her father left home and went to live in another block of flats. It is six storeys high and her father lives on the top floor, which to Stephanie's amazement is higher than the nearest tree. A few days ago she sat by the window in her father's flat, looking down into the tree and imagined herself flying out of the window and landing like a bird on one of the branches. Remembering the sensation of blissful escape, words come out in a rush. She writes about a girl who jumps from a sixth storey window, towards the nearest tree. To land in a branch looks easy, and fun! She imagines the birds fluttering high into the air when she lands, then realizing she is a friend and flying towards her, settling on her arms and legs, singing, chatting. She decides to write about this feeling, but the story takes a different course. To land in a tree is not so easy, and the girl finds herself falling, falling... To her amazement, it takes forever to reach the ground, and while she is falling birds gather around her, singing, gently tugging her clothes, as if they are trying to lift her, help her to fly ... All around her, a flurry of beaks and feathers, and she hardly notices that she is airborne ...

'Five minutes', says Mrs Wymark. Stephanie looks at the clock. It is almost time for the break and she doesn't know how to finish the story. She picks up the pen and writes: 'The girl hit the ground with a crash. All that stuff about the birds – it was just a dream she had in the back of the ambulance. When she arrived at the hospital, she was dead.'

She receives no star for this story. When the exercise book is returned, she finds that Mrs Wymark has scribbled some words she can't quite read. She is scared to ask, but she has to know, so she timidly takes her book to the front of the class and asks the teacher what she has written. 'You can't write a story like this', says Mrs Wymark. 'If the girl dies, no one will ever know what she was thinking while she was falling to the ground. It doesn't make any sense.'

A few years later, Stephanie is at the grammar school. She loves English, music and art, but she has not yet learned that history is about human beings, their tragedies and their triumphs. She thinks history is about facts, in particular, dates, and is convinced that it's not for her. The teachers are looking out for specialists, and they never press the question: why should a child with literary and artistic ability seem so indifferent to the dramas of the past?

Stephanie isn't much good at sport either, but she enjoys the weekly tennis lessons. She has been discovering that tennis isn't just about winning: it's about the thrill of a swift response to an elusive ball, the grace and power of one's limbs. She looks forward to the lessons and wants to improve. She even has a germ of a wish: to become brilliant at tennis, to be a star ...

A few weeks later she reads her end of term report. 'Stephanie plays tennis as though her legs are tied together', the teacher has written. 'She has no talent for the game.' Stephanie throws the report book across the room and resolves never to play tennis again.

Rationality in teaching

In 1993, an influential book, *Back to the Rough Ground: Practical Judgement and the Lure of Technique*, was published by Joseph Dunne. Its theme is described in the introduction as 'the nature of rationality in teaching – and indeed, beyond this, the nature of any rational practice' (p. 3). Its target is the behavioural objectives model – a conception of what it is to teach rationally, responsibly and well, encountered by Dunne in the late 1970s when he was working in a college of education. Dunne writes:

> Teachers who used it would formulate very specific goals (in terms of demonstrable changes in their pupils) for each lesson or series of lessons and then plan their teaching as a series of instrumental steps toward the achievement of these goals. The pre-specification of intended learning-outcomes would be the primary requirement for effective teaching. (p. 1)

A 'very specific goal' is a learning objective. Dunne goes on:

> Written into the concept of an objective was the requirement that the latter's achievement should be verifiable – that unequivocal evidence should be available to establish it; and confining objectives to observable behaviour ensured that this requirement could be met. The verification to be insisted on was of a kind that could be carried out by a detached observer not assumed to have any familiarity with the teacher's situation or background. The language in which objectives were to be formulated was to be precise and explicit and thus preclude the possibility of misinterpretation by removing the need for interpretation itself. (p. 3)

This conception of rational practice is scientifically inspired; whether a child has or has not learned what she was intended to learn is determined, not by judgement, but by the 'detached observation' of a neutral bystander, noting matches and mismatches between precisely formulated objectives and behaviour in ways that are immune from error. Whether objectives so described and so assessed are meaningful is not a question that proponents of the model need to raise. They are required for effective teaching, and it remains for philosophers to ask: what *is* effective teaching? What indeed is teaching?

The following passage, written in 1969 by W. James Popham and quoted by Dunne, expresses a sense of horror about the failure to meet this requirement:

> Until the last few decades, educators have been approaching the task of describing educational objectives with a hand-axe mentality … We are at the brink of a new era regarding the explication of instructional goals, an era which promises to yield fantastic improvements in the quality of instruction. One can only sympathise with the thousands of learners who had to obtain an education from an instructional system built on a muddle-minded conception of educational goals. (1993, p. 2)

One can only sympathize with learners who were denied an effective education … Stephanie, for example. Barely a decade has passed since Stephanie's teacher told her: this story doesn't make any sense. The sense of horror is understandable, as is the impulse to *re-conceptualize* education in order to 'yield fantastic improvements'. Dunne comments on the 'confidence, if not … arrogance' of Popham's commitment to the behavioural objectives model, and we can understand what he means (ibid.). But I would argue that the impulse to 'rescue' children like Stephanie – as Buber (2002) puts it, to cherish rather than squander the potentiality of the reality *child* – deserves our attention and our sympathy.

There are many horror stories about interactions between teachers and children in classrooms, not to mention between adults and children in homes and other settings. But the post-war school may be an especially good source of such stories, placed as it were between the pre-war elementary system – characterized by 'cheapness, economy, large classes, obsolete, ancient and inadequate buildings' (Galton et al. 1980) – and the rise of progressive ideas. My account of Stephanie's woes is sympathetically embroidered rather than fictitious. The 1950s class sizes was huge – over forty children were not unusual – and many teachers must have paid scant attention to children whose success *or* failure in the 11+ was assured. If 'getting them through the exam' is the priority, and you're facing a bewildering sea of faces, why waste your time on those who (it seems clear) will pass or fail whatever you do?

'Muddle-minded' isn't necessarily an unjust description of many teachers' goals during this period. Popham's conviction that a scientific-rational response is needed to 'yield fantastic improvements' persists to this day, and many teachers experience the obsession with 'unequivocal evidence' as a staggering declaration of distrust. It intrudes on their daily work in ways that are hardly tolerable, but the question remains: how do we protect children like Stephanie from indolent or soulless teaching?

The term 'potential' has been massively over-theorized, but I suggest that the *neglect* of children's potential in the 1950s and beyond is a general concern, common to a wide range of theorists, politicians, parents and professionals with different conceptions of what it is to engage responsibly with children. We are appalled by what happened, and what happens, to children like Stephanie, and the impulse to 'cherish rather than squander' their potentiality has erupted in decades of assurances that *finally* we are at the brink of a new era.

Cherishing children

The 1967 Plowden report, published just two years before Popham's call for rational educational objectives, famously responded to concerns about children's potentials: 'At the heart of the educational process lies the child' (p. 2). Children, argued Plowden, need 'individual and different attention' (p. 25). They should learn by discovery and their progress should be evaluated by teachers who do not 'assume that only what is measurable is valuable' (p. 202). These ideas might have nourished Stephanie's talents better than the curt disdain of her primary school teacher, but they did not further a political vision: that of preparing a generation of children for a competitive role in the world economy.

Fast forward thirty-six years. It is 2003, the dawn, as they say, of a new millennium. Education Secretary Charles Clarke breathes hope into a profession wearied from decades of fresh initiatives, each embodied in new sets of objectives. Teachers, says Clarke, should do 'creative and interesting things'; new research shows that literacy and numeracy will be aided by this freedom. Is this Plowden? A return to progressive ideas? Sadly, says children's writer Philip Pullman (2003), this is not the case. For consider the reality of what goes on in schools rubber-stamped by Clarke. The following is a task undertaken by 200,000 11-year-olds in their key stage 2 SATs: 'They were confronted with four crudely drawn pictures of a boy standing in a queue to buy a toy, and they then had to write a story about them, taking exactly 45 minutes' (ibid.). Pullman comments:

> It was a task of stupefying worthlessness and futility, something no one who was serious about the art of storytelling could regard with anything other than contempt ... I'd like to suggest a principle that should be a point of honour for everyone involved in education: something we ask a child to do in school should be something that is intrinsically worth doing, something we would be proud to do well.

As if to exemplify this (what it *means* to be 'serious about the art of storytelling', do something that is 'intrinsically worth doing'), Pullman tells a story about writing a story:

> Writing a story ... feels to me like fishing in a boat at night. The sea is much bigger than you are, and the light of your little lamp doesn't show you very much of it. You hope it'll attract some curious fish, but perhaps you'll sit there all night long and not get a bite.
>
> And all around you is silence. And plenty of time. You're in a calm state of mind, not at all sleepy, but calm and relaxed and attentive: truly aware, truly absorbed.
>
> Are you going to find a fish? Well, there are things you can do to improve your chances: with every voyage you learn a little about the bait these fish like; and you're practised enough to wait for a twitch on the line and not snatch at it too soon; and you've discovered that there are some areas empty of fish, and others where they are plentiful.
>
> But there's a lot you can't predict. Sometimes you will feel a tug on the line and pull in nothing but seaweed; sometimes a cunning fish will flicker at the hook

for a moment and disappear, with the bait in its mouth and the hook left bare in the water; sometimes a great fish will swim round and round, close enough to touch, and then with a flick of the tail plunge into the deeps and vanish without touching your poor bait at all.

And the sea is very big, and the weather is changeable, and you really have only the most rudimentary knowledge of what things lie in the depths. There might be monsters there that could swallow hook, and line, and lamp, and boat, and you. These powers are not interested in any rationally worked-out plans concocted far away on shore; the fears and delights of fishing at night have nothing to do with rationality.

So you set off in your little boat, your little craft of habit and intention and hope, and bait your hook, and drop it in the water, and sit and wait, calm and relaxed and aware of every faint swirl of phosphorescence, every twitch on the line, until ...

That's what it feels like to me, and that's only the beginning.
(https://www.theguardian.com/education/2003/jun/05/schools.news)

This is not a passage you are likely to find in a policy document. It is easy to recommend that teachers do 'creative and interesting things', but without a leisurely consideration of what this means – articulated in a way that is itself literary, creative – how tempting is it to suppose that hasty attention to some crude pictures and a ticking clock is 'doing something creative'? Pullman concedes that there may be 'freshness' in the educational air, but his poetic account of what it is *like* ('what it feels like to me') to write a story brings the 'stupefying worthlessness and futility' of Clarke-style creativity home to the reader. If Pullman is right, this is an ethical emergency. How, he asks Clarke, can you reconcile these scenarios – in the first of which all around you is silence, and plenty of time, in the second of which there is no time and no opportunity to be truly aware, truly absorbed? How, above all, can we talk about *education* if our terrifying ignorance about 'what things lie in the depths' is siphoned into rationally assessable tasks? Pullman's article, I would say, is a call to *cherish* children and stop squandering their precious potentialities.

Real teaching

Stephanie's essay-writing task (write a story about a tree) was not necessarily one of 'stupefying worthlessness and futility', though it may have been age-inappropriate, especially for children who were discouraged from asking questions and for whom 'instructions' were 'released into the air'. The point of this example is that the task was *reduced* to worthlessness and futility by its abrupt terminus and the teacher's silly supposition that children must learn fixed rules of essay-writing. Mrs Wymark assumed that *breaking the rules* (albeit questionable and idiosyncratic ones) is an unambiguous failure that must be communicated to a fanciful child. She failed to acknowledge or approve some thoughtful, imaginative work, indeed work that betrayed painful emotions. Whether – or to what extent – it is the business of teachers to respond to such things is a hot question today, and one that I shall explore throughout this book. Whatever one's views about the *formalization* of educational interest in children's emotions, the idea that primary school teachers should be sensitive to dark emotions in an essay about danger, hope and death would normally be accepted unhesitatingly today.

The 1950s classrooms were over-populated and under-inspected; in many cases no one outside those classrooms had much idea what was going on inside them. From one point of view, the behavioural objectives model imported a welcome commitment: to expose and put an end to pseudo-teaching. It made short work of people like Mrs Wymark, but it did so at a price. Most obviously, it left many in the ensuing decades with a sense that not only has the ethical emergency identified by Pullman *not* been resolved; it may be more pressing than it was in the 1950s. Post-war classrooms generated anxieties about idle or irresponsible teaching; the behavioural objectives model, by contrast, seemed anything but idle, not least perhaps because it generated mountains of bureaucracy. It seemed to clinch the troubled connection between educational endeavour and the transformation of children.

However, an excess of zeal can be idle in another sense. The behavioural objectives model responded to real anxieties, but it showed a willingness to *contract* our attention to truth and meaning in the service of hope, a sense of resolution. It *delivered learning* with an almost surgical precision, but what kind of learning? What did children really achieve? That they achieved *something* seemed to be clearly demonstrated: the objectives had been clearly articulated, classroom activities had taken place in ways that verifiably matched or failed to match those objectives. That there can be *idleness of meaning* is something Wittgenstein made clear: 'The confusions which occupy us arise when language is like an engine idling, not when it is doing work' (1953, para. 132). A cog is loose; a wheel spins out of control. This image captures some children's dramas in the classroom, where *outcomes* are pursued with zeal, but little attention is given to truth and meaning.

One of the crucial entry points of philosophy into the field of education was Richard Peters' acclaimed book *Ethics and Education* (1966). Like the concept of reform, Peters wrote, education implies that 'something worthwhile should be achieved.' If a father tells his son that all non-Muslims are infidels who should be beheaded, we may talk about brainwashing, indoctrination or simply abuse; 'education' seems altogether the wrong word. It may be a far cry from this to the precision engineering of the behavioural objectives model, which at worst imparts skills and knowledge that children may not need. But we could be too complacent here; a failure to achieve 'something worthwhile' on the part of educators need not be heinous for it to have an ethical dimension that should be taken seriously. Pullman's emergency is not directly about turning schools into hotbeds of radicalization; indeed, this seemed less pressing in 2003 than it does today. But giving children tasks of 'stupefying worthlessness and futility' is not only uneducational; it means *squandering potentialities* in ways that may lead to frustration and resentment, as well as the violent tendencies that are a tragic (and increasingly common) corollary of these.

I believe that Pullman's concern is pervasive. It lies deep in our culture of education, by which I mean that it is deeply buried as well as deeply felt. 1950s classrooms raised the alarm about idle teaching, but the other side of this coin is that many teachers look back on those days with nostalgia, as an era in which some of them, some of the time, were *able* to teach. They were able, that is, to communicate passionate convictions about what was truly worthwhile. The behavioural objectives model turns this into an idea that can hardly be coherently thought. 'Worthwhileness' acquires a contracted meaning. Not only are radicalization and the like excluded; so are those murky things that make us (as Pullman says) 'truly aware, truly absorbed'.

The behavioural objectives model has an obvious defect, nicely described by Philip W. Jackson in an article called 'Real Teaching' (2007, pp. 336–346). As a newly appointed principal of a nursery school, Jackson tried to learn about the institution by 'poking about the school … watching what was going on and trying to get a feel for the place'. He noticed some interesting things:

> when nursery school teachers spoke to individual children or listened to what they had to say they first descended to the child's height by bending at the knees until their faces were on a level with the child's own … when reading to pupils the nursery school teachers … propped the books they were reading on their laps with the open pages facing the students. The reason for doing so was obviously to allow the children to see the book's illustrations. But what made such a natural thing so amusing to me was that it required the teachers to develop the knack of reading upside down! (pp. 336–337)

These observations opened up some fascinating discussions with the teachers. To what extent can teaching be described in purely behavioural terms? How far can good teaching be captured in simple imperatives: you should descend to the height of young children when talking to them; you should read books upside down so that children can see the illustrations? Is it possible to *impersonate* an excellent teacher merely by mimicking her behaviour? At what point does the mimic *become* such a teacher?

Jackson and his colleagues explored these questions, with Jackson playing the part of the mimic:

> My mimicking of their behaviour amused the teachers ... But [it] turned out to be more than simply amusing. It triggered a discussion that went on far past lunch, one that we returned to on several occasions in the ensuing months ... [They] could easily imagine the person getting away with such a pretence for quite some time. They even conceded that I might succeed in doing it myself for a while. But the notion of someone pretending to be a nursery school teacher and *never* getting caught, was a condition they found puzzling. (p. 337)

This was a philosophical investigation: not philosophy in a detached or arid sense, but *engaged* philosophy that feeds off our everyday experiences and tries to make good, ethical sense of them. The teachers learned that, contrary to a powerful, everyday assumption, behaviour cannot be 'skimmed off' human beings like a layer of cream, to be rendered explicit and unambiguous in words. Bodies are not *really* separate from minds. We can 'pretend' by deliberately mismatching our behaviour and thoughts or feelings; but we can only do so in limited ways, for what emerges when we hone our attention on to human behaviour is not a skimmed-off layer but a person, a human being, whose character, intentions and feelings are exposed (as they are in a good portrait) by countless nuances of glance, gesture, response. This happens particularly when we throw away the stopwatch and give ourselves, as Pullman says, 'plenty of time'. Time, as every serious teacher and parent knows, is needed not only for children's learning, but also for us to learn about children.

Jackson summarized his discoveries in the words: 'There is no such thing as a behavioural definition of teaching and there never can be', for 'our attempt to say when a person is or is not teaching is always an act of interpretation. We are forever "readers" of human action ...' The defect of the behavioural objectives model is its failure to appreciate what this means, indeed to overcome a crude polarity between thought and behaviour, or mind and body. It is committed to the idea that, in the sphere of educational expertise, human action is not 'read' as much as 'neutrally observed', recorded, fed into an evidence base. But if anything worthwhile is ever to issue from adult relations with children – if, in Buber's fine phrase, we are to cherish rather than squander the potentialities of the reality *child* – it seems clear that 'reading' human actions and encounters, indeed human beings themselves, cannot be avoided.

This has only become more obvious since rote learning fell out of favour, and a large, ethical concept came on to the educational scene: the concept of well-being. Philosophers need to take stock in order to ensure that their *style* of thinking is sufficiently sensitive to take such a concept on. I suggest that Jackson and his colleagues set a good example, and that thinking about this topic requires the kind of engagement they demonstrate – being puzzled, amused, 'trying to get a feel' for what is going on, and being wary of (rather than ideologically opposed to) the impulse to theorize.

In 1995, a headteacher was murdered by a pupil at the gates of his school. He had been trying to help a child who was under attack, and a young gang member, aged 15, stabbed him through the heart and lung. The news generated waves of shock. One journalist wrote: 'Rarely has a killing so clearly illustrated a moral chasm separating victim and attacker.' He meant that the victim was an exemplary human being, devoted to the well-being of his pupils, family and others, whereas the killer was a member of a ruthless criminal gang. This was, however, a surprising comment. A moral chasm between victim and perpetrator is the very stuff of drama, Shakespearean, biblical, Greek, whatever. What struck the public, I believe, was not this *familiar* chasm, but the terrifying new chasm that had opened up within a hallowed national institution: the school. The perpetrator was not Judas, Iago or Cassius; it was a north London schoolboy whose simmering hatred and disaffection could hardly be imagined.

This is not primarily a historical survey, but we might trace our national obsession with children's well-being at least in part to the momentous death of Philip Lawrence. The idea of diligently tracking children's progress, viewed as measurable effects of which specific behavioural interventions were the cause, suddenly seemed unbelievably naive. Lawrence's death, and growing evidence of disaffection in schools, suggested that children's minds may not after all be spaces into which learning can be delivered with precision by experts. 'Big questions' came to the fore, driven by big anxieties and paving the way for the biggest concept of all: well-being. Are the kinds of learning that 'effective teachers' bring about in children genuinely good for them? What *is* good for children? Do we know? Have we exhibited (like Popham) an excess of confidence and hope?

One thing is sure: the 1990s were a triumph of muddle-minded thinking about education. On the one hand, as if to emphasize the newness of New Labour, there was a standards agenda trumpeted by Tony Blair and David Blunkett, in part as a response to the death of Philip Lawrence. As well as serving the interests of the economy, the agenda seems to have had two aims, neither of them especially robust. It aimed to *occupy* children, make greater demands of them, giving them less time and fewer opportunities to engage in violence; and it aimed to inspire them, through the thrill of achievement, to want to live prosperously and well. On the other hand – and flowing in precisely the opposite direction – there was the burgeoning self-esteem movement that aimed to protect children from a sense of failure, and hence from the pressure to achieve (see Cigman 2004). *All must have prizes*, for the key to learning is thinking well of oneself, *believing* one is a success, even if the belief has no basis in reality.

The effort to navigate this confusing set of ideas must have defeated many a weary teacher. This was the soil out of which emerged a grand new agenda, successor to the standards agenda and promising enhanced achievement for children *without* the sting of failure. This was the *enhancement agenda*, and it was built on several propositions. The first is that there are conditions for learning, some of which are emotional. Non-emotional conditions include things like having a decent breakfast, getting to bed at a reasonable time. Emotional conditions include resilience, optimism, confidence about one's strengths *and* weaknesses so that one can enjoy developing the former and not be crippled by the latter. For many years, self-esteem was touted as the emotional key, but studies seemed to show that this was wrong, for people with low self-esteem are often higher achievers than people with high self-esteem (Baumeister 2003, Emler 2001). Few questioned this result by trying to expose weaknesses in the concept of self-esteem itself.

The second supposition is that such conditions are very much the business of teachers. Positive emotions can and should be enhanced in schools so that children can build on their achievements with resilience, confidence and/ or (depending on your view) self-esteem. Above all, children must develop the *confidence to fail*; they must learn (as Beckett said) to fail, fail again and fail better, without succumbing to depression or anxiety (see Cigman 2001). Furthermore – and this is a third supposition – *studies show* (as they must if enhancement programmes are to be validated) that certain kinds of emotional education *are effective*. A behavioural objectives model operates here, showing that clearly articulated goals, well-trained teachers and soundly researched materials *make children better*: more willing to learn, more competent socially, more virtuous, better able to achieve without succumbing to stress.

This brings us up to date, for the idea of 'enhancing children' in scientifically validated ways is current. It takes several forms, and experts disagree about whether self-confidence, resilience or character understood in an Aristotelian sense is the 'magic bullet' of learning and well-being. Adjudicating between these theories is not my primary aim. I am interested in the *thought* that a 'magic bullet' is what we are after, so that the proper response to a moral chasm is a heightened effort to validate causal connections. Do well-being lessons or resilience training resolve the ethical emergency identified by Pullman? I doubt it, though no doubt they are helpful to some children some of the time. These simple words from Frances Lawrence, Philip Lawrence's widow, remind us of how people speak when a moral chasm suddenly opens up before them: 'My faith has been sorely tested. Forgiveness is such a complex issue, or maybe such a simple one, and I don't think I really understand it yet and I'm not sure what it is that I am meant to do.'

How should we proceed?

To what moral imperatives, principles or ideals should we commit ourselves? This book proposes a variety of answers. The basic one is that the sense of moral crisis in education is not primarily about education. At its most fundamental level, it is about the idea of goodness, and in particular what it means for one person to be good to another. The Philip Lawrence case was disturbing because it raised questions about human relationship. I don't mean the relationship between Lawrence, who was a humane teacher, and his killer. I mean something more nebulous – but important and ripe for philosophical enquiry – about the relationship between adults and children within a certain culture, which also means between the polity and the young people it confines to institutions in the service of what is called education.

Education is, or should be, a way of being good to young people, but we know that it can also be good for the economy. There is scope here for endless moral muddle: a viscous soup containing obfuscation and neglect, as well as abundant good intentions. At one level the idea of 'enhancing children' means helping them to deal with painful emotions, helping them to understand themselves and others better – and what could possibly be wrong with that? At another level, it is about making 'better people' in a sense that sounds alarm bells. As the sense of crisis deepens, ambitions soar. It is no accident that the idea of enhancement has been extended from standards to 'positive emotions' at a time when eugenics has reappeared with what many see as a new, acceptable face. Bestselling economist Richard Layard tells us that anxiety and depression are throwbacks to life in the

African savannah. We need, he says, to 'use our mastery over nature to master ourselves and to give us more of the happiness that we all want' (2006, p. 27). Many leading philosophers and scientists believe that parents should be free to choose their children's genes, not only in the interests of eliminating disease, but also in the interests of creating better human beings with (as philosopher John Harris puts it) 'increased mental powers ... as well as enhanced strength, stamina, endurance, speed of reaction, and the like'. The gap between education and genetics is closing, according to these thinkers. One day genetics may be able to achieve precisely the human enhancements that elude teachers in schools. It is as though schools will be replaced by laboratories in rather the way Victorian buildings with their quaint wooden desks have been replaced by smart new 'buildings for the future'.

So science, social or genetic, is thought to herald an era that (in the words of Popham) 'promises to yield fantastic improvements'. This way of thinking is optimistic, and misguided. I doubt whether Frances Lawrence – for whom the crisis was intimate and unbearable – ever thought of turning to science for a solution to her problem. Her stammering sentiments betray a sense of helpless bewilderment, reminiscent of Philip Pullman's sense of the sea. It is very big and you have only rudimentary knowledge of what things lie in the depths. *There might be monsters* ... Much contemporary thinking about what it is to be 'good to children' follows a scientific path, contracting the idea of 'worthwhileness' so as to exclude attention to monsters and other scary things.

This book is based on the premise that the imperative we seek is captured by Buber's fine words: *we must cherish rather than squander the potentialities of the reality child.* To submit to this imperative is to create a space for monsters, not indiscriminately, but as appropriate for the reality of *this child.* Everyone needs monsters and permission to be scared. Children's writers understand this only too well. No doubt some monsters must be avoided, the monster of sickly sentimentality for example, but let us not fear this monster so much that we embrace another: the monster of idle meaning. In this sense we must be generous to ourselves as well as children. We must take care not to squander our *own* potentialities for creative, engaged thinking in the interests of a chimera of resolution. This is the contraction I spoke of earlier, and the central idea of the book is that the contraction of our thinking not only inhibits children's learning; it seriously limits our sense of what it might mean for one person to be good to another. *That* limitation is more than sufficient to generate a sense of ethical emergency.

2

Ministering to the Good

I know nothing about education except this: that the greatest and the most important difficulty known to human learning seems to lie in that area which treats how to bring up children and how to educate them.

Montaigne (2003), p. 163

'Bodies and souls', says Socrates in the Gorgias, 'can each be in good condition, can they not?' – and he uses the medical term euexia. Real euexia must be distinguished from apparent euexia, though only a doctor or trainer may be able to detect the difference in the case of the body. In the soul, too, there is a condition which counterfeits euexia, and there are arts corresponding to the skills of the doctor and the trainer, namely the arts of the lawgiver and the judge. These arts are therapies which minister to what is best in the soul.

Anthony Kenny (1973), p. 1

Some children can't bear learning. They do everything in their power to resist and avoid it. In particular, many can't bear ethical learning. It feels like an imposition, a lie, to tell them that *this* is the right thing, when they know perfectly well that the opposite is true. It seems like a denial of who they are, who they need to be.

In many cases, we have to persist and show them that they are wrong. *We have to stop them hitting their classmates, scribbling on walls, trampling in the flowerbeds.* This sentence is intended to capture a dramatic imperative in our engagements with children. We may be confused at times about right and wrong, and this confusion may stimulate philosophy, a desire to think more clearly and deeply about our lives. But well or ill understood, the imperative is there: some children, many children perhaps, *must become better behaved and more proficient at learning.* It is our duty to ensure that this improvement comes about – and there is often desperation attached to these thoughts. There is a sense that we or others have failed, that not only must children improve, but *we* must do so too. We must work out the best, most efficient route to the enhancement of children.

This enhancement imperative resonates *with and against* other imperatives. In Chapter 1 I discussed indolent teaching: teaching that attempts to minimize the sense of drama by avoiding eye contact with children, muttering platitudes, ignoring their emotions. Whether children find learning painful or thrilling is not this kind of teacher's business. The only emotions that concern her are ones that disrupt the tedious monotony of her lessons.

I said that this kind of teaching *demands* a response; teachers must do better. There's nothing wrong with imperatives per se, and this imperative must stay. The behavioural objectives model – which has seeped into all areas of institutional life – appeared as a line of defence, seeking to replace indolence with zeal. Teachers and pupils came under scrutiny with multiple targets they had to meet. This is a kind of engineering model, in which micro-successes and micro-failures are believed to be there for all to see, and it brings a proliferation of opportunities for educational endeavour to be experienced as meaningful or meaningless, worthy or unworthy, acceptably or unacceptably imposed. It brings *conflict* between those who believe (as we discussed in the previous chapter) that there is an ethical emergency in education, and those who welcome the behavioural objectives model as a way of bringing real improvements into young people's lives.

Wittgenstein said: 'A philosophical problem has the form: I don't know my way about' (*Philosophical Investigations*, 1953, para. 123). This chapter is about disorientation, losing one's way; and we see this in the meleé of conflicting imperatives that permeate our engagements with the young. The situation is in a real sense dramatic, but who are the characters in the drama? Well, clearly, every home and classroom contains individual characters, but more than this, there are recurrent episodes, situations that play and re-play, *around* individuals. There are *dramas of learning and unlearning*, in which children resist or pursue learning in ways that may test us to the limit.

Of course, there is a sense in which every interchange, every drama, is a unique event, prompted by individuals. But there are also tendencies or repetitions from which we can learn: there are children with repertoires of evasive strategies for whom the goal of learning has been replaced by the goal of *appearing* to learn; children who seem addicted to learning in ways that both impress and disturb; children with a tendency to smash things up if they don't get their own way. For experienced teachers, these are both *templates* from which general insights may grow and *individual challenges* to be met on individual terms.

Not only are there dynamics associated with individuals and the extent to which, in responding to them, we can learn from 'similar' cases; but there are also *intellectual* dynamics, dynamics between ideas, theories, convictions, and here too the question may arise whether one idea is or is not to be assimilated to another. Consider, for example, the debate around children who disrupt classes, smash things up, beat up other children. Paul Cooper, a specialist in social, educational and behavioural difficulties (SEBD), says: 'No other educational problem [outside these kinds of difficulties] is associated with such a level of fear, anger, frustration, guilt and blame'. Into this fraught situation comes a pressing philosophical/political question: is it *just* to exclude this child from the school or classroom? Is it just even to describe him as a 'child with SEBD', or is such talk (along with other so-called labels) offensive? Should adults rather than children take responsibility for children's difficult behaviour? If I say 'adults should take responsibility', am I necessarily aligning myself with those who believe (rather romantically perhaps) that children are *never* responsible for their actions? If my judgement about a particular child collides with your theoretical outlook – so that I thought I was talking about Jasper and you thought I was talking about child-centred philosophy – there is further scope for conflict, jangled imperatives that may adversely affect our capacity to *get together* and think lucidly and practically about Jasper.

Montaigne (2003) locates the 'greatest and most important difficulty known to human learning' in the indivisible domain of upbringing and education. This is contentious; it is reminiscent of the child-centred philosophy that, in its original form at least, is broadly rejected by most philosophers of education today. Most educationists want to establish education as a discrete and respectable domain, not to be confused with therapy or the raising of children. From one point of view, this is understandable, but it also paves the way for a jangle of imperatives.

Replacing the *imperative of reticent cultivation* implicit in child-centred theory, we seem to have opened the floodgates to a harsher set of imperatives based on authority, instruction and assessment. At the present time, many teachers and parents are at war with the government, accusing it of imposing unacceptable stress on children through over-testing. One school governor talked about 'six or seven-year-old pupils who, during the testing period were crying, visibly shaking and reportedly waking up at 4 AM unable to sleep' (2016) (https://www.theguardian.com/education/2016/may/03/morgan-sats-test-children-primary-school-pupils). This is obviously worrying, but Nicky Morgan, Secretary of State for Education, was unrepentant, saying that children *must acquire good literacy and numeracy skills.* Isn't it possible, one wonders, to resolve apparently conflicting imperatives: one, don't test children to the point of making them ill, and two, teach children *well*? Many teachers, engaged with what I call dramas of learning and unlearning, appear to have good ideas about this, but the imperatives continue to clash.

In one sense, I believe, Montaigne is right. If we are to address the ethical emergency to which Pullman draws our attention (rightly, as I argued), we must look carefully at the combined domain of upbringing and education in which emotions rage, learning is often loved or hated and dramas are enacted with us, the adults, playing key roles as thinkers, actors and human beings. I am using the phrase *dramas of learning and unlearning* uncritically for now, to suggest (what seems at a certain level obvious) that there exists a *primary sphere of operation* for education and upbringing that we ignore at our peril. For me, what matters is *what goes on* in kitchens and bathrooms, streets and parklands, as well as traditional and not-so-traditional classrooms. Close attention to dramas is the starting point from which I hope to tease out some practical and philosophical insights without becoming unhelpfully anecdotal. This may sound messy but the question remains: does my on-the-ground focus improve our prospects of responding seriously to Pullman's ethical emergency?

Dramas of unlearning

In an article called 'Are some children unteachable? An approach to social, emotional and behavioural difficulties' (Cigman, 2007, pp. 158–169), Paul Cooper (mentioned earlier) discusses a boy called Nathan whom teachers and pupils find 'difficult'. He smashes things up; for example, he keeps smashing up a model that he builds for a design class, which means starting all over again in the next lesson. Cooper describes him as 'moderately disruptive', meaning that on a scale of 'externalising disruptive behaviour' he is at a midway point. His vandalism makes him more extreme than 'simply rude' children who answer back, talk out of turn etc. On the other hand, he has never acted violently to pupils or staff; he is merely 'antagonistic and defiant'. Nathan frightens and upsets people, and when he vandalizes his own work, they must wonder whether he could do something similar to another person's (or his own) body.

Cooper has some suggestions for responding to children like Nathan, whose needs, he says reasonably, 'if left unmet, will tend to escalate and multiply'. He advocates empathy and unconditional positive regard, as well as a range of 'teaching strategies'. What interests me about this example is that, beyond some fairly predictable recommendations (as Cooper says, his suggestions pick out the 'natural social styles' of many people), there are clues in Nathan's testimony (quoted by Pomeroy 2000, cited by Cooper in Cigman 2007) about *why* he resists learning:

> The lesson I was doing, the teacher was never there anyway ... I built a park five times. He used to come every lesson and say 'carry on with your park', then used to go away, and we didn't have a park. We smashed it up every lesson.
>
> I'm alright you know ... I'm not that bad ... But if I don't like somebody [i.e. a teacher], I won't do it [the work] and I'll try to wreck it and everything. But if I do like it, I'll be alright with it. I'm alright. (Cigman 2007, pp. 159–160)

Cooper describes Nathan's declaration that he is 'alright' as defensive and says that from one point of view 'Nathan is far from "alright". People who habitually respond to others in the way he describes reveal dysfunctions in the way in which they deal with other people in general' (ibid., p. 160). Maybe Nathan is dysfunctional, but I would say that the testimony doesn't necessarily suggest this. Rather it betrays a grievance that we can understand, though Cooper passes over it without comment. *The teacher was never there anyway....* . Is Nathan angry because he has an *indolent* (or absent) teacher? Is this why he resists learning? When he says 'I'm alright', is he saying that he is more than willing to work hard for a *conscientious* teacher, someone who actually teaches, rather than issuing an instruction and going away? Is the basic problem here – as far as we can tell on the basis of this testimony – that Nathan needs help recognizing that he is *angry*, as well as a frank acknowledgement of the justice of this feeling – as far as that goes – and some sensitive conversation?

Conversation isn't recommended as such, though it is certainly suggested by the bullet-pointed list of strategies recommended by Cooper:

- finding out what interests the pupil
- finding out what the pupil knows already
- allowing the pupil to teach others (including the teacher) what she/he knows about the topic
- using questions rather than statements so that pupils extend their understandings by drawing on knowledge they already possess

This is fine, but it doesn't address the question: what kind of drama of unlearning is going on here? How does Nathan feel, and is there some justification for his feeling this way? What might we possibly learn *from Nathan* if we listen carefully to what he has to say? Granted, his behaviour is immature, but Nathan is young and for all we know has experienced indolent parenting as well as indolent teaching. Instead of working methodically through a list of 'strategies', might we bring Nathan himself – a human being with a decade's worth of memories and experiences – centre stage? Could Cooper's assumption of educational expertise *inhibit* the able practitioner?

Cooper raises a pressing question: are some children unteachable? It is a question on which I hope to shed some light in this chapter by probing the ideas of teaching and learning. He also asks: should teachers be expected to put up with SEBD? Why should they be subjected to 'involuntary and uncomfortable responses, such as increased heart rate and a strong desire to flee the scene or retaliate in some way' (p. 158)? These are important questions, frequently raised, but it is vital that our efforts to address them don't degenerate into dry-as-dust theories. I have introduced the term 'drama' with a view to reflecting on the tensions and conflicts that animate our thinking. Our *first* task is to explore dramas of learning and unlearning, and the ways in which we participate or perform, rather than merely observe. We need to understand what goes on between adults and children, especially between adults and so-called difficult children. Perhaps the adults are difficult too! Perhaps their attraction to checklists is a dramatic reality of which many educationists are happily oblivious. I have no idea what I should or should not put up with independently of a frank evaluation of my own contribution to someone's dramas of unlearning.

Teaching, learning and conversation

In Chapter 1 I discussed Joseph Dunne's assault on the idea that 'rational teaching' articulates objectives for learning so lucidly, so unambiguously, that the success or failure of a lesson is easily determined. The language of objectives refers, in principle at least, to 'discrete, observable behaviours' that *anyone* can assess. Teaching becomes a community effort in which teachers can accurately evaluate each other's achievements or non-achievements by watching, listening, examining children's work, using clear markers for degrees of failure and success. Instead of one big success or failure at age 11, determined by national tests, there are endless micro-successes and micro-failures by which the community can determine 'how children are doing' and, if necessary, intervene. Education ceases to be the kind of muddle that existed, or was believed to exist, in the post-war era, when most learning was delivered and assessed in the ultra-privacy of the classroom.

As an education lecturer in the late 1970s, Dunne was struck by what I would call the imperative: teach efficiently! He saw a worrying gulf between the promise to yield 'fantastic improvements in the quality of instruction' and the reality for practitioners of micro-assessments, endless checklists and the impoverishment of learning. In a ground-breaking study, he explored the limitations of the model, setting it against a rich Aristotelian conception of practical rationality, meaning good, engaged thinking, knowledge in action. This is a hugely valuable contribution to the field, and I shall discuss it later in the book.

In a real sense, suggested Dunne, the behavioural objectives model sacrifices education on the altar of objective knowledge. It is easy enough in most cases to agree whether a child can distinguish between solids, liquids and gases, or recount the principal causes of the First World War; but what about learning that does not command consensus in this way? What is *lost* when children are treated primarily as the sum of their performances?

In this passage Dunne offers an alternative vision:

> It is through participation in conversations that arise in the context of focused tasks that people truly develop their repertoires of thinking, feeling, speaking and acting as well as reading and writing. Creating contexts that elicit and sustain such conversations is the great challenge to schools. And the great art for teachers is to be responsive not only to the opportunities and demands of the specific practice [i.e. the subject discipline – sport, music, geography etc] but also to the needs, aptitudes and difficulties of particular pupils. It is the latter requirement that makes them teachers, that is to say people competent not only in the specific practices that give substance to education, but also in the peculiar practice that is teaching itself.... To most truly teach, one must converse; to truly converse is to teach. (2005, p. 157)

It is an inspiring passage, and the last sentence offers a concise alternative to the behavioural objectives model's *teach efficiently!* Teach *conversationally*, urges Dunne: speak, listen, attend to children's 'needs, aptitudes and difficulties', hear not only what they are saying but also what they are trying to tell or avoid telling you. As far as circumstances allow, this means *taking your time*, rather as Philip Pullman urges teachers to give children the time to think, to write, to craft a story.

This brings *children themselves* into the educational picture in a profound and even bodily sense. To converse well is not simply to exchange words; it is to use gestures, smiles, sighs etc. and read these in another. When I converse with a child, I do what Mrs Wymark resisted; I look into her eyes, hear the tremor in her voice, note her tendency to fidget or tug her hair. I do these things assuming that I *can* see and hear, for avoiding the reality *this child* is alien to my intention. I speak, using the most appropriate words I can summon to convey meaning to *this child now*; and I listen, understanding that the words she utters may not quite reflect what she feels. She may be pretending to feel more confident than she does, or trying to conceal the fact that she is afraid, ashamed or angry. Such things happen when children meet the imperative: learn, or try to learn!

How far this is from the behavioural objectives model's disambiguating imperatives! The need to formalize the concepts of sameness and difference – so that a teacher in Exeter *teaches the same lesson in the same way* as a teacher in Hull – brutalizes conversation. Dunne's declaration of equivalence – true teaching and true conversation *are identical* – offers a humane and personally responsive alternative that shifts the focus from neglect and zeal, indolence and efficacy, towards a meaningful conception of education.

But is it quite right? Is it *precisely* what we need in our armoury if we are to address the sense of ethical emergency? Consider a parent with her newborn infant. There is a considerable literature on attunement and misattunement between parents and infants, expressed in the interplay of sounds, gestures, facial expressions and so on. (See 'An Intimate Conversation between Mother and Daughter', https://www.youtube.com/watch?v=9FeTK7ZXmVI.) These are passed back and forth with what appears to be a wide range of meanings, enquiry, surprise, delight, revelation and so on. Are they really conversations, as infant researchers like David E. Arredondo maintain? Not in the ordinary sense of the word, but they are certainly *conversational,* that is, rich with meanings that form patterns and progressions, understandings and misunderstandings, just like the verbal conversations of which they are precursors. Daniel Stern, psychoanalyst and empirical researcher, has filmed and analysed the split-second 'tiny behaviours' of parent–infant interaction, which he calls 'an elaborate dance choreographed by nature' (2004, pp. 2–3). Such interaction is, he says, both dance-like and musical, melodic vocalizations conveying meaning in both directions. Just as we find meaning in dance and music without vocabulary in a lexicographer's sense, so we may observe intimate meanings at play in parent–infant interactions.

Stern brings a microscopic vision to something that, in a general way, we know; human exchanges can be dense with meaning without a single exchange of words. Playful or threatening, they can be crucial arenas of learning, and this is by no means confined to infancy. The learning of older children and adults may be delicately but decisively influenced by the manner of delivery and response. Is it the case, then, that 'to most truly teach, one must converse'? Only if 'conversation' is understood as a form of interaction that can be non-verbal as well as verbal. How about the other way round? Is it the case that 'to truly converse is to teach'? The word 'teach' seems ill-suited to the intimate domestic scenes we have just been considering; it seems more natural to say that, when adults and infants are locked conversationally into each other's worlds, adults normally hope to *bring about learning*, in however ad hoc or loose a way. If they cherish their infants (as I believe most parents do) they want them to learn (amongst other things, but most importantly) about *being with* another human being, being cherished, being responsive.

There is no reason to think that Dunne would disagree with any of this. The intimate exchanges between parents and infants include – when all goes well – responsiveness to 'needs, aptitudes and difficulties' exactly as in most good teaching. It is in this *conversational responsiveness* that I think we should locate and explore Montaigne's 'greatest difficulty known to human learning' if we want to understand what goes wrong with children like Nathan or children who suffer acutely from testing. In their conversations with very young children, verbal and/or non-verbal, adults try to bring about learning at a fundamental level, and when they issue instructions before leaving the room, or homogenize children by 'teaching to the test', they may be neglecting an urgent need for conversational responsiveness. It is not turning education into therapy, or teachers into parents, to recognize this unfulfilled need and seek to address it.

Conversationally responsive parents are *inter*-responsive. They respond, amongst other things, to the child's responses to their own (the adult's) gestures, sounds and so on. Learning is continually and implicitly 'assessed' (judged, noted, wondered about) at this level; the conversationally responsive adult *follows* and *guides* the child, maybe repeating a gesture that was ignored or misread, pulling back if the child seems scared or weary, judging how far to go with this or that game, judging what is enjoyed, what is instructive and so on.

I asked whether this kind of engagement is properly called 'teaching', though as I indicated, it's not clear how much hangs on this. Wittgenstein (whose commitment to ordinary usage is frequently misunderstood and exaggerated in my view) describes 'giving a person a tip' as a kind of teaching. He does *not* withhold the word from personally embedded contexts such as helping another to judge the genuineness of an expression of feeling. A child, he says, 'has much to learn before it can pretend', and this, I am suggesting, is a *kind* of learning that is acquired through conversation at the beginning (but not only the beginning) of life. Children need to learn to distinguish, for example, between a 'genuine loving look' and a 'pretended one', and in this context what Wittgenstein calls tips (one could add hints, prompts, suggestions, reminders) can be valuable. He writes:

> Can one learn this knowledge [about the genuineness of expressions of feeling]? Yes; some can. Not, however, by taking a course in it but through 'experience'.-- Can someone else be a man's teacher in this? Certainly. From time to time he gives him the right tip.--This is what 'learning' and 'teaching' are like here.-- What one acquires is not a technique; one learns correct judgements. There are also rules, but they do not form a system, and only experienced people can apply them right.... What is most difficult here is to put this indefiniteness, correctly and unfalsified, into words. (1953, p. 227)

What happens in an education system where learning and teaching are theoretically and ideologically inhospitable to 'indefiniteness'? The answer, I think, is that some children will flourish and many will propel us into difficult ethical and political conversations. *Should we put up with them? Can we include them? May we exclude them?*

Education, practices and the acquisition of virtue

I am happy to accept that 'to truly converse is to teach' if this means that conversational responsiveness (with a significant non-verbal component) includes a kind of teaching that *brings about forms of learning that are required to understand things like pretence.* This is *learning about* in the broadest sense: learning about the world we live in and its inhabitants, learning about what is generally expected of us as human beings, learning (through many kinds of sensory engagement) about human faces, expression, dissemblance and a good deal else. We all need (or have needed) help with subtle forms of learning that enable us to develop as ethical beings, conscious not only of our own needs and interests but also those of others. We need to learn *what other people are like* – what they love and what they hate, what they need and cannot bear – and we need, at a basic level, to learn to care about the difference. Such learning is the basis for learning about ethical principles and ideas: fairness, forgiveness, reciprocity, courage and so on.

There is a great deal to explore here. If conversational responsiveness belongs, as I have suggested, to the domain in which lies Montaigne's 'greatest and most important difficulty known to human learning', there is a hole at the bottom of many theories of moral learning. Conversational responsiveness is clearly seen in infant–parent interactions, but it underpins a great deal of teaching generally, especially but not exclusively with the very young. The demands of conversational responsiveness – time, sensitivity, wisdom etc. – are great in any intimate human engagement; but this is especially so today when there is unprecedented pressure *both* to produce good academic results (for which the behavioural objectives model may seem admirably well-suited) and to 'solve' the problem of children who fail academically, not to mention increasing numbers who bully or vandalize, bring knives or radical ideologies into classrooms. The current refugee crisis and our concerns about terrorism intensify this drama considerably.

I have agreed that 'true conversation' and 'true teaching' are generally equivalent, given that both 'conversation' and 'teaching' are broadly interpreted as discussed. It is important to keep in mind, however, the purpose of this enquiry, which is to explore dramas of learning and unlearning in ways that have an intimate rather than statistical basis. The suggestion is that both the raising and educating of children involve conversational responsiveness, but it does not follow that there are no forms of teaching that stand outside the concerns of this book and do not involve conversational responsiveness as a central form of educational attention. Some teaching *breaks away* from the intimate sphere into an arena of maturity and dedication. It is often delivered in lecture theatres packed with students who are taught, and may be taught *well*, in anonymity as far as the teacher is concerned.

Here is an example. One of my colleagues has snapped up almost every award going for undergraduate teaching in her institution. She teaches medical ethics and law to student doctors, and the arrangements are such that by and large teaching is conducted in large groups. The reason she receives the awards is that, assuming her students are awake, they receive, and hugely appreciate, lucid and engaging lectures on legal case histories, ethical dilemmas and even the kinds of emotional challenges that are typically faced by doctors. When they break into groups of 15 to 20 students, of course my colleague provides conversational opportunities to seek and receive clarification; but these sessions are occasional and relatively brief, so that for most students, conversation is minimal or even absent.

Here is another example, fictitious but hardly improbable. A physics lecturer in a university achieves renown as a wonderful teacher for the most able and committed students of physics, though like my colleague, her conversation with them is limited. What she offers is the most lucid and exciting rendering of their subject that these learners have ever encountered. True, she is taking their aptitude (passion, enthusiasm, intelligence) for granted in most cases; sometimes it would be truer to say that she *stimulates* passion in those with an aptitude for the subject. It is also true that when students raise their hands and ask a question, she replies pertinently, getting straight to the point of the question, sensing the difficulty, setting the matter straight. This is hardly the back-and-forth exchange normally associated with the word 'conversation', however. Perhaps she resembles those comedians who engage in brilliant repartee with members of packed auditoriums, but retreat into mute self-consciousness in social settings. For this teacher, as for my colleague and the (possibly clichéd) comedian, *conversation is hardly the point*. What makes her a great teacher is her passion for the subject and her unusual ability to articulate and share this. Quite simply, she leaves her colleagues in the shade.

Teaching is a complex and nuanced concept. I think we may go further and say that it contains a difficult-to-negotiate polarity at its heart. Many theories of teaching cluster around two broad models. Philip Jackson, discussed in the previous chapter, distinguishes between transmission and transformation models of teaching, and British philosophers in the 1970s talked similarly about initiation into worthwhile knowledge and understanding as a *counter* to child-centred conceptions of education that aim to release the child's potential. Much of what I earlier called 'intellectual drama' revolves around the disputed merits or demerits of these models.

However, teaching has *both* transmissive and transformative aspects, and the question we should ask is not so much 'which model is superior?' as 'which comes to the fore when?' The medical students in my example are pursuing their elected careers, and the imaginary physics students are virtually specialists. These are *mature* learners, eager to receive what their teachers seek to transmit, but some secondary and even primary school pupils are eager (or can easily become eager with the right stimulation) in just this way. I suggested that it is possible to meet the challenges of transmission *outstandingly* in the admittedly less than ideal circumstances where the teacher is massively outnumbered by students. One might even go further and wonder whether it could be somewhat inappropriate to bring responsiveness to 'needs, aptitudes and difficulties' into every learning situation. Do our specialist physics students want this?

How different this is from the parent/infant scene, in which nothing particular is transmitted. There isn't a lesson plan because there isn't a hint of a lesson! The adult is responding to the moment, *being responsive*, and this may be playfully conversational, unplanned and unsystematic, with no further aim beyond assuring the child that she is cherished, her company is enjoyed and people can be happy together.

Why does Dunne talk about the 'great art for teachers', as though this encompasses teaching at levels of greatest maturity and immaturity? I have suggested that there may be *at least* two arts underlying the theoretical polarity between transmission and transformation. Undoubtedly in many or most cases these will interweave and interact, but should we not recognize that excellent teachers may have *different kinds of gift*, some being exemplary transmitters who are animated by pupils' passionate receptivity, others being exemplary transformers marked by their sensitivity to human dramas and challenging moments?

In a broad sense, children like Nathan obviously need moral education. I am talking about education in the sense discussed by Aristotle when he argued that young people need to develop a virtuous character *as required for a good or flourishing life*. Dunne, an Aristotle scholar, is concerned with this too, and aims (as I do) to explore this topic in a way that responds to its complex practical and ethical demands. Towards this end, much of his work is usefully focused on the idea of *practice* – both the practice of teaching and the disciplinary practices of geography, music-making and so on that provide the content of teaching in schools. Dunne argues that the serious, 'truly conversational' teaching of these practices is itself a form of moral education:

> To really engage with a practice [such as cabinetmaking, physics, farming, chess, computer programming, metalwork, drama production, soccer and weaving] is to acquire, in doing so, qualities such as honesty and humility (in admitting the shortcomings of one's attempts), as well as patience and courage in sticking at a task, even when it does not offer immediate gratification, and a sense of justice and generosity in cooperating with others that require a kind of partnership which overrides the rivalries of individuals precisely insofar as it responds to the demands of the practice itself. (2005, p. 153)

He continues: 'Education into a practice is … in a very strong sense a *moral* education insofar as, properly conducted, it involves … the learning not only of skills but also of virtues.'

Is this right? Is the excellent cabinetmaker, farmer, chess player or computer programmer *as such* a bearer of virtues? I think the answer is: yes and no. There is no doubt, as Dunne says, that 'real engagement' with particular practices calls for a range of virtues. What he calls 'education into a practice', meaning the often lengthy process of developing competence in, or mastery of, the rules, principles and standards that constitute the practice, *is* a kind of virtue education. Not only does it involve skills and understanding in the domain in question; it also involves, as Dunne says, the development of traits like patience, honesty and generosity. Practices are always rooted in communities of practitioners – partners in chess, fellow farmworkers or computer programmers – so cooperation and respect, rather than egotistical rivalry, are required for those who 'really engage'. This is a dual engagement – with forms of work or activity in which one aspires to excellence and with other human beings.

At one level, this resolves the problem of moral education. The key to 'making children better' is to motivate them to become good practitioners in some area or other – and perhaps the key to becoming a good practitioner is to develop one's aptitudes, explore one's passions. Excellent education, in short, becomes the key to moral education, and the implication for policymakers might be that they are barking up the wrong tree when they test children to, or beyond, a reasonable limit. Instead teachers should encourage children to 'find their own way' in an area that is likely to lead to competence or expertise in a practice. This would be quite a child-centred recommendation, focusing on the realization of individual potentialities. Is there anything wrong with this?

My concern is this. Although I agree with Dunne that 'education into practices' has a moral dimension, involving the development of virtues and so on, I disagree that this is *in a very strong sense* a moral education. I reject this *even* on the supposition that the 'education into practices' is truly conversational in the sense I described, that is, conversationally responsive to the student's needs, aptitudes and difficulties in ways that go beyond an exchange of words. I reject it because it makes no reference to dramas of unlearning, attention to which *sometimes* exceeds the remit of education into practices.

We have talked about true education and true conversation. I believe that true *moral* education – education that promotes the development of *true virtue*, rather than compliance or some sort of semblance of virtue – engages with emotion-as-drama. Although this is hardly alien to teaching in general, I am suggesting that it is possible to be an excellent 'educator into a practice' *without* engaging at this level. Some children love learning and do so with ease; others find learning painful or impossible. We see the results for the second group in poor test scores, vandalism, insomnia, bulimia and other symptoms of stress. An enhancement agenda registers the *sense of waste* consequent on dramas of unlearning – for the nation that needs an educated population, for children themselves. The concept of enhancing children is fraught with difficulty, but its foundational principle – that lives may be squandered through emotional resistance to learning, and that this situation must be addressed by educators – is one that I endorse. An enhancement agenda may turn out to be a misguided form of moral education, but it recognizes the limitations of even the most exemplary 'education into practices', and this is a strength.

The idea that 'education into practices' is moral education in a strong sense has become a kind of orthodoxy in philosophy of education. I think it places excessive and unreasonable burdens on teachers, ignoring the ways in which people can be genuinely virtuous without possessing virtue in every aspect of their characters. There's a cliché about people who have a bad day at work and go home and kick the dog. One could adapt this to talk about people who have a *good* day at work, exhibiting a range of virtues that they habitually express at work, but less habitually (or rarely) at home. There's a wonderful line in Helen Simpson's story 'Four Bare Legs in a Bed' about a married couple whose rows are 'like the weather'. They appear out of nowhere when all seems well, and the couple 'hurtle back down the decades, transformed into giant infants stamping and frowning and spouting tears of rage'. Don't most of us behave better at work than at home? Isn't this a truthful description of the transformation that most of us undergo from time to time with those we love, or purport to love? If we kick the dog at home, are we necessarily feigning virtue at work?

The following passage by Richard Smith expresses the orthodoxy (as I called it) that exemplary practitioners are virtuous in a 'very strong sense'. The practice in question is chairing a meeting:

> In chairing a meeting, she encourages one colleague to hold the floor but another to be brief. Now she attempts a summary of where the meeting has got to, but now she allows ideas to go backwards and forwards without intervening. At one point she lightens the atmosphere with a joke, at another reminds colleagues of inexorable external pressures. All this flows to a large extent from the sort of person she is: generous and good humoured, or tense, defensive and impatient. Later her colleagues are as likely to remark on her character as on her skill at chairing meetings. (2005, p. 209)

At one level, I agree: in chairing a meeting, one exhibits 'the sort of person' one is. If one has a habit of interrupting speakers, this is reasonably seen as a mark against one's character, as the skilful defusing of aggression between speakers is a mark in its favour. Another example of a person in a prominent position might be a soloist – a pianist, let's say – performing a concerto with an orchestra. In both cases, various virtues are on display – patience, respect and so on – but it takes little imagination to elaborate the story. The excellent chair is generous and good-humoured with her colleagues, but mean and humourless with her children or friends. The virtuoso pianist treats her orchestral colleagues with respect, but privately gloats over their less than dazzling careers.

We are talking about character ('the sort of person' one is), and I am drawing attention to something that may seem quite obvious: most human beings, as they acquire any kind of learning and history, become complex and prism-like. They *appear differently* in different lights, different settings, to themselves as well as others. The appearance of a person's character is not the same as its reality, though in many cases these will be well aligned. It is one of the peculiarities of our species that appearance and reality can be distinct on all sorts of levels: socialization requires a kind of refinement of appearance, which may be benign or deceitful, hard or easy to decipher. The point is not that the excellent chair or pianist described above *lacks* the virtues she displays; at one level, of course she possesses these virtues. What is crucial, I suggest, is a recognition of what we might call the dramatic compromise at the heart of human character and emotion, and the demand this makes on our powers of perception and judgement. People are not always (entirely) as they seem; the challenge will be to bring this simple platitude into a vision of what it means to guide the young.

The idea of a ministrative practice

The idea of a practice is immensely rich, with roots in the philosophies of Aristotle and Wittgenstein. It has been modified and elaborated in recent years by Alasdair MacIntyre (1982) and Joseph Dunne (1993), and I shall follow them in using this idea as a frame within which to explore certain ethical engagements with others. The idea of education as a practice points inescapably to the realities of what people do, feel and think, and my hope is to get deeper into what this means in order to illuminate the aspiration to enhance or improve others, or lead them towards better lives.

Dunne is concerned with teaching as an ethical engagement that is susceptible to violation or derailment. This is reminiscent of Pullman's sense of ethical emergency in education, as discussed in Chapter 1. The task of writing a story in 45 minutes to illustrate some 'crudely drawn pictures' is, says Pullman, one of 'stupefying worthlessness and futility', though it was presented by then Education Minister Charles Clarke as a breath of creative fresh air. As a point of honour, Pullman adds, we should be committed to the principle that the tasks we set for children are 'intrinsically worth doing'. Dunne's work is moved, as

I understand it, by a similar concern, which he explores (predominantly but not exclusively) through the work of Aristotle and MacIntyre.

Praxis, for Aristotle, is an ethical concept, referring to good and bad, admirable and unadmirable actions. Our daily interactions with others are forms of *praxis* in this sense, and Aristotle distinguished them from *poiesis*, another kind of action that involves making or fabricating things (pots, buildings, meals etc.) *Praxis*, then, is a *type of action* that is irreducibly ethical.

MacIntyre's development of this idea involved the introduction of the article: terms like 'a' and 'the' that suggest a *plurality* of specific practices, rather than a mode of acting in the world. Architecture is a practice, as are music-making, farming, chess, painting, banking and so on. These are domains of cooperative activity with their own rules, standards, principles of excellence, and MacIntyre's revision breaks down the Aristotelian distinction between *praxis* and *poiesis* (architecture and painting, for example, being practices, or forms of *praxis*, that involve 'making or fabricating things'). This introduces the educationally significant thought that there are ethical and non-ethical ways of 'making or fabricating', as well as acting in a broader sense. The distinctness of practices is not absolute. There are likely to be overlaps between them, and the boundaries will in many cases shift over time, as the practice of painting in modern times has morphed into (but continues to overlap) photography, installation, performance art and so on. To say that there are different practices is not, or should not be, to say that they are isolated or independent.

The lifelong hermit or solipsist is beyond their reach. A solitary individual isn't in a position to achieve what rule-governance requires, namely, common understanding – understanding shared with others – about whether or to what extent something is done well or badly. All practices involve standards of excellence that are generally, if not uncontroversially, agreed.

MacIntyre and Dunne describe these standards of excellence as internal goods, and the important point about practices is that they may be deflected into an effort to achieve external goods instead. MacIntyre illustrates the difference between internal and external goods by distinguishing between two chess-playing children. One child plays chess in order to enjoy the goods internal to the practice: analytic skill, strategic imagination, friendly rivalry. The practice of chess involves a cooperative engagement with these goods, and includes some personal qualities. This child displays persistence, determination and respect for her partner; she has no inclination to cheat. The other child plays chess with a different motive; she has been promised candy if she can master the rules and focus on the game. These children may be indistinguishable to a bystander, but we know that the candy-seeking child has an external rather than internal motive for playing the game, and as far as this goes, no particular reason *not* to cheat.

Now compare two teachers. The first, let us say, is pained by the thought that many children in today's education system fail to develop their potentialities in valuable ways. Maybe her own education was poor; maybe she is a reader of Martin Buber, awed by a sense of human possibility. This teacher is moved by the desire to 'cherish rather than squander' children's potentialities. The second teacher, having tried her hand at a few careers, wants a regular salary and the prospect of promotion to a senior position. She sees her job as a means to the end of an improved life for herself, and she may in addition have a political motive: to boost attainment as a way of helping to restore national prosperity. This teacher is motivated primarily by external goods, and there are potential losses to children when education is conceived this way.

Joseph Dunne (2006) makes the point through an ecological metaphor:

> For decades now the greatest dangers to living species have come from environmental changes caused by human intervention and assault. And practices have their own similar ecology: they too are exposed to drastic changes in their human environments that threaten their continuing viability. 'Viability' here, however, is not a matter of mere survival; one can perhaps better speak of 'integrity', which introduces a necessary moral inflection and makes one look to other analogies, as, for example, when the integrity of a national territory is at risk from colonising forces, or a person's artistic integrity is compromised by commercial pressures. (p. 367)

Loss of integrity is the danger faced by education when it is instrumentalized or steered towards external ends. Many policymakers see the practice of education primarily as a route to national prosperity and global prominence, and the point is not that education should be dissociated from these external goods, but that its internal goods must be respected and pursued if its integrity is to be preserved. Philosophy has an important role to play here, articulating these goods and explaining why they matter.

The internal good of education relates, as Dunne says, to the development of children's powers or potentialities. In a general way, the task of the educator – teacher or parent – is to stimulate or strengthen engagement with worthwhile practices. It is to help and encourage students to *care* about the difference between conducting themselves badly and well within various domains, so that they may aspire to 'do well' and hopefully enrich their lives through continued learning and achievement. I said in Chapter 1 (rather simplistically but as a way of preparing the ground) that education is a *way of being good to people*, and I want to express this slightly differently now by saying that educational practitioners with integrity (meaning good parents as well as teachers) attempt to *minister* to the good of others. Education's distinctive mode of ministry involves stimulating a caring and responsible engagement with practices beyond itself, and this is normally achieved through a kind of care and responsibility towards the learner. Education, says Dunne, belongs to a group of practices, 'whose ends reside in changes in human beings who are themselves engaged more or less actively in the (inter-) activity that constitutes the practice … we may consider the caring work of doctors, nurses and social workers, and the educational work of various kinds and levels of teaching' (p. 370). The ministrative practice of education, then, like those of medicine, nursing and social work (not to mention psychotherapy, which I shall discuss presently), aims to produce 'changes in human beings' who are *also* involved with the practice. The sought-after changes are naturally expected to be good, and it is the desire to bring these about *independently of desirable changes elsewhere* that indicates a concern with internal rather than external goods.

If I have, in the previous paragraph, sketched the idea of education's internal good, this only pushes the question back. What *is* it to minister to the good of another? I hope in the course of the book to engage helpfully with this question, which is a large and difficult one. The first part of my proposed answer will be objectionable to many philosophers: we must *believe in* the idea of the good. Ministrative practitioners must, in short, commit themselves to an idea that many philosophers find dubious, fantastical or obscure. Or rather – to put this another way – I would say that this is what good ministrative practitioners *actually do*. They occupy a zone, as it were, between individuals in all their personal and sensory detail and this perplexing abstraction, the idea of the good. Particularly in the domains of education, upbringing and psychotherapy (sadly, practices like medicine currently operate within such tight constraints that what I am calling ministry is often a nostalgic ideal), it is the willingness to engage with this abstraction in a way that is and remains finely focused on individuals that *makes* a practitioner good.

This, at any rate, will be my somewhat startling argument: startling because it appears to make of humble teachers, parents and therapists a kind of contemplative philosopher. What I am rejecting here is the spirit in which Mary Warnock succumbs to the difficulties posed by the idea of the good:

> Nor can we be blamed if we sometimes seem ignorant or uncertain about what the good of the child may be. For evidence is extremely difficult to come by in

such fields; and we are all to a greater or lesser extent governed by prejudices or beliefs not much better than old wives' tales about what will or will not, in general, turn out to be good for children. (1992, p. 77)

It may seem generous for a philosopher to submit frankly to the relativism of our age, claiming no privilege over spinners of old wives' tales. And Warnock is right: we are often extremely ignorant about the good for children. We send them to the school or holiday camp that we think will serve them well, and they come back with heightened arrogance or a new set of phobias. It doesn't follow from this that we are condemned to prejudice when we reflect on the good for others. It doesn't mean we can't *learn more* both about what this good consists in and our own defects of vision.

This book is concerned with human intimacy. It is, in particular, about our intimate engagements with others and the feelings and reflections that render these genuinely ministrative. It is about the concepts on which we draw, the manner in which we think, the temptations to which we are prey. It is, inevitably, about the perplexity and dramatic uncertainties that arise from time to time, as well as the willingness to *rest* with these in a manner that may be called contemplative or philosophical (though in many cases our reflections are doubtless inarticulate or unexpressed). In this sense I do think that good parents, like teachers and therapists, encounter and accept a kind of philosophical challenge, though they will not normally describe it as such. This is the challenge of 'believing in' the huge abstraction we call goodness, as a *reality* to which human beings can aspire on others' behalves. Distasteful as this may sound to some academic philosophers, I shall argue that it is at the heart of the attitude I call cherishing.

What does it mean for one person to cherish another? As an initial outline, I have suggested that the person who cherishes believes in the 'possibility of the good' for another, and is committed to ministering to this. She is committed, not to an empirical conception of the good – which may in principle be established by science – but to a truly ethical conception. Part of what this means is that the idea of the good *demands* an ethical engagement, in the manner that I outlined earlier. There *will be* perplexity and there *will be* uncertainty: to engage ethically is to be willing to think and feel, wait and act, as the good of another requires. A scientific answer – the good of this child will be fulfilled by certain criteria – may be reasonable enough up to a point, but the ethical work of enquiry and reflection on the vicissitudes of *this individual* remains to be done.

To 'believe in' the idea of the good is to believe that the good is in no way relative (as Warnock seems to believe) to your or my opinion. To say that it is *real* is to say that we can *really* get it wrong, and this in a highly specific sense. What I am doing here is locating Plato's metaphysics (particularly as presented by Simone Weil and Iris Murdoch) at the heart of our ministrative practices. From this perspective the idea of the good is no mere abstraction, subject to criticisms that most philosophy undergraduates can recount in their sleep. What is needed, as Murdoch says (and this could have been Wittgenstein), is an appreciation of 'the place where the concept of good lives'. It lives, I am suggesting, in the midst of our ministrative practices, where we frequently *get things wrong*, misperceiving and misreading other people's realities, grieving over such failures and endeavouring to remedy them. 'The idea of "objective reality"', says Murdoch, ' undergoes important modifications when it is to be understood, not in relation to "the world described by science", but in relation to the progressing life of a person' (1970, p. 26). Here 'the good' is more than an object of contemplation; it is an activity, an engagement, a task (as Murdoch says) of 'infinite difficulty', involving the struggle to apprehend 'a magnetic but inexhaustible reality' (ibid., p. 42). The person I am calling a ministrative practitioner is *drawn* to the other person's good as though it were a magnet, understanding that it will never be 'fully apprehended' (let alone captured in a report or document), but intent on doing all she can to support and enhance it.

I call this cherishing. It might be said, quite reasonably, that teachers, nurses, therapists etc. can't possibly cherish every child, patient or client. What they can do, I would argue, is regard every recipient of their ministry as unconditionally *cherishworthy*, and in this sense entrusted to them for a qualified or temporary kind of cherishing. This is not an insignificant conclusion. Good-enough parents *do* cherish their children, and I believe that in such parenting we find a kind of paradigm of ministrative practice. This is also a paradigm of what it means to lead an ethical life, and it is within this frame that we shall hopefully illuminate perplexing concepts like happiness, virtue and flourishing.

A Wittgensteinian reminder

It is a Wittgensteinian insight that philosophers and other thinkers often issue imperatives without acknowledging the concern, anxiety or purpose by which the sense of urgency is driven. *Something must be done* is the cry of the imperatival thinker, or *something must be true, something must exist*. There *must be something frightful* accompanying my cry of pain – pain *must be* an inner something. Much of Wittgenstein's work explores the anxieties driving such imperatives, and his responses are sometimes surprising. *Who are you informing of this? On what occasions? For what purposes? What gives you the impression that we wanted to deny anything?* (1953, paras 296–305).

If philosophy is to contribute well to the way people live, we must watch our imperatives and sometimes trace their demands to an anxious source. The source may be someone else's philosophical denial: for example, there is no inner world, no mind as such; there is only behaviour. Naturally, this makes us anxious, inclined to respond: *there must be an inner world, I experience it all the time!* Of course, says Wittgenstein with a shrug. Only who are you informing of this? And by the way, don't underestimate the dangers of responding this way to a claim that is, let's face it, nonsensical. You are in danger of thinking like Descartes: believing in a 'space' called mind that contains mental rather than physical objects, and is knowable by no-one but its owner. What's the use of such a picture? What does it contribute to our lives? What do we learn from it?

The tracing of imperatives to an anxious source allows us to raise a significant question: is this the best or only way to address our anxiety? Anxieties about children have intensified in recent decades, sealed in the present century by the UNICEF well-being report (2007) that placed UK children at the bottom of a league of 22 countries, and the more recent Children's Worlds well-being survey that placed English children 14th out of 15 countries. *We must enhance children* ('make them better') is the guiding imperative that responds to these anxieties. In Chapters 3 through 7, I explore a succession of sub-imperatives: we must make them happier; we must equip them for twenty-first-century life; we must build character through evidence-based interventions; we must foster respect and self-respect through inclusion.

I have no doubt that these imperatives are motivated in most cases by sincere concern about children. There is a desire to respond humanely to indications that children are unhappy and struggling to learn, setting this against imperatives that seek to *make* them learn in order to boost national prosperity. It is no part of my argument that children have not been and will not continue to be helped by this significant shift of focus. But I think we can *and must* go further if we are to help children as they deserve to be helped. We need to think, with Pullman and Dunne, about true teaching, true conversation, not to mention true virtue and truly good lives. *This* is ethics, and commendable as much recent effort is, I do not think we have adequately pressed the question: what does ethics *mean*? How should we distinguish between real and apparent virtue, a truly good life and its semblances? We shall address such questions throughout the book, and particularly in Part Three.

Part Two

Enhancing Children

3

Should We Try to Make Children Happy?

What is the objective mark of the happy, harmonious life? Here it is again clear that there cannot be any such mark, that can be described.
Wittgenstein, Notebooks 1914–1916, p. 78e

It seems like a silly idea: *adults can make children happy*. But the opposite idea – *adults can make children unhappy* – is not only sensible but corresponds to a depressing and widespread reality. Small insensitivities, gross abuse and simple neglect are, if not guaranteed, fairly reliable ways (especially as regular occurrences in the lives of the young) to set people on a path to misery.

This asymmetry in our power over the young, and indeed over anyone who depends on our ministry, tells us a good deal about the endlessly recurring debates and disagreements around the idea of happiness. We know all too well what *unhappiness* is, and if we trade in neglect or abuse of vulnerable others, we have the power easily to bring it about. We know what it is and are often quite good at recognizing its malign and intractable forms. What is happiness? This is a question, it seems, without an answer beyond 'make up your mind about what it means to you'.

Many policymakers and statisticians proceed from here. Happiness, they believe, is what the nation says it is, as declared by individuals on questionnaires. An amalgam of opinions on the meaning of happiness produces an authoritative consensual definition. And accurate statistics on how happy each of us *feels* can be pooled with reports from other nations to produce a global happiness hierarchy in which every nation is assigned a place.

Despite the promises of science, however, happiness continues to trouble us. Confidence in ranking people, cities or nations meets protests and objections. Some are epistemological; they concern the reliability of the knowledge that questionnaires allegedly yield. Some are ethical, charging happiness-obsessives with sentimentalizing or trivializing life. The famous pursuit of happiness is criticized from this angle, with the suggestion that one has to be woefully self-serving to devote one's energies to such an end. Other concerns about happiness fall less easily into a category like 'dubious knowledge' or 'dubious ethics'. The preoccupation with happiness *makes some people uneasy*; they regard it with suspicion and distrust.

In this chapter I review efforts in contrary directions: efforts to accord happiness a supreme role in human life; and efforts to prick the bubble of hope and expectation by relegating happiness to the margins. One side says we must think carefully about happiness, analyse the concept, review its preconditions, try to enhance (or 'achieve') it in others as well as ourselves. The other side says that happiness is (as its etymology suggests) a *happening* that you may enjoy or be denied. There is a bigger picture, continues this argument, which includes being decent, being properly educated, being helpful to others, living a worthwhile life. Combined with the ideas of pursuit or enhancement, the emphasis on happiness is basically an error.

I tend towards the latter view – with qualifications I shall discuss later on. Turning our own happiness into a lifelong project (as many do), not only are we pursuing a chimera, but we are likely to become narcissistic to a point where (to our own great detriment) true friendship and intimacy are impossible. Thinking about happiness on other people's behalves is different, I believe, and this is not because *adults can and therefore should make children happy*; as I said, I think their power to do so is questionable, and happiness – understood in an everyday sense – is something of a misfit in our ethical lives. It is more about the power we have to make children *unhappy* in ways that may be intractable.

In the last chapter I introduced the idea of a ministrative practice, in which the idea of guiding others towards 'the good' plays a key role. This doesn't (I am suggesting) include happiness in any straightforward sense, but it seems clear that a good-enough ministrative practitioner (we shall return to this phrase, good-enough) takes seriously, and wants to avoid causing, *serious harm* to those who fall within her ministry. This includes not any kind of unhappiness, but the profound and often enduring kinds that we call trauma, deep distress, the experience of abuse. These sometimes manifest as dramas of unlearning, since they have the power to inhibit valuable learning, or pervert its course. Children who sabotage achievement or are addicted to its glories may signal a kind of unhappiness that requires attention from teachers as well as parents.

The present Conservative government, led by Theresa May, professes to be concerned about children's unhappiness. The rhetoric of this concern is typical of what I call enhancement agendas. Unhappiness is noted, rather as I have noted it, as something that requires serious attention (I suggested that this is true, at least, of certain kinds of unhappiness). The assumed corollaries are, first, that children need 'happiness lessons' and, second, that substantial resources must be devoted to the building of an evidence base that will ensure success in converting unhappiness into happiness. The latter may strike us as a woolly concept, but the *science* of happiness transforms it into a construct on which causal operations may be tested with rigour.

This is from is a recent Guardian article about May's project:

> Eight year-old children will be given lessons on happiness and teenagers will be instructed on combating anxiety and suicidal thoughts under government projects due to be trialled. The government for education is inviting bidders for multi-million pound contracts to offer mental health training to more than 200 schools. Typical mindfulness lessons will reportedly encourage children to think of disturbing thoughts as 'buses' that will move away.
>
> https://www.theguardian.com/society/2017/mar/12/schools-to-trial-happiness-lessons-for-eight-year-olds

So happiness lessons, rolled out to schools nationally, are to relieve the miseries of suicidal teenagers, as though these painful feelings belong at the bottom of a scale, and can be nudged higher, and higher still, by expert happiness-boosters. But if the origin of these miseries is a deep problem of trust – perhaps the child has been abused or neglected – she is unlikely to be reassured by the current object of her distrust, a teacher say, who has been trained to cast her difficulty as a 'disturbing thought' that (like a bus) will obligingly move on. If the child is terrified of exams, or ashamed of her disability, she is similarly unlikely to be comforted by a metaphor that is pressed upon her in the pretence that these stubborn realities will magically disappear. A recent study showed that academic pressures are the most common antecedents to teenage suicide, and it is hard to see a connection between itinerant vehicles and what feels to many children like a permanent threat of being held to account. There is, to say the least, a sense of *wishful thinking* in the idea that unhappiness – especially the serious or enduring kind – may be reliably alleviated by classroom instruction on 'combating anxiety and suicidal thoughts'.

It is tempting to think of unhappiness and happiness as simple binaries, like the negative and positive poles of a magnet. You are *either* happy *or* unhappy, and subtle mixtures of the two – like being happily unhappy, or unhappily happy, or somehow content and desperate at the same time – are distracting conceptual riddles. Yet it is often by recognizing such mixtures that conversationally responsive adults learn about and guide the young. An enhancement agenda is committed to a binary conceptualization, and it is supplemented in some cases by the idea that scientifically validated intervention is a proper mode of engagement between adults and young people, in preference to emotionally guided, well-judged responsiveness. Part Two of the book calls these assumptions into question.

Emotional matters are far more complicated than proponents of enhancement agendas are willing to admit. A proper concern about a person's unhappiness does *not* necessarily have as a flipside the compensatory desire to 'enhance her happiness'. I have noted an asymmetry – we recognize unhappiness, on the whole, better than happiness – and this is, I believe, a significant difference. The enhancement agendist's fixation on positivity as an antidote to negativity is misguided, but our reflections on this error will hopefully illuminate the largest positivity of all: the idea of the good. In this chapter, we shall consider ways in which alleviating unhappiness and (possibly) promoting happiness may be implicated in its meaning.

The positivity turn

I suggested in Chapter 1 that, at a basic level, education is a way of being good to people. Here, at least, is a proper (if abstract) use for the concept of the good. If we forget this and think of education as a set of techniques for making children learn, or making them do things, not to mention making them *feel* things, we will have lost our way. Education is not, of course, the only way of being good to people. I spoke about its 'distinctive mode of ministry', which is (as I put it) to stimulate 'a caring and responsible engagement with practices beyond itself… through a kind of care and responsibility towards the learner.' I suggested we should think of this 'care and responsibility' as a form of cherishing, and particularly 'cherishing rather than squandering' the potentialities of the reality *child*. We need to add flesh to these bones.

I also discussed Montaigne's thought that 'the greatest and most important difficulty known to human learning' belongs to the indivisible domain of raising and educating the young. This supports Joseph Dunne's suggestion that 'true teaching' and 'true conversation' are equivalent, or at least (as I amended it slightly) intimately connected (coming apart, if at all, only with mature, committed learners, who may be 'well taught' by excellent lectures rather than as they are by excellent books). If, as I suggested, such thoughts are properly understood as *descriptive* of our ministrative practices, *descriptive* of the manners in which good-enough ministrative practitioners reflect and engage, we can understand the unease that many are likely to experience about the idea that children need *classroom instruction* on how to combat their anxious and suicidal tendencies. Can teachers really teach children how to be happy (or happier) in ways that are also caring and responsible? Can they do this in classes of 30 or so children – settings in which some may be adept at faking their moods, pleasing their teachers, blending with the crowd? Might not some children use happiness questionnaires as a hopeful experiment and distraction from pain? (*If, like my classmates, I say that I'm happy, perhaps happy is what I shall feel…*)

My aims in posing such questions are not especially radical. I do not want to deny that excellent, conversationally responsive teachers may guide the young *towards* sources of lasting happiness, or *away from* sources of lasting unhappiness. By sharing their sense of what is not only worthwhile but wonderful, they can of course inspire joyful learning, learning that may endure and grow. By sharing (and in some cases having difficult conversations about) their sense of what it means (for example) to *succumb to addiction*, they may divert children who are heading towards lives of lonely, screen-based fantasy, because they feel more comfortable with avatars than human beings. Adults, I suggested, can hardly *make children happy*, but they do, nonetheless, have powers over children's happiness that we need to understand.

Philosophers are forever telling us how complex happiness is. (French philosopher Pascal Bruckner writes: 'It is in the nature of this notion to be an enigma, a permanent source of debates, a fluid that can take every form, but which no form exhausts.') All the more reason, surely, for drawing lines in the sand, creating some basic contours for thinking. One of the first things that comes to mind is that, while we cannot *make children happy* in any serious sense, we can offer opportunities and inspiration in directions where happiness may be found. *Music* makes many people happy (famously so), as do long walks in nature. For others, it is blissful to wander around cities with a camera, observing and recording human stories. Part of the complexity of this topic is a feature that some call 'subjectivity', but I would call (more informatively, I think) its embeddedness in personal desire. *Different things make different people happy*; indeed, this seems like one of the most basic things we can say about happiness. Aristotle wavered over whether true happiness was to be found in the contemplative or the practical/political life. Though he said much of interest about happiness (or rather, *eudaimonia*, sometimes translated as happiness, sometimes as well-being or flourishing), I don't think we should be detained by Aristotle's difficulty here. *Some* people, clearly, find great happiness in contemplation, whereas others must be forever *doing*. They must be swimming, throwing a javelin, interviewing interesting people, scratching shapes into wood, visiting the elderly, making cupcakes and a host of other things. 'What makes us happy', says psychoanalyst Adam Phillips, 'is a kind of key to our sense of ourselves' (2011, p. 88). Adults cannot hand children this key, still less make them accept and use it; but they *can* assist and guide them towards its discovery. This seems like a crucial aspect of the cherishing engagement.

They can also, I have suggested, be alert to serious unhappiness, judging whether or how this might be alleviated through conversation with themselves or someone else (e.g. a counsellor). Unhappiness has been miscast in recent years as the culprit behind most social and educational ills. Except when stimulated by real misfortune, it is (economist Richard Layard suggests) a recidivist habit, an evolutionary throwback to 'life on the savannah', over which we should attempt to obtain 'mastery'. *Unhappiness is (almost) always bad; happiness is (almost) always good*. Or: *happiness is the default state towards which we should aim; unhappiness is the state we should try to avoid*. If unhappiness deflection and happiness promotion are somehow implicated in 'the good' towards which ministrative practitioners aspire, they will not (I am arguing) rest on these simple platitudes. The task we face is more like tracing a path through a heavily mined terrain.

Happiness is, after all, as Bruckner notes, 'a fluid that can take every form, but which no form exhausts'. That we should choose happiness over unhappiness as a default state seems in some sense right *and* wrong. I remember as a philosophically inclined child pondering this matter. I had two thoughts that did not sit easily together. The first was that my life was reasonably good, better than many; I was sufficiently attuned to the world to know that this was true. (For one thing, there was always food on the table.) The second was that I sometimes felt miserable, inconsolably so, and this seemed anomalous, if not ungrateful. How could I be miserable (*logically*, as it were) when I knew that children who didn't have food on their tables would be in paradise if, as a sudden gift of fate, they were routinely *fed* as I was fed? My thought was that happiness must be conscious of itself, and I wondered why no one had ever explained this to me. If adults want children to be happy, they shouldn't simply give them food to eat, houses to live in, schools to attend (though they should certainly attempt to do these things). They should help them to *reflect* on happiness, which means reflecting on desire, reflecting on life, who they are, who they might have been, who they might become.

Many years later I learned about a fictional child called Verruca Salt (a Roald Dahl character), who had her parents at her beck and call, was given everything she asked for and more and was permanently dissatisfied. This, obviously, was an unenviable child on course for a miserable life. As usual in Roald Dahl's stories, she contained a moral lesson: a lesson about how happiness can be craved for ourselves, guiltily nurtured in children and tantalizingly elusive. I believe I was right as a child to come to the realization that happiness is, or ought to be, an object of reflection. It has serious and unserious forms. It is understood in one way by young children, and quite another by older children or adults who have become aware of the limitations of what we might call the childish conception of happiness. Young children, after all, *know* what happiness is, *know* that they are entitled to it and *know* that all will be well if only their stubborn parents would (on demand) give them some cash or hand over the biscuits. The happiness question – my question in this chapter – is about how and why we must think more deeply.

The science of happiness

Imagine that your 8-year-old child comes home from school bubbling over about her day. 'We played tag, we read a story about a wolf, and we measured things!'

'What things did you measure?' you ask.

'Pencils, feet, pieces of toast. And guess what. We measured the cat. It's six and a half!'

'Six and a half *what*?' you ask, bemused. Is she talking about centimetres, inches, kilos? Did they measure the cat or her *tail*?

'Dunno', she says, turning on her iPad. 'Just six and a half.'

'Were you measuring how *long* the cat is?' you persist. 'How heavy? How wide?'

But your daughter is zooming up the highway on her screen, and she's lost interest in your questions.

Is this the kind of thing that happens when scientists measure happiness? Do they know what they are measuring?

Let's consider what measuring means ordinarily. It is a practice that takes place within a setting. In this setting we normally know quite a lot about what we are measuring before we take out the tape measure, blood pressure monitor, thermometer, scales or whatever. *I know that my dog is looking plump.* I've also noticed that when she walks across the room, the floorboards creak. (They never used to.) From these two directions, then, I have confirmatory suspicions of excess weight. I put her on the scales and my suspicions are confirmed: She weighs almost 3 kg more than the last time she was weighed.

Normally when we measure things, we are looking for more precise knowledge of something that, in a general way, we know. *Measurement specifies knowledge –* or if not knowledge, suspicion, and if not suspicion, an enquiry about something, the nature of which is reasonably well understood (like blood pressure or glucose in the blood). The practice of happiness measurement departs from these conditions. When people fill in happiness questionnaires, the results may be fed into computers by people who don't know Tom or Dick or Harry and have no idea how seriously they are taking the questions. (Perhaps they see it as fun, light relief after a maths lesson.) Maybe the scientists are not quite sure what happiness is, but they take comfort in the fact that others seem to know and are confident that they can measure it. They are willing to accept that results are 'accurate' and 'reliable' even as the enigmatic nature of happiness is acknowledged.

In the next section, I shall probe this idea, happiness. I shall suggest that, while at one level happiness and unhappiness may be seen as simple binaries (think of young children, whose quicksilver fluctuations of mood are registered by laughter and tears, smiles and scowls), at another level, happiness is more mysterious than unhappiness and more challenging not only for philosophers but also for those who want it on behalf of others. I don't want to suggest that unhappiness is straightforward; it is not. But the motivation to *relieve* unhappiness is, I believe, more straightforward than the motivation to promote happiness. We are 'hurt' by other people's unhappiness, and moved to alleviate it; this is a proper aspect of our ministrative practices (although it can, of course, be excessive), and it is on the whole clearer, less problematic, than the wish to make another happy. Why should this be?

In an interesting small book called *The Ethics of Memory* (2002), philosopher Avishai Margalit explores the asymmetry (as he sees it) between negative and positive. What hurts us into politics? he asks, and his tentative answer is this. 'Is it not injustice rather than justice? And tyranny rather than freedom, poverty rather than equality, humiliation rather than dignity?' This, he says, is not a 'stylistic preference but a strategy'. The strategy is to stress negative emotions over positive ones: '... humiliation rather than pride, rejection rather than being recognised and accepted, feeling estranged rather than feeling at home. On many occasions we recognise what is wrong with something without having a clear idea, or any idea at all, about what is right with it' (pp. 112–114).

This perspective comes from negative theology: the shift, as Margalit says, in the 'language of theology from attributing positive traits to God to expressing attributes that God does not have. The idea behind it was that nothing positive can be known about God, for He has nothing in common with other beings'. Here is the crux: 'The gain from such an interpretative move is not new knowledge about God but rather the loss of the illusion of ever attaining such knowledge.' This is reminiscent of Iris Murdoch's remark about 'the good', quoted in the previous chapter: 'Good is indefinable... because of the infinite difficulty of the task of apprehending a magnetic but inexhaustible reality' (1970, p. 42). Both philosophers warn us against supposing we may apprehend something we will never fully apprehend: the good for another. This is, I suggest, something that good-enough ministrative practitioners affirm continually in the course of their engagements with others.

From this perspective, enhancement agendas rest on an illusion of epistemological finality: the assumption that we can *know* what is good for another in a total sense (or what will make another happy) as a flipside to recognizing and being 'hurt' by what is bad (or makes them unhappy). We can 'make children better' by nudging them up a scale that exhibits *consistency of meaning*. The scale merely distinguishes between more and less, positive and negative; unhappiness fills the space that happiness sometimes leaves vacant, and vice versa. The same is true of low and high self-esteem.

Margalit's argument isn't simply about knowledge; it is about the proper focus of our *efforts*, political and ethical, on behalf of others. He is right to say that there is no smooth transition from a hatred of humiliation and cruelty to a love of respect and kindness. Respect doesn't *follow* from the elimination of disrespect in any straightforward way, as kindness doesn't *follow* from the elimination of cruelty. To laugh at a beggar or steal her change is obviously disrespectful and unkind, but it is (Margalit implies) a further, *independent* question what respect and kindness mean, practically as well as semantically. How *do* we speak respectfully to someone who has nothing and is begging on the street? How *do* we show kindness? Is it kind to give money, and kinder to hand over banknotes than loose change? Or should charity be avoided because it is an *appearance* of kindness that reinforces dependency on others? Is extreme generosity to someone who has nothing ostentatious rather than kind?

Rather like Pullman, discussed in Chapter 1, Margalit conveys a sense of ethical urgency:

> Eradicating cruelty and humiliation is more urgent than promoting and creating positive well-being. Thus, the politics of dignity should in my account be understood not as positive politics but rather as negative politics. It should not

address the question of how institutions can promote dignity in every human being by virtue of his or her being human, but rather it should ask how to stop humiliation. (ibid., p. 114)

Suppose Margalit is right, and suppose that these thoughts capture something significant not only about political concepts, but also about good and bad, right and wrong, happy and unhappy. *On many occasions* (he says) *we recognize what is wrong with something without having a clear idea, or any idea at all, about what is right with it.* If we lack a 'clear idea, or any idea at all' of what happiness means and what it means to promote it, scientists are whistling in the dark when they claim to measure happiness. There is a problem, moreover, with enhancement agendas generally, for these are forms of positive ethics, positive education, positive policy. They claim to convert negative traits into positive ones.

Measurement, I said, *specifies knowledge*, and 'unclear ideas' signify ignorance, doubt, uncertainty, in short, unclear knowledge. If I tell you that Tom is less happy than he was last week by 15 per cent, but happier than poor Harry, whose suicidal tendencies make him 30 per cent less happy than Tom, you may accuse me of joking about serious matters. But the possibility of ranking nations, cities and individuals – creating a happiness hierarchy – requires us to suppose that such comparisons are meaningful and may even be accurate.

The concept of happiness has been subjected to a good deal of analysis, presumably because its unclarity seems like an affront to its importance. One of the principles of this book is that analysis is less useful when we are considering difficult, ethical concepts than dropping words and phrases into human settings, and reflecting on the light they bring or fail to bring. Literature can be helpful in this regard, for it provides settings to which we have common access between the covers of a book. I shall soon attempt, not to *analyse* the meaning of happiness as much as *present* this idea (up and running as it were) in the context of human lives.

Deepening understanding

But first, some further thoughts from Iris Murdoch, this time on the nature of meaning:

We have a different image of courage at forty from that which we had at twenty ... A deepening process, at any rate an altering and complicating process, takes place. There are two senses of 'knowing what a word means', one connected with ordinary language and the other very much less so. Knowledge of a value concept is something to be understood, as it were, in depth, and not in terms of switching onto some given impersonal network. (1970, p. 29)

The idea of happiness is under consideration as a 'value concept', associated with the 'good' to which ministrative practitioners aspire on behalf of others. As such, one would expect it to be loosely connected with ordinary language in the sense described here. A *deepening* process is required. Consider how this works with courage. It is surely correct to say that, all being well, our understanding of courage deepens as we grow older. Children don't normally use the word 'courage' but they certainly use the word 'brave', which they are taught to associate with queueing for a tetanus shot or waiting for the dentist. Adults normally face more complex challenges. Should I stay with or leave a difficult partner? they might ask. Either choice might be the courageous one, and their eventual decision may rest on their judgement about the directions in which courage and cowardice lie. Should I struggle with or exclude a difficult pupil? This too may be a question of courage in either direction, depending on many factors and circumstances, including a person's honesty about the difference between the child's interests and her own.

I suggested earlier that children *know* what happiness is; I meant of course that they *believe* they know. It takes time for this 'knowledge' to become 'problematized' as children discover that the anticipation of bliss may bring indigestion instead, and it is sometimes better 'in the long term' to defer than seize satisfaction. None of these difficulties are recognized by Richard Layard, who says 'by happiness I mean feeling good – enjoying life and wanting the feeling to be maintained. By unhappiness I mean feeling bad and wishing things were different' (Layard 2005). This is not *wrong*, exactly, but it is far from complete. It treats the idea of happiness as if it had no deeper meaning than that which is grasped by children. It can be fed into a simple algorithm of 'more' (getting my own way) and 'less' (submitting to incomprehensible adult demands). Layard owes his conception to Jeremy Bentham. 'Nature has placed mankind under the governance of two sovereign masters, *pain and pleasure*,' wrote Bentham. 'It is for them alone to point out what we ought to do, as well as to determine what we shall do' (Mill, 1962, p. 33). Unhappiness and happiness, for Bentham, simply *are* pain and pleasure, understood as opposing motives and guides to action, like a signpost that forks in two directions.

Bentham was, however, according to his disciple J. S. Mill, a 'boy to the last'. He was an empiricist 'who has had little experience':

> He never knew prosperity and adversity, passion nor satiety: he never had even the experiences which sickness gives; he lived from childhood to the age of eighty-five in boyish health. He knew no dejection, no heaviness of heart. He never felt life a sore and weary burthen. (1962, pp. 96–97)

In short, Bentham *hardly grew up*, and it is not surprising that his conception of happiness seems simple. He would have had difficulty, I think, understanding the 'deeper' conception that the following examples hopefully bring to light.

Wanting happiness on behalf of another

Imagine or recall the feelings and sensations of a woman who has just given birth to her first child. By 'sensations', I don't mean aches and pains; I mean the feelings she experiences at a basic level, physical and sensory as well as cognitive. It is obviously hard to put these into words; it includes the smell of the infant, the sense of the infant's comfort or discomfort, agitation, curiosity, stillness. I am talking, not about any mother, but about one who is destined to be 'good-enough'. She is attuned. She has formed a bond with this child, or is about to do so. She cherishes, or will soon cherish, the child. I think it is reasonable to use the word 'awe' to describe this encounter.

In his passionate essay 'Education', Martin Buber expresses a sense of awe before what he calls the 'primal potential might' of the young.

> This potentiality ... is the reality *child*: this phenomenon of uniqueness, which is more than just begetting and birth, this grace of beginning again and ever again.
>
> What greater care could we cherish or discuss than that this grace may not henceforth be squandered as before, that the might of newness may be preserved for renewal? (2002, p. 99)

He writes lyrically about the responsibilities of dialogue with the young:

> In our life and experience we are addressed; by thought and speech and action, by producing and by influencing we are able to answer. For the most part we do not listen to the address, or we break into it with chatter. But if the word comes to us and the answer proceeds from us then human life exists, though brokenly, in the world. The kindling of the response in that 'spark' of the soul,

the blazing up of the response, which occurs time and again, to the unexpectedly approaching speech, we term responsibility. (p. 109)

This kind of writing is not to everyone's taste. Philosopher Raimond Gaita would describe it as 'language at full stretch', and in Part Three of the book, we shall consider different stylistic and linguistic tendencies of philosophers. I shall suggest that 'language at full stretch' must be taken seriously if we are to think fruitfully about our engagements with the young.

The new mother, I have suggested, experiences awe, and we might add that she is fearful about the responsibilities of conversational responsiveness. *For the most part*, says Buber, *we do not listen to the address…* I am placing this failure – which is inevitable for us all, to some degree and at certain times – at the heart of our ethical enquiry into education and upbringing. Fear and awe are *appropriate* responses to the young, and they typically explode after a birth. For births bring heightened awareness, transformation and reverie, far from the mind-numbing mundanities of everyday life. I believe we shall fail to appreciate Buber's point if we are sceptical about happiness.

I only want my child to be happy, say many parents, and the concern seems to be that, without moral vigilance, they could be tempted to pursue lesser ambitions on behalf of their child. Fame, brilliance, success in a conventional sense: many parents are seduced by such prospects, though good-enough parents understand the perils of such seduction. One frequently hears this kind of thing from parents of disabled children. She will never be a Prime Minister, professor or CEO, they say, but who cares? I only want her to be happy.

This suggests that such parents undergo a moral reality check as they confront the demise of conventional dreams. They may be accused of self-deception, but there is another possibility: they are alert to what is important, what really matters and released from common delusions. The term 'happiness' seems right and unsubstitutable here, and I am suggesting that the happy-making wish in a serious sense belongs to the good-enough parent's intense first encounter with her child. She wants happiness in a deep sense. She may wince when her child is in pain and glow when the child experiences pleasure, but she knows that happiness means a good deal more than pleasure and the absence of pain. This mother may be so lost in her reverie that she is *all feeling*, with little to say beyond the mutterings of practicalities. But I am suggesting that the happy-making wish is stirring within her, bound to the new life that is no longer stirring within her. This is the idea of happiness that I hope to rescue from sentimentality, triviality or oblivion.

The scenario I have described finds a place for happiness or, more specifically, *hopes* for happiness, within a powerful human encounter. A fragment of dialogue from Ibsen's *A Doll's House* makes a similar point:

> Nora. Eight whole years – no, ever since we first knew each other – and never have we exchanged one serious word about serious things...
>
> Helmer. Nora, how unreasonable... How ungrateful you are! Haven't you been happy here?
>
> Nora. No, never. I thought I was, but I wasn't really.
>
> Helmer. Not... not happy!
>
> Nora. No, just gay, and you've always been so kind to me. But our house has never been anything but a playroom. I have been your doll wife, just as at home I was daddy's doll child. And the children in turn have been my dolls. I thought it was fun when you came and played with me just as they thought it was fun when I went and played with them. That's been our marriage, Torwald.

This is a turning point in the play. We have by now witnessed some private jokes and mincing animal games in which Nora's submissiveness before her husband is acted out. Nora does not say: 'I wasn't happy; I was miserable'; in fact, she seems to have had fun. She enjoyed herself, and for this she is appreciative ('you've always been so kind to me'), but 'happy', she suggests, has a deeper meaning. You cannot be happy when you are living a lie, when *pretence* belongs at the heart of a relationship, rather than at its frivolous margins. In these circumstances, the question of enjoyment becomes irrelevant and may even be an embarrassment. Nora was not happy; she was 'just gay'. Happiness in a serious sense was what she sought, and for the sake of this, she believed, she must leave her family.

Here is another example to consider briefly. Judith Kerr, the well-known children's writer, described her father's dying words to her mother in an interview on Radio 4. 'Be happy!' he said, and there was no suggestion that she must not also grieve and be unhappy about her loss. It may seem presumptuous to suppose that we can grasp his intention here, but I would venture to suggest that Kerr's father was urging his wife to try to find the *courage* that real happiness, difficult happiness perhaps, requires. Happiness in this sense is an ethical concept, grounded in virtue, particularly the virtues of courage and truthfulness. It is, as Adam Phillips says, a 'kind of key to our sense of ourselves', and it is opposed, not by unhappiness, but by reticence: a fear of being ourselves and living by our own lights.

This interpretation fits all three of my examples. The new parent, overwhelmed by the life she has created, hopes that her infant will have integrity, the courage to *become herself*, rather than the person others want her to be. Ibsen's Nora sought exactly the same thing, and I have suggested that a dying man's call on his wife to 'be happy' urges her to find the courage to live her own life, rather than settle mournfully into her dead husband's shadow. If I am right to connect courage and truthfulness (including 'being true to oneself') with a deeper conception of happiness, we may add that happiness in this sense is associated with cherishing: a kind of engagement with people, practices and objects that can be difficult, joyful and sometimes traumatic. It is the best we can be and do.

'Happiness is not the goal of life'

In a recent publication, *Happiness, Hope, and Despair: Rethinking the Role of Education*, Peter Roberts challenges what he sees as the unquestioned assumption that:

> education should make us feel better, not worse, and that teachers have a responsibility to prepare students to become happy, well integrated, contributing citizens in their lives beyond schools.
>
> The idea that education might, at least in part, be concerned with promoting unhappiness – and perhaps even a certain kind of despair – is very much at odds with the spirit of our age… Education, I maintain, is meant to create a state of discomfort, and to this extent may also make us unhappy, but is all the more important for that. (2016, pp. 1–3)

What follows is a fascinating essay around the thought that education is 'meant to create a state of discomfort'. Despite the prominence of the word 'happiness' in the book's title, this is not a book about happiness. Happiness is critiqued – especially as an object of obsession (p. 117) – but the 'importance' of happiness gets little more than a double negative:

> This is not to suggest that happiness is unimportant; nor does it imply a position 'against' happiness. Happiness, for most of us, is a vital component of a good life – but it need not be *the* goal to which we should always aspire.

Roberts is not a happiness sceptic, but he has little to say about *why* happiness might be a vital component of a good life. Like many people today, he is a child (and critic) of the Enlightenment, and it seems natural to him to associate the idea of happiness with the shift from a sacred to a secular perspective on life. For Enlightenment thinkers, happiness is a this-worldly entitlement rather than an other-worldly reward for virtuous conduct during our mortal careers. This was in many respects a valuable shift, associated not only with the decline of religion but also with the abolition of slavery and the crusade against pernicious forms of hierarchy; it allowed *human beings as such* to take ownership over their lives, rather than handing these to the rich and powerful (including God). But as we know only too well, the Enlightenment also brought unwelcome freedoms, including the freedom to turn happiness (along with much else) into a commodity that may be bought and sold without reference to the *care for others* that I am emphasizing in this chapter. Self-help gurus typically 'make people happier' for a fee, and they don't have to worry about difficult issues like courage and truthfulness. They may support happiness by praising people's courage, whether they are courageous or not!

Roberts turns all this on its head. He is (he says) 'at odds' with the spirit of the age, including ideas about what education is 'meant' to create, namely happy, well-integrated children. We should recall, however, that this is landmined territory, hard to navigate around without prompting doubt or dissent. Much of Roberts' work is about 'complicating' simple assumptions, not to mention (as in the title of his final chapter) the curriculum, so it may be unfair to examine a smattering of thoughts out of context. But I think we should feel as uneasy about the project of turning Enlightenment assumptions about happiness on their head as we do about those assumptions themselves. Why should education be 'meant to create' happiness *or* unhappiness? Is it 'meant to create' anything at all? Why *shouldn't* teachers help children to have 'happy, well-integrated' lives, so long as they *also* help them to learn, reflect and refine their childish understandings?

Above all, I think we should feel uneasy about the subversive thought that education should create unhappiness and despair. *It depends what is meant by this*, as our acceptance or rejection of the converse – that education might be concerned with promoting happiness – *depends on what is meant*. But then we can no more dismiss the latter *as such* than we can affirm the former *as such*, and 'it depends' is a phrase to which we must repeatedly return. We must guard against critiques of the idea that 'education should make children happy' as though this prescription can *only* mean: 'education must assist children in the pursuit of happiness'. There are other ways in which happiness may play a part in education and upbringing, as I have suggested.

Part of what Roberts means by his 'subversive thought' is that we should resist the modern impulse always to try to put smiles on children's faces or 'cure' their unhappiness through therapy. He is right about this, and about the fact that our efforts to 'make children happy' are often more about making ourselves happy (or 'guilt-free'). Roberts sees the capacity to endure and 'work with' despair without taking flight into quick-fix fantasies as a crucial aspect of education. This is also important, and it resonates with Iris Murdoch's ideas about deepening and complicating understanding. A 'complicated' conception of courage may help us (amongst other things) to *despair* courageously, instead of converting despair into trivial or distracting modes of 'feeling happy'.

Like Roberts, philosopher Sara Ahmed overturns Enlightenment motifs about happiness: 'I do not want to offer an alternative definition of happiness (a good happiness that can be rescued from bad happiness), as this would keep in place the very idea that happiness is what we should promote' (2010, p. 217). She then offers a beautiful piece of writing to describe or remind us what 'a good happiness' might be:

> If we think of happiness as a possibility that does not exhaust what is possible, if we lighten the load of happiness, then we can open things up. When happiness is no longer presumed to be a good thing, as what we aim for, or as what we should aim for, then we can witness happiness as a possibility that acquires significance by being a possibility alongside others. We can value happiness for its precariousness, as something that comes and goes, as life does.
>
> When I think of what makes happiness 'happy' I think of moments. Moments of happiness create texture, shared impressions: a sense of lightness in possibility.

'Lightening the load of happiness' means removing the ethics as well as the instrumental rationality from happiness. Ahmed has just said: 'I want to conclude with a reflection on how happiness can acquire significance if it is taken outside the domain of ethics.' 'Good' or 'light' happiness is no longer 'aimed for', let alone contrived or 'made to happen' through evidence-based interventions. This is reminiscent of John Stuart Mill, who famously said, 'those only are happy who have their minds fixed on some object other than their own happiness. Aiming thus at something else, they find happiness by the way' (1960, p. 100). Ahmed deflects the *sense of mastery* implicit in the happiness enhancement agenda, suggesting that happiness should be more 'precarious' than this.

I believe she is right, or mostly right. Happiness, she says, comes and goes 'as life does'; we should receive and accept it rather than strive to make it happen. I think she is wrong to try to take the ethics out of happiness, however. She is rightly concerned about a moral obsession: that each of us should pursue happiness for ourselves, and must endeavour to realize and maximize this imperative. This is obviously a form of utilitarian thinking, and it is as though there can be no gentler ethics that includes a desire for other people's happiness in a deep and unobtrusive sense that belongs to our reflections on a good life. This, I am suggesting, is the ethics of the good-enough parent or dying husband whose desire for happiness for another is nestled discreetly within the feelings and attitudes of cherishing. It is true: the term 'happiness' may and often does produce false gods. But it is not necessarily the *wrong* word to choose, and I think we must be as careful about concept-scepticism as we are about concept-obsession. (The concept of self-esteem has suffered from both fates in ways I find generally unhelpful.) Meaning, as Wittgenstein insisted, is embedded in use, which means that the word 'happiness' works well or badly for us depending on the contexts in which it appears, the thoughts it is used to express.

To want happiness for another is, as Ahmed says, to want moments of happiness, moments of possibility. I want to add: it is also to want some honest, if precarious, unfolding of these moments into fulfilling work, loving relationships and so on. It is no easy task to cultivate the kind of receptivity that allows such moments to occur, but this is part of what good-enough ministrative practitioners want for those they cherish. It is in this gentler domain that I hope to find the meaning not only of cherishing, but also of *intolerable* (from the perspective of one who cherishes) unhappiness or despair.

Happy moments

Happy moments in Ahmed's sense are normally quite rare. They aren't strung together in a utilitarian manner, as described by Richard Layard:

> is your happiness something, a bit like your temperature, that is always there, fluctuating away whether you think about it or not? If so, can I compare my happiness with yours?
> The answer to all these questions is essentially yes. (2006, p. 12)

Two entirely different conceptions of happiness. One: it fluctuates constantly on a positive/ negative scale. Two: it appears unbidden (and probably infrequently), if we are ready to receive it. The problem with the first conception is that, apart from being *nice*, we have no idea why happiness might be important for human beings. Despite her intention to remove happiness from the domain of ethics, Ahmed's conception responds to this question. We value happiness because it 'opens things up' and, particularly, opens us up to life.

I once knew a successful cellist who, after rehearsing Schubert or Beethoven with his quartet, would say things like 'it was divine'. Apart from the tedium of travel, he seemed to have had a perfect life in which 'happy moments' were indeed strung together rather as Layard describes. These moments were not simply 'nice'. We may use a variety of words to describe utilitarian happiness (cheerful, satisfied, contented etc.), and we may arguably use numbers. (Consider Martin Seligman: 'Lying awake at night, you probably ponder, as I have, how to go from plus two to plus seven in your life, not just how to go from minus five to minus three and feel a little less miserable day by day.') Happy moments in the sense that interests me here seem to *require* the word 'happy', if not another (like 'divine') that takes us further down the road to ecstasy. Numbers (e.g. 10 out of 10) seem ridiculous in this context, and it is the richness of happiness in Ahmed's sense that points not only *to*, but also *through*, ethics in a direction one might call aesthetic. Happy moments bring *beauty* into our lives, and I shall later suggest that the Greek word for beautiful, 'kalon', should be *permitted* to bring aesthetics into ethics. Many scholars, translating 'kalon' as 'noble' or 'fine' when speaking about ethics, make it impossible for readers of Aristotle in English translation to grasp this connection. (We shall return to this.)

Marilynne Robinson's novel *Home* (2012) is a literary masterpiece in which the joys and agonies of cherishing others are poetically explored. I want to quote a passage in which the term 'happiness' appears with the beauty, the resonance and virtual *untranslatability* that we sometimes associate with the experience. This passage illustrates the way in which the *word* 'happiness' may resonate in a text in rather the way that 'happy moments' resonate in a life. It is not (as many philosophers argue) substitutable by words like 'flourishing' or 'well-being', which lack the quality of fleeting but unsurpassable beauty that gives sense to the thought that happiness is something we ought to want for others.

Home is a novel about a Presbyterian family with nine adult children, seven of whom are leading conventionally successful lives away from the parental home, with partners, jobs, children and so on. Only Glory and Jack remain at home with their elderly father. (Their mother died many years ago.) All we need to know in order to understand the following passage is that Glory cherishes Jack, Jack suffers acutely, and Jack is 'bad' (he has done 'bad things' that landed him in jail), but also 'good' (he aspires to be 'good') and even 'beautiful'. At one point, Glory wanted to tell her brother 'how beautiful it was to have taken up his father in his arms that way'. This is Aristotle's conception of ethical beauty (*kalon*).

One day, Glory buys some clothes for Jack, washes them and hangs them on the line. Jack sees her hanging the clothes and asks, 'Those for me?'

A conversation ensues in which Glory's passionate care for her brother is present in every remark, every gesture. The text continues:

> Why hadn't she bought clothes for him weeks ago? Because he was a stranger she was afraid of offending with so personal an attention. Because her buying clothes for him would allude to his poverty and offend him. Because it might seem like a subject of conversation for people who saw her buying them and this would embarrass and offend him. Because he was vain, and particular, and Jack. Cheap, sturdy work clothes were not the kind of thing he thought he should wear, and they would offend him. But in fact she saw him check the clothes on the line several times, and when one of them was dry enough, he brought it in and ironed it and put it on. The pants were heavier and took longer to dry. She saw him check them, too, then walk over by the orchard, pick a fallen apple off the ground, throw it up on the barn roof, and wait and catch it when it came down, and throw it again. Her brothers all did that when they were boys. Jack looked a little stiff, as if he were making an experiment in attempting this lonely game after so many years. Tentative as he was, it might have meant happiness. (p. 203)

It might have meant... This is subjunctive happiness, happiness as a possibility, and it is also happiness associated with (the title of the book) *home*. This passage illustrates many of the ideas we are exploring here. *Why hadn't Glory bought clothes for him weeks ago?* For a multitude of reasons relating to the fine line between cherishing and condescending, Glory gives her 'particular brother' Jack ('bad' as he is) the gift of her efforts to do the former without inadvertently doing the latter. 'It might have meant happiness' offers a *tentative* clarification, embedded in 'attempting this lonely game after so many years', of the *unclear* idea of happiness. And it is no accident, as I said, that Jack seems to have been 'experimenting' with the idea of home. For this idea – along with the ideas of return, recovery and indeed 'finding oneself' – touches on what we want for others when we 'want them to be happy'.

I have not tried to define the word 'happiness'. I have talked about childish and deeper conceptions of happiness, linking these with the idea of *growing up*, about which I will say more in later chapters. Unclear as the deeper conception is, I have offered what I hope is a partial clarification by identifying the happy-making wish with two things. The first and most important is that we want others to cherish. We want them to find value outside themselves, in people, practices, nature, objects, in the special sense that is yet to be explored in detail, but for which 'cherishing' is a pointer. If music makes someone blissfully happy, and if she is willing to engage with it seriously and be honest about her talents or capacities, then she should have every opportunity to create a life for herself of numerous 'divine moments'. These will not, on the whole, be 'unbidden'; they are associated with the discovery of what makes her *deeply* happy. Education should certainly play a part in helping the young to learn about themselves in this way.

But they should also be 'open' to beautiful or joyful moments that could never have been anticipated. These are moments that stand outside one's chosen engagements, moments of grace perhaps. One of the ways in which adults cultivate 'openness' in the young is by opposing what I earlier called *intolerable* unhappiness and despair. Negative emotions are certainly an aspect of every human life, but some people get stuck; their learning is, or can be, permanently inhibited by fear, shame, anxiety, depression. Instead of being open, they become closed, shut off. I want to close with some remarks about what this means.

What is wrong with unhappiness?

In *The Drama of the Gifted Child* (1983), Alice Miller relates the following:

> I was out for a walk and noticed a young couple a few steps ahead, both tall; they had a little boy with them, about two years old, who was running alongside and whining.... The two had just bought themselves ice cream bars on sticks from the kiosk and were licking them with enjoyment. The little boy wanted one, too. His mother said affectionately, 'Look, you can have a bite of mine, a whole one is too cold for you.' The child did not want just one bite but held out his hand for the whole ice, which his mother took out of his reach again. He cried in despair, and soon exactly the same thing was repeated with his father: 'There you are, my pet,' said his father affectionately, 'you can have a bite of mine.' 'No, no,' cried the child and ran ahead again, trying to distract himself. Soon he came back again and gazed enviously and sadly up at the two grown-ups, who were enjoying their ice creams contentedly and at one. Time and again he held out his little hand the whole ice cream bar, but the adult hand with its treasure was withdrawn again.
>
> The more the child cried, the more it amused his parents. It made them laugh a lot and they hoped to humour him along with their laughter, too: 'Look, it isn't so important, what a fuss you're making.' Once the child sat down on the ground and began to throw little stones over his shoulder in his mother's direction, but then he suddenly got up again and looked around anxiously, making sure that his parents were still there. When his father had completely finished his ice cream, he gave the stick to the child and walked on. The little boy licked the bit of wood expectantly, looked at it, threw it away, wanted to pick it up again but

did not do so, and a deep sob of loneliness and disappointment shook his small body. Then he trotted obediently after his parents. (pp. 86–87)

Why is this disturbing? Of course, if we want to leave no ethical stone unturned, we may reserve judgement about the possibility that this was a one-off event in which two 'affectionate' parents (for some reason unusually absorbed with each other) inadvertently humiliated their little boy. Perhaps they realized what they were doing, picked him up and did their best to console him. Or perhaps 'father' was not really a father at all; he was an exciting new lover and this child's normally good-enough mother quickly understood that on this occasion, she had not been good-enough at all.

Setting these possibilities aside, this scenario paints a picture of a child whose unhappiness should be relieved as a matter of urgency. He may, as an adult, surmount the experience of being (let us suppose) routinely humiliated by his parents, but he may *not* surmount this, and there may be indications throughout his childhood that *as a consequence* he lacks the resources to learn, discover what will 'make him happy', build a decent life. Perceptive teachers may understand that this child's dramas of unlearning are *rooted* in habitual humiliation, but they will be under pressure, if they speak about this, to defer to empirical evidence and refrain from 'blaming the parents'. In some cases, however, their judgement will be right.

'Every child', says Alice Miller, 'has a legitimate narcissistic need to be noticed, understood, taken seriously, and respected by his mother' (1983, p. 49). We can take it that this means 'by his father' too, as well as any other adults (e.g. teachers) with whom he has prolonged contact. The need to be 'noticed, understood, taken seriously, respected' is common to us all, and I think it is safe to assume that the younger a child is, the more profound is this need.

The last statement may sound controversial, and one of my aims in this book is to draw attention to the striking indifference of most philosophers – including those who are involved with ethics, education, emotion – to the phenomenon of infancy as understood by psychoanalysis. Notable exceptions are Martha Nussbaum and Nancy Sherman (both distinguished philosophers and classical scholars), and I agree with the former when she says 'adult human emotions cannot be understood without understanding their history in infancy and childhood'. There are many reasons for dismissing this view, but they are not, I think, good ones, as we are reminded by Iris Murdoch's point about deepening. This is not simply about a point about our grasp of *concepts*; it is about the deepening of moral and emotional insights. And of all things, it seems plain as day that emotions require deep rather than shallow understanding, which I take to mean understanding beyond familiar cognitive and non-cognitive models. For this, I shall argue that psychoanalytic insights are not only valuable but also needed. But we are not at this point yet.

The little boy in Miller's scenario suffered unacceptably as people suffer when they are bullied, ostracized, discriminated against for the colour of their skin, their disability and so on. He was humiliated and condescended to by, of all people, his parents, and it seems likely that this was a regular occurrence. Psychoanalyst Donald Winnicott writes beautifully about the infant's discovery of herself or himself through the 'mirror' of her/his mother's/father's face (which includes tone of voice, physical holding and so on). The infant is *all sensation*, and this is the foundation from which lasting emotions are created and formed. One who does not experience what I call cherishing – meaning, at this stage, the intimate *sensations* of being cherished – is likely to experience lasting (not necessarily permanent) unhappiness. Not the enhancement of happiness, but wise attention to a history of confused, distracted or unloving mirroring is what adults must offer children.

4

Should We Equip Children for
Twenty-First-Century Life?

We will completely overhaul the curriculum – to ensure that the acquisition of knowledge within rigorous subject disciplines is properly valued and cherished.

Michael Gove MP (2009)

Why introduce children to the best literature, history, science or mathematics unless this is in some way personally beneficial to themselves or to others?

John White (2011), p. 121

What should children feel? Which emotions should we encourage them to have, and which should we discourage? In the previous chapter I discussed a popular answer: they should feel happy rather than unhappy. Coming from scientists and philosophers as it frequently does, this answer reinforces a parental desire that seems, at one level, natural and right. I don't mind what kind of person she is, say enlightened parents. I'm not ambitious for my child and have no stake in her being clever, famous, beautiful or athletic. I only want her to be happy!

We saw that philosopher Nel Noddings supports this view. 'Children learn best when they are happy', she declares. 'Happy people are rarely mean, violent, or cruel.' William James – forerunner of the positive psychology movement – tells us *why* the 'attitude of unhappiness' is bad: it is 'not only painful, it is mean and ugly'. But 'children should feel happy' is not a sustainable imperative, and for all his severity towards the 'attitude of unhappiness', James was clear about this. He warned us not to take flight into its more attractive alternative, for happiness imports its own dangers. It may include 'blindness and insensibility to opposing facts', an unwillingness to acknowledge and engage with the painful realities of life.

What does this mean? How far should children be expected to suffer in the service of valuable learning? What *is* valuable learning, and why should it be assumed that this must mean academic learning? Readers will be familiar with the progressive idea that we should attempt to 'enhance children' by offering a curriculum that is relevant rather than irrelevant, engaging rather than alienating, true to the natures of media-savvy, streetwise, ethnically diverse and often mentally fragile twenty-first-century kids. Why should valuable learning mean facing the 'painful realities of life', as traditionally conceived for a privileged elite? Why waste time with Latin and Shakespeare, geometry and mediaeval history, when you could be honing children's life skills, enhancing their capacities to flourish in a twenty-first-century setting? An unexamined life, said Plato, is not worth living, and it is in a spirit of kindness as well as fearless philosophy that some have extended the thought: an unexamined curriculum – inherited rather than designed – is not worth teaching.

Philosopher John White, for example, says: 'Schools should be mainly about equipping people to lead a fulfilling life…. In one way, this sounds banal: isn't this what we all expect of them? In another, it is anything but. If we were *really* aiming at fulfilment and had a blank sheet to plan how we went about it, schools, especially secondary schools, would become very different places (p.1)'. This is a radical thought invoking the philosophical tabula rasa with a distinctly digital resonance. *Delete* that file. *Open* a new one. Think creatively, think afresh. *Why* should we teach subjects like literature, history, science or mathematics if children are unlikely to benefit personally from this education?

As with happiness, this seems to belong to an enlightened rather than unenlightened worldview. The standard school curriculum, with its emphasis on academic rather than practical or physical learning, is (it is said) antiquated and regressive. It bears no relation to the well-being or flourishing of twenty-first-century citizens, and it entrenches class differences by rewarding intellectual tendencies that are cultivated by wealth and leisure. What's the point of school? asks this brand of educationist. What are, or should be, the *proper* aims of education? The enlightened answer seems simple and obvious: education must promote the flourishing or well-being of all.

By rejecting a lazy reliance on tradition, the progressive view taps into the argument we were exploring in Part One of the book: that education has an ethical core, and we must reflect carefully on what this means. But is it 'lazy' to suppose (as Matthew Arnold famously argued) that children should have an opportunity to experience the 'best'? The best thinking, the best poetry, the best accounts we have of ourselves as human beings, of nature and the universe? What does it *mean* to relativize the curriculum to 'personal benefit', as White suggests?

I hope it is clear to readers that the recycling of traditional norms is far from my aim; on the contrary, I am exploring ways in which we can restore *people* with their dramas of learning and unlearning to our ministrative practices of education and upbringing. But the curriculum is a policymaker's creation and makes no reference to what is suitable or appropriate for this or that child. Ancient history, Latin or quadratic equations may be hellish for Sohail or Fred, but paradise for Toni or Jade.

In *War and Peace*, Tolstoy airs the thought that we *ought to believe in happiness*. He meant, of course, happiness in a serious, life-affirming sense, and he reminds us that believing in one thing often means doubting or disbelieving in another. '[Natasha] was at that highest pitch of bliss when one becomes completely good and kind, and cannot believe in the existence or possibility of evil, unhappiness or sorrow' (pp. 542–543). Many educational debates (like religious ones) seem to turn a similar question: what do I, should I, believe in? What should I *dis*believe in?

Ought we to 'believe in' Latin as a focus of study? Or advanced mathematics or the history of civilizations? Should we 'disbelieve in' film studies or sport psychology? There is a great deal to worry us in the political rhetoric of 'rigorous subject disciplines', especially when this is allied, as by Michael Gove when he was Education Secretary, with the rhetoric of 'plummeting in the rankings' of global educational achievement. Gove's emphasis on academic rigour threatened something much worse than irrelevance, namely mental illness. Research indicated an explosion of psychiatric problems in the young during Gove's period of power, and this was attributed to the focus on both traditional subject learning and rigour. Not only were children forced to learn subjects they found uninteresting or irrelevant; their progress was finely monitored, with 'failure' a terrifying and ever-present prospect.

There is a significant gap between our *legitimate* concerns about all this and the idea that we should 'disbelieve in' Latin, Greek or quadratic equations – or relegate them, as I shall say, to a curricular scrapheap. I think we should listen carefully to the sceptical tone of philosophers and educationalists who respond to Gove-like policies with the equivalent of a digital cleanup: empty your hard drive and start again.

This is a political response to a political folly, and it ignores individuals with their own potentialities and sources of happiness, expressed in the dramas of human life. One may 'believe in' Latin and Greek, not as an elitist reverence for a hallowed tradition, but as a source of fulfilment *for some*. This seems perfectly obvious, and my concern in this chapter echoes my concern throughout the book: that our efforts to guide and educate the young often suffer from generality. 'The young' may be an ineliminable policymaker's concept, but teachers and parents must attempt to *think well* about individual human beings.

Some people 'believe in' a classical education rather as Tolstoy's Natasha believed in happiness: it makes them *feel* good. Their erudition will (they suppose) inspire envy, admiration and awe, easing their own unhappiness by stimulating it in others. These people are not to be admired, but throw their classical education on to the scrapheap and you will prevent *some children* – who may be rich or poor, able-bodied or disabled, immigrants or UK citizens – from ever coming to cherish the history, philosophy or poetry of ancient civilizations. This is a loss, and it contravenes the spirit and integrity of education. Let's look more closely at the arguments.

What's the point of school?

Guy Claxton opens his book *What's the point of school?* (2008) like this:

> The purpose of education is to prepare young people for the future. Schools should be helping young people to develop the capacities they will need to thrive. What they need, and want, is the confidence to talk to try things out, to handle tricky situations, to stand up for themselves, to ask for help, to think new thoughts.... But they are not getting it. There is no evidence that being able to solve simultaneous equations, or discuss the plot of Hamlet, equips young people to deal with life. (2008, p. vi)

This book predates an interesting speech in 2011 by Education Minister Michael Gove. Claxton and Gove are engaged in a single conversation, a single debate, approached from opposite angles. What's the point of school? What is it for? From one direction, education's purpose is to initiate the young into 'the best that has been thought and said'. From the other, it is to prepare young people for the future. But are the conversational partners really listening to one another? Must Shakespeare, Greek or advanced mathematics *impede* preparation for future?

During his watch as education minister, Gove produced some exceedingly bad arguments. Consider this (Gove 2011):

> When Zuckerburg [Facebook's founder] applied to college he was asked what languages he could speak and write. As well as English he listed French, Hebrew, Latin and ancient Greek. He also studied maths and science at school. He would have done very well in our English baccalaureate. And the breakthroughs

his rigorously academic education helped create are now providing new opportunities for billions. Which is why we need schools that equip its students with the intellectual capital to make the most of these opportunities. Critically that means giving every child a profound level of mathematical and scientific knowledge, as well as deep immersion in the reasoning skills generated by subjects such as history and modern foreign languages.

https://www.gov.uk/government/speeches/michael-gove-to-twyford-church-of-england-high-school

There is a resounding inferential error in this argument. Gove draws a universal conclusion (we need schools that equip students with intellectual capital) from two particular premises (Zuckerburg had a rigorously academic education; Zuckerburg provided new opportunities for billions). The phrase 'which is why' in the middle of the paragraph fails to establish the conclusion to which Gove is committed. A good rejoinder might be: what about Steve Jobs? He was a college dropout who took courses in subjects like calligraphy, but he was no less successful than Zuckerburg.

What about this child? What about that? Such questions naturally occur to teachers, whether or not they are familiar with the technicalities of bad argumentation. Little Samuel acquired a passion for Roman history through the Horrible History books he found in the school library and has a habit of shouting 'ecce homo!' in the middle of football matches. Charlie *listens* to his classmates speaking Swahili or Pashto, and is curious about the vocabulary and grammatical structures of these languages. These are white working-class boys who are expected to take up apprenticeships at age 16, but might they benefit from a highly academic curriculum? Why should the reasonable aspiration to prepare children for twenty-first-century life (requiring, as Claxton says, the confidence to try things out, handle tricky situations, stand up for themselves etc.) undermine the traditional educational 'belief in' interesting knowledge that achieves little beyond the enrichment of life? For budgetary and other reasons, it may be impossible to include classical languages and history on Samuel's school curriculum, but we shouldn't pretend that Samuel may not be the loser.

It would be misleading to suggest that proponents of 'twenty-first-century flourishing' are necessarily hostile to academic learning. As children differ, so do these proponents, and John White for one has made it perfectly clear that he is no enemy of such learning. He calls for a brave conversation: I have called this radical, which means that we should banish complacency and examine cherished assumptions. I agree. What concerns me is, as I said, a *tone* of scepticism that presents certain ideas, certain concepts, as suspicious. One of these is the idea of knowledge without clear practical or social benefits, such as knowledge of ancient or mediaeval history. White refers to this as 'knowledge for its own sake', contrasting it with 'knowledge for flourishing or well-being'. He reminds us that it is *useful* to understand our political and financial systems, not to mention the risks associated with drugs and sex, and he suggests that schools should impart knowledge that will help children to *function well* in these domains. The 'point' of certain historical knowledge, like the 'point' of certain language learning, is far murkier and should (White argues) open up a discussion.

Nothing wrong with this, but where I differ from White is that I fervently hope the discussion will lead in a certain direction: towards a recognition that *cherishing what is good* – in addition to functioning well in banks and polling stations – belongs to the ethical core of education and upbringing. The idea of 'knowledge for its own sake' introduces a polarity between, to put it crudely, useful and useless knowledge, from which perspective *cherishing what is good* may appear utterly useless. It is impossible to think in terms of this polarity without advancing sternly on the idea of 'uselessness'. This is particularly so at the current time, when many children suffer acutely from educational pressures and we are desperate to alleviate their suffering. 'Knowledge for its own sake' sounds like a luxury for the elite and a cruel burden on twenty-first-century children.

Education for well-being, which aims to enhance well-being or flourishing in adult life through curricular reform, sends 'knowledge for its own sake' into the naughty corner and promotes thoughtful attention to children's well-being that cuts through Gove-like obsessions with global ranking. In many ways this should be applauded, but we should also be concerned about the losses that ensue – or so I argue – from polarized thinking. This project of well-being-inspired curricular reform points in two directions: towards *additional* classes devoted entirely to well-being (these may focus on qualities like resilience, grit or happiness) and towards the *elimination* of subjects like Latin or mediaeval history that are believed to fail the well-being test. Both developments should concern us.

Is emotional education risky?

In a report called *Grit: The Skills for Success and How They Are Grown*, Yvonne Roberts urges us to include 'education for grit' on the school curriculum. 'Grit', it seems, is a gritty word for describing what positive psychologists usually refer to as resilience. Roberts' argument is summed up by policymaker Geoff Mulgan in the preface of the report:

> Over the last two decades a gulf has opened up between what education systems provide and what children need. Education systems rightly provide children with skills in numeracy and literacy and academic qualifications. But the emphasis on a set of core academic skills, and a culture of intensive testing, has too often squeezed out another set of skills – how to think creatively, how to collaborate, how to empathise – at the very time when they are needed more than ever. (2009, p. 6)

The idea of a gulf between provision and need is a familiar feature of this discussion. Guy Claxton, as we saw, distinguishes similarly between 'what children need' and 'what children are getting'. Basing her argument on wide-ranging research, including research in positive psychology, Roberts explores the theme of *life skills*, particularly skills needed for twenty-first-century life, of which she argues grit is key. We can see her point. In an age of economic turbulence and emotional instability, the capacities to get up, carry on, fail again and fail better may be crucial for survival. But what *is* grit? Why are some children devastated by failure, terrified of defeat? Will 'education for grit' help or hinder? Could it even make things worse?

Discussing the Penn Resiliency Programme, Roberts writes:

> It is a cognitive behavioural intervention for adolescents that teaches [children] gradually to change the beliefs that are fuelling their maladaptive emotions (or more colloquially, to control the volume of their 'internal radio station – one that plays nothing but you 24/7'). It encourages them to keep a sense of perspective; to 'think outside the box' and more flexibly about the multiple and varied causes of problems ('self disputing') and to restrict the tendency to 'catastrophise' that fuels negative thoughts. (2009, pp. 21–22)

I have no doubt that, as its proponents claim, this programme has helped some children, at least temporarily. Roberts herself approves the programme unreservedly, but reading on, one may wonder why. She goes on to talk about children who are *falling behind* in their developmental abilities:

> What protective or competence-enhancing factors might help to build resilience in children so far behind in their developmental abilities? [Researchers] argue that there are no universal protective factors. Instead, these may vary according to the age of the child and developmental outcome being targeted. 'Paradoxically, the promotive processes in one context may prove to be risky in another,' they

say.... The researchers conclude: 'The major implication of multiple risk models is that interventions need to be as complex as development itself.' This view echoes.... John Dewey's belief that learning is the interaction between a young person and their environment, which means that the experience is different for each individual. (ibid., p. 39)

Paradoxically, the promotive processes in one context may prove to be risky in another. This is only paradoxical if one is thinking at a high level of generality, as Roberts clearly is. There is no paradox in the thought that certain plants enhance the health of one species while posing risks to another, or that certain drugs are beneficial for you but dangerous for your child. Thinking contextually allows us to understand this without difficulty, as we understand that a project of national enhancement through evidence-based intervention must be approached with care.

Positive psychology promotes what seems on the face of it a worthy ideal: focus on the bright side of life, concentrate on 'what goes right', instead of dwelling neurotically (as Freud-inspired psychologists are said to do) on 'what goes wrong'. But this assumes a robust distinction between good and bad emotions, what goes right and what goes wrong. Such distinctions are idealized and especially unsuitable for application to classrooms full of children. Most classrooms contain children at different developmental levels, and teachers are not always able to discern these levels clearly or determine which children are vulnerable to which interventions. This is not the job for which they were trained. It is one thing to say that teachers should aim to be conversationally responsive, particularly when children are young and vulnerable. It is another to say that they are responsible for raising the moral bar, so that a graph-like enhancement of qualities like grit or resilience can be demonstrated. Good teachers are always alert to and concerned about the potential for harm to their pupils. We shall return to this thorny issue in Chapter 6.

Aristotle would have shared these concerns. To be a good or wise human being, on his view, one must be able to judge what is going on in particular circumstances. The moral education of children must be responsive to individuals, and adults who undertake this in group settings should, by implication, be alert to developmental immaturity. This is often a consequence of inadequate emotional education in the early years: being raised by mothers who are themselves children, living in poverty or war zones. This can bring not only unhappiness but also grandiose and even radicalized solutions.

Aristotle was not optimistic about the prospects for emotionally undeveloped children, and it is a serious and under-explored question how far classroom teaching should be expected to 'enhance' the desperately emotionally immature.

When resilience is 'taught' as a 'life skill', we may be missing the vital detail, the rage or shame or terror that renders some children anything but resilient. They may, as Roberts observes, have a tendency to 'catastrophize', but could this be because they have experienced and continue to experience catastrophes in their own homes or countries? An emotionally stable child may be responsive to your efforts to curb her tendencies towards what William James calls the 'pining, puling, mumping mood'. ('What', James asks, 'is more injurious to others? What less helpful as a way out of the difficulty?' (1971, p. 102)). An unstable child may become *more* anxious and depressed as she realizes that she *can't* curb her gloomy moods, or convert them, as positive psychologists recommend, into cheerful or happy ones.

Emotional education is complex and potentially hazardous. At the very least, it requires a sensitive conception of emotion that does not polarize good and bad. It is assumed by positive psychologists that resilience, like self-esteem, is a positive attribute, and no doubt this is often the case. Thinking physically, we know that resilient materials withstand shocks, retain or resume their original state on impact, are resistant to foreign bodies. But how resilient should we be? How would you feel if your resilient spouse withstood not only the misery of his own chemotherapy, but also the misery of yours? Just like materials, resilient people can be tough, and from an emotional point of view this may not be ideal. It is human sometimes to weep and accept vulnerability. When, where and why is resilience good? How can resilience programmes gauge and monitor such things? How can we feel at ease with them if they fail to do so? How can we be sure that their effects are truly beneficial?

What do children need and what do schools provide?

The discourse of need and provision is hopelessly blunt. If we talk about need, we need to ask: for what purpose, towards what end? There are many needs, and most are unclassifiable. They belong to teachers as well as children, and in the medial space are played out dramas of learning and unlearning in which subject-disciplines are loved and hated, rejected and tolerated, and sometimes gradually, painstakingly, through strenuous effort on both sides, accepted and even cherished. What matters is the detail, the variation, and good policy is built on the recognition that this must be so. There are of course questions about 'what schools provide', amongst them questions about the curriculum. But there are also pressing questions about *how* schools provide what they provide, how teachers respond conversationally to what Joseph Dunne calls the 'needs, aptitudes and difficulties' of students. My concern about the curricular scrapheap is that it discourages us from recognizing this, stigmatizing subjects like ancient history that are believed to fail the most curious of tests: the so-called well-being test.

Why should such a test exist? Human passions are endlessly diverse, just as temperaments, dispositions and abilities are endlessly diverse. The crucial curricular issue, it seems to me, is one of threatened loss, as tight budgets limit our capacity to 'cherish rather than squander' the passions, or potentialities, of the young. This is a regrettable fact, and it is supplemented at the present time by a culture of nihilism. I would say that the radical well-being agenda – delete the old file, start anew – betrays an unwillingness to *cherish what is good*. It is easier to *doubt* that this phrase has meaning than it is, first, to 'believe in' its meaning and, second, to articulate what it means.

Philosopher Richard Peters was a traditionalist; he characterized education as the transmission of intrinsically valuable knowledge. He made it clear that this dry-sounding idea is actually about passion and our 'quality of living':

> 'There is a quality of life which lies always beyond the mere fact of life'. The great teacher is he who can convey this sense of quality to another, so that it haunts his every endeavor and makes him sweat and yearn to fix what he thinks and feels in a fitting form.... It is education that provides that touch of eternity under the aspect of which endurance can pass into dignified, wry acceptance, and animal enjoyment into a quality of living. (2010, p. 74)

For Peters, the gulf that matters in education differs subtly from the one that concerns Mulgan and Claxton. Children, says Peters, need to discover a 'quality of living' and there is a lamentable gulf between this and the provision by teachers of information, pedantry, dry facts. Remember Gradgrind, who trained children to define 'horse' thus:

> Quadruped. Graminivorous. Forty teeth, namely twenty-four grinders, four eye-teeth, and twelve incisive. Sheds coat in the spring; in marshy countries, sheds hoofs, too. Hoofs hard, but requiring to be shod with iron. Age known by marks in mouth.

Here the extremes of dry, factual education are richly satirized by Dickens. A. N. Whitehead, a mathematician whose book *The Aims of Education* (1967) influenced Peters, also attacks the tendency to *desiccate* knowledge:

> There is no royal road to learning through an airy path of brilliant generalisations.... There is only one subject matter for education, and that is

Life in all its manifestations. Instead of this single unity, we offer children – Algebra, from which nothing follows; Geometry, from which nothing follows; Science, from which nothing follows; History, from which nothing follows; a Couple of Languages, never mastered; and lastly, most dreary of all, Literature, represented by plays of Shakespeare, with philological notes and short analyses of plot and character to be in substance committed to memory. (pp. 6–7)

What is striking about this passage is that it captures an ideal that virtually everyone shares. Education should be about 'Life in all its manifestations': this is what children need to learn about, what many schools do not provide. Given our testing obsessions at the present time, the passage prompts us to ask whether we have progressed very far beyond Gradgrind after all. Are we teaching a kind of geometry, history, literature, *from which nothing follows*? The answer, from almost everyone who currently claims an interest in education, is a resounding 'yes'. *Much* of the time, we agree, this is what teaching has been reduced to; and recent educational policies are responsible for this.

We are unanimous, then, about the baneful gulf between Life and Education, and as we realize this, the idea of a well-being test that subject disciplines may pass or fail appears increasingly odd. Not only traditionalists like Peters, but also so-called progressive thinkers like Claxton, Mulgan, Roberts and White must applaud Whitehead's argument in this passage. Whitehead is not suggesting that algebra, history, Shakespeare etc. are useless. He distinguishes, rather, between different *manners* in which knowledge is imparted and received, whether this is done 'ertly or inertly':

In training a child to activity of thought, above all things we must beware of what I will call 'inert ideas' – that is to say, ideas that are merely received into the mind without being utilised, or tested, or thrown into fresh combinations.

In the history of education, the most striking phenomenon is that schools of learning, which at one epoch are alive with a ferment of genius, in a succeeding generation exhibit merely pedantry and routine. The reason is, that they are overladen with inert ideas. (ibid., p. 1)

Whitehead does not prompt us to ask: should we teach history or IT? Literature or media studies? Natural history or sport psychology? He prompts us to consider whether we transmit knowledge in lively or moribund, ert or inert ways. It is not Hamlet that is useless; it is Hamlet as plot summary, philological notes, imagery grid, testable KS3 resource. Shakespeare as rich poetic drama has the power to enhance our lives 'perennially', as Wordsworth did for utilitarian JS Mill when this arithmetical philosophy led to an emotional breakdown.

When we consider the manner in which knowledge is dished up to GCSE and A Level students, it seems obvious that ertia and inertia, rather than enhancive and unenhancive knowledge content, is the distinction educators and policy-makers need to examine. Children are bored and depressed by high-stakes bullet pointed lists, which desiccate fascinating material, present hoops to jump through and place pupils in terrifying competition with one another. It is my belief that if we could address this problem clear-sightedly, the debate about which knowledge passes and fails the well-being test would be seen as pointless, as it is. The problem is that no-one appears to have a clue what the test amounts to. How do we *decide* and *agree* which knowledge content has and has not the power to enhance well-being? Whose well-being are we talking about?

It is interesting that, on the last point, left wing journalist Melissa Benn and Conservative Education Minister Michael Gove concur. It is unsurprising that Gove favours a knowledge agenda; more surprising is the discovery that egalitarian Benn does the same:

> Young people need not just efficient instruction but the opportunity for exploration – of ideas, history, literature, poetry, music, art, film, politics. These are the things that make and keep us human, and if we don't learn how to begin to think about these things when young, we may never return to them as adults. (2011)

Benn is not asking us to put these subjects on hold while we debate their enhancive powers. She believes they are valuable in rather the way Mill, Peters and Whitehead believe they are valuable: because they are rooted in our humanity. Implicit here is a willingness to identify certain knowledge as *intrinsically* valuable, which enhancement thinkers are unwilling to do. The question posed by the latter – which kinds of knowledge content enhance well-being? – risks cutting the connection with individual lives through over-generalization. As Benn implies, placing traditional knowledge on the curricular scrapheap because it is believed to fail the well-being test can mean loss and deprivation for countless individuals whose lives will never be enriched by it.

Disciplines and Discipline

I have presented contemporary educational discourse as polarized between the ideas of well-being enhancement and knowledge for its own sake (or intrinsically valuable knowledge). Enhancement thinkers see well-being as the *overriding* educational aim; they mount an assault on the idea of knowledge for its own sake, which is cast as a luxury for the elite unless it is shown to serve enhancive aims. Knowledge advocates are not so exclusive. They agree that well-being (happiness in a perennial sense, quality of living, Life with a capital L) is at the heart of education, and say that knowledge in its richest, most *emotional* sense is bound up with this.

Note that the knowledge agenda does not depend on instrumental thinking, though it can sometimes sound this way (as when Mill talks about poetry as 'medicine for the mind'). Rather, it says that intrinsically valuable knowledge *enriches* life. This is a humanistic educational aim that does not pretend to be scientific. We can agree that this is important without being tempted to conduct a survey, for it rests ultimately on our thoughts and judgements about what makes human lives worthwhile. We shall return to this point.

So we have knowledge as a humanistic educational aim in one column – here well-being has a central place – and well-being as an overriding educational aim, to which knowledge aims are beholden, in the other. The latter lends itself to science; it encourages the question 'which kinds of knowledge do/ do not enhance well-being?' which I have suggested is obscure and possibly meaningless. It is expressed in Claxton's idea that equations, Hamlet and much else besides *fail to equip young people for life*. This prompts further questions: which young people? How do you know? What does it mean to 'equip young people for life'?

The exclusivity of the enhancement agenda, by contrast with the inclusivity of the knowledge agenda, betrays something of philosophical importance. Advocates of the first are clearly *uncomfortable* with the idea of intrinsically valuable knowledge. For the philosopher Wittgenstein, discomfort with ideas should be the mainspring of philosophy, that is, of fruitful reflection. It should prompt what he called 'philosophical investigations' rather than leading directly to conclusions with which we feel more (as we now say) in our comfort zone. He thought that, without examining the underlying discomfort, the latter are likely to be misguided. (See, e.g., Wittgenstein 1953.)

Geoff Mulgan says in the Preface to Yvonne Roberts' report:

> There is a remarkably broad consensus on what would be in the curriculum if it started with children's present and future needs rather than what's familiar to policymakers and teachers. What's required includes systematic reasoning, creativity, collaboration and the ability to communicate as well as mastery of the disciplines. (ibid., pp. 7–8)

This is like John White's point about starting with a blank sheet, though the idea of a 'remarkably broad consensus' about what to put here might strike many as optimistic. What mainly interests me about this passage is the last phrase, mastery of the disciplines. It has a tacked-on, uncomfortable feel, and examining the report that follows, one understands why. Disciplines are not discussed by Roberts, though the life skills of *discipline* and *self-discipline* are discussed a great deal. From an enhancement perspective, disciplines are antediluvian things that have not been submitted to the rigours of the well-being test (particularly the twenty-first-century well-being test). They are based on the quaint idea of intrinsically valuable knowledge, knowledge for its own sake, which lacks a sound rationale in the modern world.

It lacks this, or is believed to do so, for two reasons. One is discomfort with the ideas of moral objectivity or absolutism, expressed in protests like: who's to say that Shakespeare is valuable? Why Shakespeare rather than Tsegaye Gebre-Medhin of Ethiopia or Chinua Achebe of Nigeria? This protest combines the idea that *nothing* is intrinsically valuable, for values are relative, with the idea that cultures other than our own may produce poets whose work is *as* valuable as that produced in the West. That these ideas do not sit easily together is clearly a problem; many philosophers, as a consequence, see relativism as a self-defeating position (see, e.g., Williams 1985, chapter 9).

Children in UK schools often demand a clear understanding of why they are learning what. Many simply refuse to engage with learning if they cannot 'see the point', and our awareness of this difficult and in many ways counter-educational situation cannot but influence our reflections about the 'point' of school. Not only must we convince ourselves; we must also convince children that there is some 'point' to what we are teaching them. The authority required to impart this conviction is often strenuously challenged.

Whitehead says:

> All practical teachers know that education is a patient process of the mastery of details, minute by minute, hour by hour, day by day. (ibid., p. 6)

I agree that teachers know this (it is at least *part* of what education involves), but how hard is their task when children cannot see the point of this process, when our testing obsessions make our educational offerings moribund, when many teachers are so paralysed by relativist and cultural inhibitions that *they* are often doubtful about the point of traditional disciplines? How, in these circumstances, can we expect children to endure the 'patient process' that Whitehead describes?

Positive psychology teaches us to avoid pain unless its rewards are pretty much guaranteed ('evidence-based'), but the humanistic enrichment of life guarantees nothing. It vaguely assures us that there are likely to be rewards, no more, and what kind of argument is this for nihilistic, impatient, anti-authoritarian and frequently depressed children?

Yet we all know that, hard as learning may be, it can also be unbelievably exciting. The quaint idea of 'mastery of disciplines' will not go away – even Mulgan cannot quite give it up – for engagement with Shakespeare or Wordsworth can be not only arduous, not only 'useless', but also thrilling and life-enhancing (as the depressed Mill was to discover). It can take us over, lift our moods, do what positive psychologists *rightly* draw attention to when they talk about 'flow'. The crucial point is that educational disciplines must be taught ertly rather than inertly, and there are countless extraordinary teachers today, passionate about their disciplines, struggling to engage children with 'Life in all its manifestations'. For an outstanding teacher this effort, as Peters says (quoted above), 'haunts his every endeavor and makes him sweat and yearn to fix what he thinks and feels in a fitting form'. The enhancement agenda's denigration of disciplines, of *intrinsically* valuable knowledge, is a denigration of such a teacher's lifelong passion.

The polarization of enhancement and knowledge casts a shadow over educational policy and debate. It is potentially damaging to children – it makes many into casualties of misguided generalizations – and it threatens the future society that enhancement thinkers are so anxious to serve. I have suggested that at the heart of this situation is discomfort with the idea of intrinsically valuable knowledge. Enhancement thinkers try to shock us out of our complacency about traditional disciplines (as they see it) by asking: what ends do they serve? If not the ultimate end of promoting well-being, why bother with them at all? The demand for justification cultivates doubt about educational experiences that set people alight, and generates a kind of nihilism that does teachers and pupils no good at all.

Fortunately, the demand often has no purchase, because poetry, history, fine arts etc. enrich many people's lives in inestimable ways. If something enriches your life, you may be unable to articulate what this means or describe your feelings to others, but the demand for justification loses its sting. It may, however, undermine your confidence as a teacher, and this can have devastating implications for future generations. What we know is that disciplinary knowledge fails to enrich every life; that knowledge and ideas are easily desiccated by educators; that intense testing makes desiccation virtually inevitable; that the *main* casualties of all this tend to be children with social and economic disadvantages; that disaffection, which can be toxic, often ensues.

I want to close this chapter with two suggestions. First, we should pay more attention to the idea of mastery, uncomfortable though its associations may be. (For a start, it is offensively gendered.) One can be a master of anything that involves the gradual acquisition of knowledge and skill: car mechanics and tree surgery as well as medieval literature. This acquisition may be more or less arduous and painful, but it is valuable for virtually everyone. It requires the personal qualities beloved by John White and others (patience, self-discipline, resilience etc.), without prioritizing these over knowledge in meaningless ways. Learning, acquiring mastery, *is* sometimes painful, but it can also be infinitely pleasurable and satisfying, as well as bringing self-respect and economic rewards. The question we need to ask is whether the enhancement agenda is not a distraction from the patient engagement with learning that we should aspire to for children. This can bring the lasting satisfactions of mastery – a crucial aspect, for many, of well-being – and is an ideal site for the Aristotelian cultivation of feeling that lies at the heart of his conception of the good life.

My second suggestion is that we can only pursue such questions if we stand up to nihilism, expressed in Claxton's idea that Hamlet lacks educational value because it fails to equip children for life. Take this idea into a classroom, and you will no doubt find a bunch of bored and disaffected children who, like yourself, cannot see the point of Shakespeare. Take Peters' 'sweat and yearning' to convey a 'quality of living', and Hamlet could change their lives. The *conviction of value* is essential for teachers, who will only help children to aspire to mastery and tolerate painstaking learning if they can transmit this. These issues need urgent examination.

I want to end with Mill (the disaffected Utilitarian), describing the effects of Wordsworth on his life. I use this passage to suggest that the enhancement theorist's sceptical demand for justification can be met in one way only. It is met *humanistically*, by listening carefully to what people say about the importance of certain knowledge in their lives. The demand for justification comes from Enlightenment, science-based thinking, and it cannot be assumed that questions of intrinsic value will yield to this demand. Hamlet is not *justified*; it is reflected on, responded to and, above all, accepted or rejected as a source of learning. My suggestion is that, as we learn from Hamlet if we allow ourselves to, so we may learn a great deal about education from passages like the following:

> What made Wordsworth's poems a medicine for my state of mind, was that they expressed, not mere outward beauty, but states of feeling, and of thought coloured by feeling, under the excitement of beauty. They seemed to be the very culture of the feelings, which I was in quest of. In them I seemed to draw a source of inward joy, of sympathetic and imaginative pleasure, which could be shared in by all human beings. (1960, p. 104)

5

Should We Promote Flourishing Through Virtue?

An enhancement agenda, as I have presented it, engages with a thought that seems to many people pressing: *we must make children better*. In its scientific variants, it tries to respond to this thought efficiently and with precision. It asks what kind of *mental ingredient*, if enhanced, is likely to fulfil this aim. It *closes in* on promising answers by operationalizing concepts through which the presence or absence of the ingredient in question is reliably determined. It conducts *pre-tests and post-tests,* mediated by *interventions*, in order to discover through measurement whether ingredient-enhancement is successfully achieved by this method. This is the general form of much research on the enhancement of attributes like self-esteem and happiness.

There are also non-scientific enhancement agendas, like the one discussed in Chapter 4, whereby an up-to-date curriculum that equips children for twenty-first-century life is regarded as the proper route to making children 'better'. In the next chapter, I shall discuss a further non-scientific example: the enhancement of children through *educational inclusion*, meaning the inclusion of *all* children – irrespective of whether or not they are able learners or communicators, do or do not need aids to walk, see, hear etc. – in the same institutions. There is a distinctly political flavour to both these variants, which aim to overturn traditional notions of superiority and inferiority. An up-to-date curriculum is one that refuses to serve a leisured elite by teaching dead languages and other 'useless' subjects as a matter of course. It opposes what is seen as an *academic bias* in education today that is anachronistic and unfair. Inclusive school arrangements, similarly, do not serve able-bodied and able-minded children by banishing their less able (and often troublesome) peers to separate buildings and institutions. We become 'better', on both these views, not by removing ourselves from society, setting ourselves above and apart, but by becoming respectfully attuned to the diverse and practical realities of life. This enriches us not only by strengthening and broadening our personal associations, but also by grounding us securely in the pluralistic, technological culture to which we belong.

In this chapter I discuss an enhancement agenda that is both scientific and, like the political agendas just described, finely focused on what it means to lead a good or admirable life. It is not so much political as ethical, drawing on an aspect of the Aristotelian vision that I believe we must applaud. To live well, on this view, is not simply to live happily, in the sense of satisfying one's desires, enjoying life. It should include these things to some extent, but it also needs to be a life of which we or those near to us might feel proud. A life spent happily counting grains of sand or blades of grass is not eudaimonic in Aristotle's sense. The classical concept of *eudaimonia* – popularly translated nowadays as flourishing, well-being or a 'good life' – is a *big* idea, *inherently* unclear in Margalit's sense, as discussed in Chapter 3. Aristotle sets it before us as the ultimate end of all our desires, the 'thing' to which we aim as an end-in-itself, rather than a means to something else. However, we don't (without mature reflection) know what it is; we have (as I describe this) a *happiness predicament*, and in regard to cherished others, a *ministrative happiness predicament*. We want it for ourselves and others, and we usually want it badly, but our childhood conception of happiness must be wisely refined. Aristotle believes that this requires a kind of philosophical or reflective work, and I think he is right on the whole. This is especially pertinent in our commercialized, highly verbose modern world, driven by seductive conceptions of happiness that young people must (if they hope to live well) submit to questioning.

This chapter's topic is character education in the modern sense of enhancing or inculcating virtue through evidence-based interventions in schools. The project takes the idea of 'making children better' in a familiar or literal sense. If such education works, children will become more admirable human beings: more courageous, more generous, more considerate, more conscientious, more just, more temperate with their appetites and 'better-tempered' generally. They will feel angry when it is appropriate to feel angry, enraged when it is appropriate to feel enraged. When anger or rage is inappropriate to the situations in which they find themselves, they will be gentle or mild-tempered. They will feel afraid when it is appropriate to do so: for example, the night before an exam that must be passed if one is to proceed to the course on which one's heart is set. Their fear will be measured and appropriate, however, rather than paralysingly intense. Balance and appropriateness are key, and this is not, as Bernard Williams complains, because Aristotle holds a 'substantively depressing doctrine in favour of moderation' (1993a, p. 36), but because habitual *immoderation* can devastate and disrupt our aspirations to live well. (So too can a dogged attachment to moderation.) You can be *too* frightened, *too* angry, *too* generous, *too* patient for the circumstances you are in, as well as insufficiently frightened, angry, generous, patient and so on. What I have called dramas of unlearning often build up and spiral out of control as a consequence of such excesses and deficiencies.

Aristotle's doctrine of the mean is about the many ways in which emotions can misfire, or be inappropriate to the circumstances in which they occur and, to this extent, irrational. This is not about moderation, and nor is it empty moralism; it is about the ways in which, through untutored feeling, we may obstruct our own desire for happiness or a good life. If we are constitutionally bad-tempered, flying off the handle at the slightest thing, not only will we make those around us miserable; we shall be miserable ourselves. If we are impatient, stingy or chronically ashamed, we may benefit from a caring teacher, parent or friend who undertakes the difficult task of trying to bring greater balance to our emotional lives. This will involve seeing the world more clearly, thinking more reasonably, making better choices about whether to submit to certain impulses or note them, wonder about them, submit them to reflection.

Aristotle captures the *quantitative* idiom in which we tend to conceptualize this misfiring of emotion. Emotions build up, intensify, recede and subside; they may be 'too much' or 'not enough'. There may even be measurable correlates in the form of blood pressure or pulse rate. It is characteristic of children to fluctuate between excesses and deficiencies of feeling relative to circumstances, and adults often work hard to 'attune them' to what they see as the 'right amount' of anger, fear and so on. Children must become more angry *and* less angry, more fearful *and* less fearful, as the varied situations in which they find themselves demand. Adults guide, model and sometimes explicitly teach children about emotions, which means helping them to discriminate justly between circumstances that may appear similar, and respond appropriately at the levels of feeling and action.

This is, of course, only a sketch of Aristotle's theory of emotion, but I think it resonates with the experiences of adults with children, not to mention adults with their emotionally wayward friends or indeed their wayward selves. Character educators who draw on Aristotle are on the right track; to make children 'better' is not simply to enhance their self-esteem, confidence or resilience, for in themselves such qualities are (as character educators frequently observe) compatible with all manner of wickedness and dysfunctionality. (Think of Donald Trump if you want to understand why confidence isn't an unqualified good.) What we aspire to when we aim to make children 'better' is to make them braver, more just, more even-tempered, less timid, less self-effacing and so on. In short, we want them to become emotionally more mature: less fearful of things that can't possibly hurt them, less aggrieved when no wrong has been done, less ashamed when they have nothing to be ashamed of. This is moral education, Aristotle-style, and it is a far cry from the moralism of Victorian teachers, authoritarian parents and others who see it as their duty to instil obedience to a moral code.

Some, however, find it more sinister than the stark brutality of Victorian moralism. Aristotelian moral education is in no small part *emotional* education, and may seem like a subtle exercise of power by the strong over the weak. Is the moral educator a person who brainwashes the young? How, one might ask, can one presume to know and teach what is the 'right amount' of anger or fear for another?

These are reasonable concerns, and we cannot respond to them without going deeper into notions like emotion, self, virtue, practical reason, well-being, education and upbringing. In particular, we need to find out how emotional education, far from being a form of brainwashing, may belong to a thoroughly ethical engagement with others: an engagement, as I put it, of cherishing. The brainwashing objection is about coercive intrusion into the intimate recesses of selfhood, as represented by the life of feeling. And it is certainly true that we are who we are, at a deep level, largely because of what and how we feel. It is assumed by purveyors of this objection that there is a *difference of principle* between teaching children about the world beyond them (ethically legitimate) and teaching them how to shape and refine their inner worlds (ethically illegitimate). But this division of inner and outer is impossible to sustain, and one of the reasons for turning to Aristotle is that his moral theory does not attempt to sustain it.

Emotions, for Aristotle, are not merely 'inner events'; they are (as Nancy Sherman concisely puts it) 'modes of attention enabling us to notice what is morally salient, important, or urgent in ourselves and our surroundings. They help us track the morally relevant "news"' (1999, p. 40). Thus adults do not simply teach children about the existence of beggars on the street, or describe their bleak economic circumstances. They convey the 'news' that other people's sorrow is in some sense our own; some feelings are, others are not, *appropriate* to an encounter with a beggar. This is not to suggest that beggars should never arouse suspicion, but the earliest lesson should, most would agree, be one of sympathy and respect rather than contempt. At the beginning of life human beings are ripe and ready for this kind of teaching, and require the kind of guidance that Aristotle calls habituation, whereby learning to *perceive justly* and *respond appropriately* are integral. Such learning comes about through guided repetition, persuasion and encouragement; it is normally supported by a great deal of sensitive conversation.

Here then is a somewhat complex introduction to character education. Today's character scientists – including some philosophers of education – are on the right track when they appeal to Aristotelian theory, but mistaken, as I shall argue, in their efforts to 'reconstruct' this theory for modern usage. I said that character educators of this ilk aim for efficiency and precision; they take pride in what they see as a thoroughly practical, *because scientifically validated*, approach to moral education. I shall take issue with this, preferring to ground our enquiry in the exploration of what we recognize as good ministrative practice. Aristotle urged us, rightly I believe, to depart from 'what is known to us'. This places us from the outset on an ethical rather than scientific footing, a perspective from which we *discriminate* between good-enough and not-good-enough ministrative practitioners: teachers, parents, friends and so on. It is not, I shall argue, so much to reconstruct as to *distort* Aristotle's thought if we reject this ethical grounding (which is not to deny that we sometimes disagree and make mistakes). We are trying to understand what good-enough ministrative practice *means*, how it looks and how notions like emotion, self, virtue and so on must be construed if they are to illuminate rather than darken our understanding.

Ministrative practices are, I maintain, the *primary setting* in which we try to develop and enhance other people's characters. In this setting, our emotions as well as theirs are at stake. It is important, therefore, to think clearly about the nature of feeling, the refinement, cultivation and possible *transformation* of feeling, the cherishing of one person by another. While Aristotle was on the right track, his account is not (as I suggested in Chapter 3) complete. He knew that human beings are 'ripe and ready' (as I put it earlier) for emotional education from the start of life, and he knew that such education is, in part, both chronologically and structurally *alogon*, or non-cognitive, non-rational, non-verbal. It is hardly surprising, given the era and culture in which he lived, that he failed to appreciate what it is to nurture the very young, refining feeling through feeling, habit through habit, character through character. In his discussion of friendship (a form of ministrative practice), he comes closest to a recognition of what this means.

My aim in this chapter is not so much to present an argument *against* the science of character education as to make a case *for* the primacy of ethics, *for* a careful enquiry into what this means, *for* attention to both the spirit and limitations of Aristotle.

Aristotelian Character Education

In his book *Aristotelian Character Education*, a chapter is devoted to what Kristján Kristjánsson calls 'character education's profoundest problem: *how do we measure (Aristotelian) virtue in people in general and in young moral learners in particular?*' It is a remarkable suggestion. The 'profoundest problem' is not the meaning of virtue in a 'deep' rather than 'superficial' sense. Nor is it the nature of feeling, reason, action or desire, which for Aristotle are centrally implicated in virtue. It is not human nature itself, with its constituent concept of excellence; if, as Aristotle believes, human beings have a nature, there must be such a thing as its realization or excellent expression, i.e. a good or flourishing human life.

Kristjánsson's concern seems to be character education's *most challenging problem at the present time*, as he sees it. Measurement presents itself as the 'urgent issue' given considerable philosophical consensus about the nature of virtue, the *practical* need to improve attitudes to learning and uncertainties about how this is to be achieved. Many people – myself amongst them – will reject this assessment of character education's profoundest problem, but as always, I want to approach this issue by considering the *purposes* for which Kristjánsson's claim is made.

The following passage provides a good part of the answer:

> When character educationists start to suggest specific interventions aimed at cultivating character in schools, those have to compete with a host of other suggestions about what schools can do to promote pro-social ends. Nowadays, a common requirement of such suggestions is that they offer pre-tests and post-tests of the success of implementation, ideally conducted via a randomised controlled trial: the platinum bar of school-based research. In the present context, the demand will be to measure students' virtues before and after the proposed implementation and to demonstrate that the moral character of those who received it has truly improved, compared to a control group. Otherwise, the rationale of the intervention is in danger of being deemed dead in the water. (2015, p. 60)

This passage contains an implicit imperative: *researchers must win the confidence of policymakers*. The latter are envisaged (no doubt justly much of the time) as bringing an attitude of doubt, if not cynicism, to the table. The project of evidence-based character education responds to doubt by submitting to specific imperatives. Character educationists *have to compete*. The competition *requires* pre-tests and post-tests, and a *demonstration* that 'character has truly improved'. Proposed interventions must do these things *on pain of being deemed dead in the water*. Aristotelian character education, then, as promoted by Kristjánsson, makes unnegotiable methodological demands on researchers.

The background to this situation is, as we know, decades of failed enhancement policy: self-esteem, emotional intelligence, resilience and so on, successively touted as the magic bullet of improvement, only to bring evidence-driven disappointment. Kristjánsson seeks to inspire, in part, by being inspired; Aristotelian moral theory, he says, 'inspires confidence in those who, like me, enter the field of character education from a philosophical side path' (p. 24). He suggests that 'if Aristotle were alive today', he would, as an 'evidential naturalist', have signed up to the virtue measurement that inspires confidence in contemporary policymakers and scientists (p. 62). This is debatable, but Kristjánsson argues the point minutely, aiming to respond confidently and persuasively to scepticism.

In this sense, evidence-based character education belongs not only to the field of ethics or moral philosophy; by frankly purporting to refute *systemic doubt*, it occupies a place in the field of epistemology, or theory of knowledge. The provenance of this way of thinking is, I would argue, more Cartesian than Aristotelian. It is well-known that Descartes' conception of mind and reality was painstakingly built on a foundation of devastating ignorance. He famously claimed *not to know* whether we have bodies, whether objects exist, whether we have human companions with whom to think and speak or indeed any companions at all.

Kristjánsson is no solipsist, and he is not at all attracted to Descartes' brutal vision of psychic isolation. But he is, along with many influential colleagues, attracted to *something* that is not inherently philosophical. He is attracted to – feels compelled to respond to – the unyielding demands of politicians who are anxious to *do something constructive* about difficult or unteachable children. Not only this: he places this attraction, this compulsion, at the heart of his project. This is why measurement is character education's 'profoundest problem': he needs an epistemological foundation and a body of knowledge that are so secure, so impeccably researched, that they are immune to doubt.

I do not mean to sound cynical. When I say that Kristjánsson (with colleagues) feels compelled to respond to political demands, I am not suggesting that the desire to help children to live and learn 'better' is negligible or insincere on their part. My personal encounters with many character educators have assured me that this is not the case. What concerns me is the derailing of a project about which many of us – including evidence-based character educators – care deeply. And so we should, for the expression 'character education' captures a basic and unassailable ethical project, as I indicated earlier. Unlike the projects of boosting happiness or self-esteem, the project of improving character is about making people wiser, kinder, braver and so on, as appropriate to the circumstances in which they find themselves. It is, in short, about becoming emotionally and intellectually (these dimensions in harmony with each other) more mature. To attempt to bring this about is undeniably the business of teachers, parents and other educators of the young.

Around these basic ideas of what character education is *about,* I believe that useful work has come out of the project of evidence-based character education, particularly in relation to literature and personal reflection (including, for example, unstructured journal writing prompted by fictional characters and their stories). We shall return to this; my current concern is with a temptation to which, in my view, many character educators are prey. The temptation is captured by the characterization of the field as having measurement as its profoundest problem. This brings epistemological concerns – the need to respond to doubt through measurement – to the fore, and the worrying corollary (inevitably I believe) is that ethical concerns recede.

We see this from some passing remarks by Kristjánsson. It can easily escape one's notice that, in the 'imperatival' passage quoted above, the idea of promoting virtue in schools has undergone a shift: the issue here is not virtue precisely, but 'what schools can do to promote pro-social ends'. In the same vein Kristjánsson speaks elsewhere about the need to 'enhance the pro-social functioning of the young'. It is a telling contraction; virtue has become 'pro-social functioning' and, by implication, a reduction of 'anti-social functioning'. The latter, if we are honest, is what most policymakers passionately seek and easily understand. If I was a policymaker without a background in philosophy, I would no doubt be happy to descend from the dizzy heights of classical virtue to the familiar valleys of human decency, in which children become less insolent, less disruptive, less aggressive to teachers, more receptive and attentive in classrooms. This may seem a trifle exegetical (which is not really our purpose here), but I think it is worth noting that the phrase 'pro-social ends' appears in a paragraph that submits frankly to the requirements of science, offering reassurance rather than philosophical reflection.

This, it seems, is how character education aims to be truly and usefully practical. But what, precisely, are its practical implications? The following passage provides a worrying glimpse into this kind of character educator's classroom:

> It remains disconcerting how many moral educationists seem to be smugly satisfied with relying on their gut feelings that a real change has taken place as a result of a classroom intervention. (2015, p. 153)

The suggestion seems to be that 'real change' is properly determined by scientific studies rather than classroom experience. I don't for a moment think that Kristjánsson believes this. He is an Aristotelian (albeit 'reconstructed'), and he understands the Aristotelian concept of *phronesis*, meaning practical reason or judgement, essential in Aristotle's view for a good, engaged life. *Phronesis* enables us to judge which feelings are appropriate when, and Aristotle rightly places this capacity at the heart of our ethical lives. The reference to gut feelings suggests, as many philosophers and scientists believe, that our deepest convictions are worthless unless they are in some sense *subordinate* to reason, and it is a suggestion that is likely to reassure policymakers who, unlike Aristotle, see reason and feeling as independent, competing faculties, with science – the embodiment of reason – *prevailing* in an ordered, efficiently run classroom. Kristjánsson, I am suggesting, does not always avoid this simplistic picture, despite his Aristotelian provenance.

Teachers do and must often rely on feelings; these are, as I put it earlier, essential sources of 'moral news'. The question is not *whether* we rely on (or learn from) our feelings, but *how* we do so, how refined they are, how attached we are to feelings that support complacency or bias. I have agreed with Philip Jackson and Joseph Dunne that in our engagements with others – and particularly what I call our ministrative practices – we *read* human behaviour and intentions, rather than identify and classify actions; *judge* what people feel, though it may be different from what they purport to feel; and our own feelings are inevitably engaged. We make errors, and in some cases do so frequently, which is why we may be tempted to deride 'gut feelings' and demand something more robust and objective as a route to personal enhancement.

This reading and judging and respect for feelings that we know to be fallible is *how it is* for those who are attracted practically and emotionally to the 'magnetic, inexhaustible reality' (as Iris Murdoch puts it) of another person's good. This good, I suggested, includes their *happiness* in a serious or Solonic sense, which is part of what Aristotle means by *eudaimonia* (the retrospective part, as it were). Kristjánsson offers an Aristotelian account of character education, but I have suggested that *epistemologically* he is closer to Descartes than Aristotle, passing swiftly over Aristotle's famous reminder 'not to look for precision in the same way in all things, but in accordance with the underlying material in each case' (2002a, 1098a 9–11). This is fundamental, and it is common to Wittgenstein and Winnicott (both of whom will be discussed in greater detail in Part Three) as well as Aristotle. We cannot sensibly aspire to identical standards of accuracy when we move from domains like mathematics, physics or engineering to the domain of human well-being. This book explores a 'discourse that is in accord with' this irreducibly human domain.

Policymakers and practitioners may learn a great deal from Kristjánsson book. They may learn that Aristotelian moral education is not to be confused with Victorian moralism, which is the popular idea of what moral education means. They may be surprised and enlightened by the Aristotelian conception of habituation, according to which early habits of feeling and responding are gradually refined by conversation, criticism and reflection. All this is admirably presented by Kristjánsson book, but I have suggested that he sounds a dissonant (not to mention un-Aristotelian) note when he submits to scepticism by absorbing its supposedly redeeming imperatives. He sounds another when he tries to 'nail' the concept of flourishing in what he calls 'a *general blueprint* of the good life that can be conveyed through teaching: a consciously accessible, comprehensive and systematic conception of what makes a human life go well' (2015, p. 99). It is important to understand what is right and what is wrong with this idea. I turn to this now.

People and kinds of people

What is flourishing and what kinds of education or upbringing are likely to promote it? Kristjánsson approaches this question through the time-honoured method of storytelling: he discusses three fictional women whose lives end at age 82 and invites us to compare them. Questions are raised about *whether* each person flourished, *how much* they flourished and in what respects. Readers are prompted to reflect, not on an abstraction called 'flourishing' (or a 'good life'), but on individual lives and whether they went badly or well (or badly in some respects, well in others). They are supplied, moreover, with considerable detail, so their reflections are supported by imaginative engagement with the characters: the families they came from, the kinds of work they did, the relationships they formed, the people they loved and how things stood with them as their lives drew to a close.

This kind of enquiry is a starting point for ethical reflection in a deep and unqualified sense. Kristjánsson does not (like the Office of National Statistics a few years ago) conduct a survey with a view to establishing *what most people believe flourishing means*. The ONS was responding to David Cameron's call in 2008 to put GWB – *general well-being* – rather than GNP at the heart of public policy. The effort to resolve difficult ethical questions through surveys, bringing confidence through quantitative analysis, has appeared repeatedly in the history of enhancement policy and has repeatedly failed or been quietly dropped.

In his discussion of flourishing, Kristjánsson speaks directly to his readers, inviting them in time-honoured *philosophical* fashion to reflect. I am extending my already lengthy discussion of Kristjánsson's work because I see his quest for a 'blueprint for flourishing' or 'a good life' as an instructive failure. I want to suggest that, despite the welcome detail in his narratives, Kristjánsson invites us to think about *kinds* of people, rather than people. It is a serious (and under-explored) question, how far philosophy is willing and able to stray in the latter direction, which is as difficult as it is necessary.

Joseph Dunne's book (from which I have quoted several times) is entitled *Back to the Rough Ground*. The phrase comes from Wittgenstein's *Philosophical Investigations*, which is concerned with the difficulties of thinking and the temptation to resolve these by avoiding the 'rough ground' of everyday life. These are Wittgenstein's words:

> Here it is difficult as it were to keep our heads up, – to see that we must stick to the subjects of our everyday thinking, and not go astray.... We feel as if we had to repair a torn spider's web with our fingers.
>
> We have got on to slippery ice where there is no friction and so in a certain sense the conditions are ideal, but also, just because of that, we are unable to walk. We want to walk: so we need *friction*. Back to the rough ground! (1953, paras 106–107)

Wittgenstein is interested here in the supposed 'purity of logic', to which many philosophers aspire when they are frustrated with everyday thinking. There is a parallel attraction to the 'purity of science', and like Dunne, I hope to restore faith in the rough ground of everyday life, which is populated with *people* rather than *kinds of people*. In order to explain this, let's proceed to Kristjánsson's fictional women.

Anne's story is the most straightforward: her life was all but exemplary (marred only in contemporary fashion by 'not enough "me-time"' (2015, p. 106)). She was born into a large, loving family, did well at school and with 'care, compassion and kindness bred into her bones from an early age' had a worthwhile career and devoted family. I shall pass over her story (which poses no awkward philosophical questions) and go straight to the comparison between Cecilia and Beth. It is this comparison that most interests Kristjánsson, for reasons that will become clear.

Cecilia was born into a troubled family; her father was an alcoholic and her mother was mentally ill. She went off the rails as a teenager, and this lends support to a familiar belief: that troubled childhoods often form the causal background to emotional disturbance (including – I would add – the 'dramas of unlearning' that are the focus of this book). This principle lies at the heart of many therapies, but it is also Aristotelian. In a grammatically fascinating turn of phrase, Aristotle asserts that if human beings are going to live well – which includes being able to *learn* to live well ('listen adequately to discourses about things that are beautiful and just') – they 'need to have been beautifully brought up by means of habits' (2002a 1095B 4–7). Cecilia lacked such an upbringing and her prospects of flourishing were therefore, as far as Aristotle is concerned, dim or non-existent.

Despite her unpropitious beginnings, however, Cecilia did well in life. Partly through luck and partly (it seems) through resilience or resolve, she became a 'true paragon of moral virtue'. Luck appeared in the form of a friendship that profoundly influenced her sense of what matters in life, as well as a philosophy course on Aristotle's *Nichomachean Ethics* (no surprises there), from which she learned about the 'intrinsic value of leading a virtuous life'. Cecilia 'died well', and this is an important Solonic and Aristotelian marker for 'living (i.e. having lived) well'. *Call no man happy until he is dead,* said Solon famously, and his thought was that a miserable, protracted or undignified end mars what might have been the beauty or nobility of a life. (We shall return to this interesting idea.) Cecilia was surrounded by 'beloved friends and family who mourned and missed her deeply' (ibid., p. 107).

Cue Beth, who appears as a narrative foil to Cecilia. Beth was born into a loving family. Her father devoted his life to charitable causes and was a role model for his daughter. Beth formed good friendships and other relationships and was, Kristjánsson says, 'generally considered to be a model businesswoman, mother, wife and friend'. There is, however, a fly in her eudaimonic ointment. Although she had good relationships generally, she had a 'slightly withdrawn personality' and at age 50 found expression for this by going to Nepal, where she dedicated her life to a personal guru. She spent most of her remaining years on retreat 'meditating and reflecting upon life with her fellow disciples' (ibid., p. 106).

Aristotle, according to Kristjánsson, would have described Beth's life as 'the most completely flourishing life of the three'. This is because he saw contemplative activity as essential for a satisfying life, and the pinnacle of human flourishing. He was wrong about this, argues Kristjánsson, suggesting on the contrary that in retreating to Nepal, Beth lost her moral compass, or abandoned it to some degree. *We* understand, contra Aristotle, that good social and emotional relationships are the basis of human flourishing, and we withdraw from them at our peril. Beth had it all initially: a good upbringing that enabled her to form good relationships and achieve success as a charitable businesswoman. But she left her loved ones and other commitments to follow a guru many thousands of miles away. The implication, for Kristjánsson, is that: 'some vital ingredient went missing through the gradual disengagement from her personal and social network' (ibid., p. 107). We (the readers) are expected to agree with her loved ones: Beth's retreat into religion was 'slightly indulgent'.

Aristotle would have been wrong, then, to award the 'prize' for flourishing to Beth. The 'modern' view, Kristjánsson suggests, is un-Aristotelian in two respects. First, as indicated, we tend to give priority to social and emotional engagement over a contemplative life. Second, we reject the idea that moral neglect in the early years precludes a virtuous life. Cecilia, sadly, remained vulnerable to 'choking self-doubt and unexplained bouts of anger'; she had less *tranquillity* than Beth, and would probably receive a lower score for 'happiness' on a Benthamite utilitarian test. However, her life was *more praiseworthy* than Beth's, and indeed more praiseworthy than most; she 'overcame the effects of her damaging upbringing and became a model for other early-years sufferers to follow'. If we moderns were to choose between Beth and Cecilia, we would say that Cecilia's life was 'best'.

Thus argues Kristjánsson, and he goes on to pose an obvious question: is Cecilia's radical self-change psychologically unrealistic? He returns a brief and anecdotal answer:

> The trouble with this thesis [i.e. Aristotle's thesis that, if human beings are to live well, they 'need to have been beautifully brought up by means of habits'] is that many of us will contend to know examples of individuals who, despite gruelling circumstances in their upbringing and a lack of moral role models, have nevertheless succeeded in transcending those conditions and acquiring a virtuous moral character. (ibid., p. 104)

This, it appears, *settles* a series of questions that many centuries of philosophy and over a century of psychoanalysis have brought to the fore. How much power do human beings really have to *transform their own emotions?* In what sense are we the *agents* of our own lives, as opposed to 'patients', often ignorant and bewildered? How do we *become* agents, and what part does reason play in this development? How do we teach reason to others, or bring about *reasoned learning*, and how, if we have not been recipients of such teaching, do we teach ourselves? What resources might there be, within or without us, to 'get on track' if we go off the rails?

Cecilia's story is intended as a significant response to such questions. I want to suggest, however, that Cecilia and Beth are not *characters* in a serious sense, and cannot therefore stimulate the kind of reflection that the *large, unclear* idea of flourishing deserves and requires. They are *snapshots* of characters. Despite the welcome detail of their stories (which I have not tried to reproduce), they are essentially *illustrations of markers for flourishing*, as extracted from Aristotle's philosophy. A poor upbringing is a strong predictive marker for (if not a determinant of) non-flourishing. A contemplative life is a marker for flourishing. Both are overturned, but this is done, primarily, by inviting assent to a 'modern' (but conspicuously non-therapeutic) way of looking at things, rather than careful reflection.

I call this *unpopulated philosophy*. It is no more inhabited by convincing human beings than a Tom and Jerry cartoon is inhabited by a cat and a mouse. A picture (it is said) is worth a thousand words, but there is an important rejoinder: it depends on the picture and the purpose it is intended to serve. When I say that Cecilia and Beth are snapshots, I mean that something *resembling* human beings has been appended to an argument about markers. In his book *The Singular Self: An Introduction to the Psychology of Personhood* (1998), philosopher of science Rom Harré draws our attention to the error of thinking this way, and he does so, in part, pictorially. The book's frontispiece contains a New Yorker cartoon depicting two young women chatting in a bar. One says to the other: 'He's the *guy* I'm interested in. He is not just the *kind* of guy I'm interested in.' *This* picture is worth a great many words.

The people we are interested in in a serious way – friends, lovers, family members – are not *kinds of people*: they are people. If you go to a dating website, you may suffer many frustrations while you learn about the difference. If you are lucky, a 'kind of person' will turn into a 'person' you can respect and eventually love. If you are unlucky, checklist after checklist of perfectly matching characteristics may prove to be bitter disappointments.

Beth's family thought she was 'indulgent'; they were, it seems, aggrieved by her departure for Nepal and critical of the path she chose. Should we agree? If we think of Beth as a person, rather than a kind of person, I would argue that we haven't the slightest idea. A couple of meaty paragraphs that don't pretend to explore layers of meaning, or feelings, motives and desires in any depth, hardly hint at trustworthy answers. We have in this kind of picture the *wrong kind of epistemological foundation* for judging human beings. We need more than facts, more even than detailed descriptions of the facts; we need sensitive human encounters or, in the realm of storytelling, acutely observed accounts of psychology and meaning, presented with the reticence that is due to human beings who are leading rich and complex lives. It is not as though Beth has committed a massacre. She has chosen a religious path, and she has done so for reasons of which we know nothing.

Of course, there are different ways of thinking about philosophy. In an article entitled 'Having a Rough Story about What Moral Philosophy Is', Cora Diamond (1995) discusses different views of the subject, suggesting that the 'richest and most satisfying' sees moral philosophy as 'concerned with a world whose deepest difficulties include difficulties of description' (p. 378). Understood thus, philosophy invites attention to examples from substantial works of literature, in which the *difficulties of describing* human experiences and encounters are artistically rather than analytically addressed. It might be said that populated moral philosophy becomes possible when fictional characters are described rather as real human beings are *with difficulty* described, and may even be cherished rather as we cherish real human beings. This represents a significant departure from character snapshots and moral markers. We shall return to this topic in Part Three.

Consider Cecilia. We are *told* that she had a terrible childhood; *told* that she became a paragon of virtue. It is recommended that we pass over the reserve of Aristotle and many others about the difficulty of such a transition. Instead, we hear about 'examples of individuals' many of us will 'contend to know' – people who allegedly triumphed over early disadvantage. Are we sure? Do we have the *impression* that this happened? How well do we know them, or know about their disadvantages? Might there have been a 'guardian angel' in Cecilia's early life – a grandfather, a family friend, an aunt – who was aware of her predicament, spent wise, compassionate time with her and contributed towards a complex and turbulent disposition? Might Cecilia have been luckier than she knew, inspired as a young child with the thought of 'developing rather than squandering her potentialities', though she was apt to forget this? If Cecilia appeared in a novel by George Eliot, we might deepen and explore our judgements by reflecting on nuances of the text. As a character presented in support of a philosophical argument, we have no such opportunity.

Human beings, I suggested in Chapter 2, are 'prismatic'; they appear differently in different lights, from near and from afar, and these differences include the light and the colour of our own sensitivity and understanding. I have been suggesting that we cannot seriously evaluate a life without focusing on a person, rather than a kind of person. We should be circumspect with our comparisons, and this is a problem for so-called Aristotelian character education, which aims to make *confident* quantitative comparisons. It is my view that Aristotle would have been on board with these concerns, and I have accordingly rejected Kristjánsson's assertion that Aristotle's 'verdict would.... be that Beth's was the most completely flourishing life of the three'. This is not the Aristotle I know, famed for his repeated insistence that 'the judgement is in the perceiving'. Good storytellers understand this, unless their purposes are purely didactic; they famously 'show rather than tell'. Good philosophical storytellers, who issue invitations to reflect rather than reform, defer to this principle in distinctive philosophical ways.

How wise was Solon, really?

Human beings need to have been beautifully brought up by means of habits. Aristotle's construction is passive, and the need is directed towards a past rather than future state-of-affairs. This construction (which appears more than once in his texts) suggests a reciprocity that contemporary thinkers need to explore between psychoanalysis or psychotherapy and Aristotelian moral education. If we *need to have had an upbringing* that we did not have, it should be an open question whether, like Aristotle, we impose closure on this need because it refers to an unrecoverable past, or whether a response from a teacher, parent, friend or therapist may somehow redeem the loss.

In *The Histories,* Herodotus relates an interesting encounter between the 'wise Athenian' Solon and King Croesus. We know that Aristotle was impressed by Solon's wisdom, particularly his thought that *eudaimonia* cannot be properly assessed until the end of life 'or even beyond'. However, the thought is complex – it may seem wise and improbable by turns – and Aristotle's reflections on its meaning are rich and uneasy. He is particularly uneasy about the idea of *tracking people's fortunes*, and asks whether this might be in some way misconceived.

According to Herodotus, King Croesus was proud of his wealth, and having escorted Solon around his splendid palace, sought his wise verdict on who was the happiest man alive, fully expecting it to be himself. To his astonishment, Solon replied: 'Tellus of Athens, sir.' Tellus, apparently, had not only enjoyed worldly good fortune – good, handsome children, a comfortable life etc. – but had also died gloriously on the battlefield and received the highest public honours at his funeral. Who is the second happiest? ventured Croesus, and he received a similar answer about a man who lived and died well. It turned out, of course, that Solon refused to consider whether Croesus' life was happy or unhappy until it had come to an end. It was this refusal to do so that earned him his reputation for wisdom, but we might ask (with due consideration of the story's mythical status), what was Solon doing *ranking* lives this way?

We need not pursue this question. We know very little about Solon, and anyway Herodotus does not advance an argument about ranking; this is more like a meditation on the nature of life, death and wisdom. Kristjánsson and others *do* advance such an argument, and they mean to be taken seriously. Aristotle would have considered Beth's life the 'best' of the three; 'we' rate Cecilia's life more highly. On this basis, researchers can advance their project of articulating a 'blueprint for flourishing' for schools.

I want to close the chapter with some preliminary remarks (to be developed in later chapters) about the *style of thinking* that is on display here. In Chapter 4, I discussed Avishai Margalit's helpful distinction between positive and negative theology and politics. (I extended this to ethics and philosophy of education.) Margalit's basic political question is not 'how do we promote respect, freedom, well-being?', but rather 'what *hurts* us into politics?' The pressing issue, he says, is what kinds of conditions (e.g. humiliation, disrespect) we abhor and seek to oppose. The point is not that we shouldn't think 'positively' about what dignity and respect mean. It is that such concepts, like the 'right' and the 'good', are *difficult, unclear ideas* that don't simply fill the vacuum created by *identifying and opposing* what is humiliating, disrespectful, wrong or bad. I am suggesting that this asymmetry is neglected by character educators who hope to construct a positive blueprint by analysing and revising Aristotle's markers.

My argument in this chapter is an extension of Margalit's insight. If we are to advance our thinking about the 'difficult, unclear idea of the good' (and by implication a good, flourishing life), we need to accept the 'difficult challenges' of thinking positively rather than negatively. We need to consider how best to proceed, how we might lose our way. In this regard, another distinction must be recognized, and it is one that goes to the heart of this book, as well (I would argue) as the philosophies of Wittgenstein and Aristotle. Margalit characterizes it neatly as a distinction between i.e. and e.g. styles of thinking, or the explicating and illustrating styles. This is what he says:

There are two styles of philosophers – illustrators and explicators. Illustrators trust, first and foremost, striking examples, in contrast with explicators, who trust, first and foremost, definitions and general principles. Explicators may use examples, but their examples are stylised and are more like those that appear after i.e. than the genuine examples that follow e.g. The illustrators, for their part, run the risk of using examples as little more than anecdotes that serve little philosophical purpose. The dangers of each style are clear; yet, I believe that style in philosophy matters greatly. When examples are apt, they are illuminations, not just didactic illustrations. When definitions are good, they are explications, not mere stipulations. I see merit in both styles. (2002, p. ix)

The word that stands out in this passage is 'trust'. E.g. thinkers *trust examples*; indeed, they see them as ineliminable sources of learning. The examples must be genuine: 'striking and illuminating', rather than merely didactic. I.e. thinkers use *stylized* examples, or what I called snapshots. These are supplementary to the real sources of trust and learning, namely 'definitions and general principles'. 'Striking and illuminating' examples, such as passages from literature or detailed reminiscences, are likely to be *distrusted* by i.e. thinkers, because (rather like 'gut feelings') they express a personal perspective. The arguments of i.e. thinkers, then, are essentially stand-alone. They may be *supported* by pictures or stories that engage our imaginations, but from a strictly philosophical point of view, these are ornamental, bringing risks that should put us on our epistemological guard.

Both styles, says Margalit, have attendant risks, and they are risks that need to be faced. I see this as a crucial insight. One of the principles of this book is that we are less rather than more likely to help children ethically if we are acutely risk-averse. The solution is not to ignore potential dangers; Margalit's point is the entirely Aristotelian one that there are dangers in *two* directions, not just one. The e.g. style risks muddying the waters by over-personalizing the issues. The i.e. style carries the opposite risk: becoming dry and ultimately meaningless as it shuns any vestige of a personal perspective. In this respect, there is an intellectual as well as practical mean, a midway point between trusting our judgements too little and too much. The endeavour somehow to find this balance must lie at the heart not only of philosophy, but also of good judgement, good ethical thinking in a general sense. The *effort and determination* to achieve this – to think well rather than badly on behalf of others – is at the heart of the attitude I call cherishing, irrespective of whether we succeed or fail.

Whether we are talking about ancient history, contemporary funding policy or philosophical snapshots, *competitions* are essentially conducted in the i.e. style. When one candidate is ranked against another, significant aspects of her life or character are inevitably lost from view. This hardly matters if our aims are to edify or inspire through fables or cautionary tales. Aristotelian character education, however, aims to *transform emotions*, and emotions are attributes of people rather than kinds of people. For this, we must occupy Wittgenstein's rough ground, understanding that what makes it rough is its human population, which is accessible to 'blueprints' only in limited ways. The stories of Anne, Beth and Cecilia are, I have suggested, too idealized, too explicatory, to illuminate the difficult dramas that often occupy us in this domain.

The 'profoundest problem' of character education is not the challenge of offering a confident, because evidence-based, response to anxious imperatives. It is exactly what it has always been: how to distinguish between genuine and counterfeit virtue, *real* courage, generosity, justice etc., as opposed to its compliant, insincere or submissive semblances. If we don't tackle *this* problem, I believe we are on course to harm as well as help, i.e. harm those for whom one or another form of compliance seems like a clever solution to an otherwise irresolvable problem. The question is whether philosophers can bring *people* with their often perplexing and complex emotional histories into the arena of our enquiries. In the next chapter, we shall hopefully take a step in this direction.

Closing remarks: Thinking about reason and knowledge

Readers may be disappointed by my tendency in this chapter to treat weighty concepts – for example, reason and knowledge – as having little more than passing interest. I briefly mentioned Aristotle's idea of irrational emotions as 'inappropriate to the circumstances in which they occur'. I mentioned 'devastating ignorance', as conceived by Descartes, and I boldly (and perhaps intemperately) aligned the Cartesian and modern character educator's projects of allaying systemic doubt. What I have avoided doing thus far is engaging directly with philosophical debates in which the history of these ideas is brought to the fore and attempts are made to defend or explicate certain meanings.

I turn to such matters in Part Three, though even there, the theoretically committed philosopher may continue to be disappointed. I am less interested in conceptual explication in this book than in *setting the scene*, getting to grips with what is important in our ministrative practices, and from this point allowing concepts to fall 'naturally' into place. In an earlier chapter, I quoted Donald Winnicott's remark (1960c, in Winnicott 1985, p. 158): 'An idea like "self" naturally knows more than we do; it uses us, and can command us.' This notion of 'naturalness' should, I believe, inform ethical enquiry at the deepest level. Not only does it indicate a commitment to an everyday grounding for thought; it is imbued with *respect* for the lives human beings lead and the practical and ethical insights they develop. Respect is another word that resists easy explication (it will become our focus in the next chapter), but it seems undeniable that it should play a central role *both* in our conception of a life well lived and in our efforts to articulate such a conception.

Philosopher Charles Taylor writes:

> Disengaged reason [is].... . reasoning which can turn on its own proceedings and examine them for accuracy and reliability. We can scrutinise these proceedings to any degree of clarity, even up to the undeniably binding. This is the great contribution of Descartes, which he expressed in terms of les idées claires et distinctes. Disengaged reason is opposed to uses of reason which try to get a good purchase on some domain analogous to perception, but also to discerning the qualities of a piece of music, being able to tell what people are about, how they stand to the matter and to you, and so on..... . Disengaged reason means that we cease to rely on our engaged sense, our familiarity with some domain, and take a reflexive turn. We put our trust in a method, a procedure of operation. (1996, pp. 6–7)

This suggests that philosophers are inescapably confronted with alternative objects of trust. Should we trust our experiences in domains that are 'analogous to perception' (music, personal encounter etc.) or should we trust 'methods and procedures'? Posing the question this way suggests that *we have a choice*, and even – as Margalit accepts – that the ground for trusting in one way or another is, at least in part, temperamentally induced. *Here* is a good use for the phrase 'kind of person': you may be the kind of person who naturally *trusts or distrusts* appeals to examples as aids to deeper understanding. Margalit says: 'by temperament if not conviction I subscribe to e.g. philosophy', and with due consideration of the fact that he sees 'merit in both styles', I think his work points *towards* a willingness to trust examples, *away from* a systemic distrust of the deliverances of perception that may have brought one into philosophy in the first place.

Such deliverances do not, to be sure, have a 'natural' role in philosophy, which is weighted towards the i.e. style. Instead of unifying us under the banner of universal reason, they seem to disperse us into the parochial worlds from which philosophy appeared to be a place of intellectual refuge. But then all the more reason, or so I would argue, for bringing these questions under the spotlight of reflection. For although dispersal into our personal worlds may present a difficult challenge to philosophers – particularly those who wish to present a compelling and united front to policymakers – temperamentally induced distrust may adversely inhibit efforts to make sense of our ethical lives with others.

I subscribe, obviously, to the principles of engaged reason. These inform the endeavour to *make* sense and *find* sense (meaning, coherence) in our lives. My guiding question throughout this book is: how can one person 'make another better'? Or: How can adults guide children or other adults towards 'better lives', more decent human interactions, greater emotional maturity? While I have taken care not to criticize the science of psychology in a general way, there is, or should be, proper caution against the idea of using science to *make* children into one or another kind of person. The phrase 'making people better' is a dual (and partly ironic) reference to attitudes underlying our ministrative engagements with others. On the one hand, we sometimes dearly wish that we *could* 'make' our children or pupils into wise and diligent human beings. How much easier my life would have been if I could have magically transformed my three-year-old thus! On the other hand, we are neither tyrants nor fools. Under stress, we sometimes indulge fantasies that we know to be coping mechanisms, forms of escape. I cannot *make* a person wise or diligent as I can *make* a pot or meal, and nor do I wish to in any serious way, for the very idea is imbued with disrespect. On the other hand, we raise and educate children, as we sometimes guide and influence our friends, and we do these things with their 'good' or 'happiness' within our sights. We are flawed and we are well-wishing. We are ambitious and we are humble. We may be persuasive, inspirational and even a little coercive at times in the interests of making people see or feel things that could (we believe) help them along. It is within this complex ethical setting that ideas like reason and knowledge will hopefully find a place.

6

Should We Foster Respect
Through Inclusion?

At the time of writing, national and local government favour a policy of inclusion; special-needs children should be included in mainstream schools if at all possible. I believe this policy to be wrong; wrong as in misguided, and in some cases wrong as in immoral.

Charlotte Moore (2005), p. 170

In the summer of 2005, I found myself at the eye of a storm. I had recently joined the editorial board of the Impact pamphlet series published by the Philosophy of Education Society of Great Britain, and my first self-imposed assignment was to invite Baroness Warnock to review her ideas on special education. To my great surprise, she came back swiftly and affirmatively. A few weeks later, an A4 envelope containing a bulky typescript – written on a typewriter, corrected with Tippex – appeared in my pigeonhole. It was the first draft of the document that became known as her U-turn: *Special Educational Needs: A New Look.*

With colleagues, I invited some speakers to the launch, which was to be held in London University's Senate House. Amongst those who accepted was a young Conservative MP called David Cameron, who was known to us for not a great deal except that he had a severely disabled child and strong views about special education. He left the launch early to go to the House of Commons and throw his hat into the ring as Leader of the Opposition. Several of us politely wished him luck.

I wasn't prepared for what happened at the launch. Pickets in wheelchairs tried to refuse Mary Warnock, myself and other colleagues entry into the hall. Leaflets were handed out urging people not to attend the event, in which (it was claimed) Warnock was going to push for a return to segregated education. The hall was packed and a quick glance showed that many people had disabilities.

There were frequent disruptions, including angry efforts to silence the speakers as they made their opening remarks. As chair it was my responsibility to deal with these, and I'm afraid that, unprepared as I was, I wasn't as forceful as I might have been. For me the climax came when a young man with cerebral palsy spoke. He was at the front of the hall and jumped to his feet when I invited him to speak. He looked directly into the eyes of the panel, particularly those of Mary Warnock herself, and argued passionately against her view, as he saw it, that children should be segregated into 'ordinary' and 'special' schools.

Many people in the hall believed that he misunderstood her, and I shall return to this shortly. People should obviously be free to air misunderstandings in debates, but several things made the young man's address especially challenging. His speech was almost incomprehensible; what came across was the gist of a message (he had suffered terribly in a special school) rather than sentences that might have been transcribed. He resisted my efforts (mild as they were) to draw his speech to a close, and must have spoken for almost 15 minutes. During that time, the audience became increasingly restless, and their bottled-up frustration intensified the emotional atmosphere considerably. Shortly afterwards, the mother of an autistic child broke down from the back of the hall as she described her thwarted efforts to get her child *into* a special school, because she had been so miserable (and bullied) in a mainstream school.

When the launch was over, I was both congratulated and criticized by friends and colleagues. I was congratulated for maintaining some equanimity in such a heated and volatile debate; and I was criticized for allowing one person to dominate the discussion for such a long time. Some felt that I had no choice; it would have been crass and disrespectful to demand that an obviously disabled young man observe a protocol that was suitable for most. Others felt that I had been hopelessly weak, allowing him to manipulate the proceedings towards his own ends.

Should I have intervened? Part of the difficulty was that the young man's disability could not have been more visible. In the area of speech, at least, not only was his disability excruciatingly exposed, but we too were made to suffer its sting for an uncomfortable length of time. I have no doubt that, at some level, this was intended. We suddenly saw ourselves (or many did) through his eyes, as a bunch of smug intellectuals with no notable disabilities of our own, who thought we knew better than disabled people themselves what was best for them. We were *thrown back on ourselves*, and one of the reasons for *not* interrupting the young man's speech was that, irrespective of misunderstandings, we had an opportunity to experience the young man's frustrations and reflect on our possible complacency.

On the other hand, he radically distorted Warnock's message, and Jonathan Dimbleby or Jeremy Paxman would have confronted him skilfully on precisely this point. Warnock was not calling for a return to the segregated education of the post-war period. She was making a passionate plea on behalf of a minority of children whose lives had been (as she believed) made impossible by her own policy interventions in the 1970s. She spoke from personal experience, particularly conversations with parents who were at the end of their tether, and was not (as accused) speaking from on high. Her argument could hardly have been more humble. She described it as a 'personal conviction' and called for 'hard evidence' because 'one person's conviction is not enough'. Her opponents ignored these comments, accusing her of having a 'monstrous ego' and thinking 'she is always right'.

Thinking back later on, I was reminded of the dramatic climax of Yasmina Reza's play *Art*, in which a character who has been rubbishing the blank white canvas that was presented as art is invited to enact his derision by scribbling on it with a felt pen. In his hesitation, we are aware of our own apprehension: is he about to desecrate something? Would *we* be willing to take this step, converting disbelief into destructive action? Do we, perhaps, need to think longer, harder and more imaginatively?

As with art, there are conflicting views about special education. Some people have no difficulty with the concept of 'specialness' that was Mary Warnock's famous contribution to the field in the 1970s. Everyone (she said) has needs and difficulties. In some cases these are easily or relatively easily met in the course of everyday life and education. In others, they pose considerable difficulties, requiring 'special provision': a special educational needs teacher, a statement of special educational need etc. 'Special' *can* be an honorific term, and Warnock's early hope was that it might be viewed this way, so that children who had been unceremoniously excluded from ordinary schools because they had so-called handicaps might be treated as bringing something valuable to educational institutions. Unfortunately 'special' can also mean 'different', 'defective' or 'especially vulnerable', and many disabled people – by no means all – are sensitive to these connotations.

The young man with cerebral palsy was being provocative. Many wouldn't have cared, but I knew that if I seriously tried to interrupt him, I would have provoked precisely the grievance that he was trying to convey to the dignitaries and intellectuals in the room. *She tried to exclude me. She didn't make allowance for my disability. She denied me the extra time I needed because speech is so terribly difficult for me. She dismissed my* **special conversational needs**, *humiliating me just as others have done.* Like the man in the play, I hesitated, fearful of going this route.

Special conversational needs

In Chapter 2 I discussed Joseph Dunne's claim: 'To most truly teach, one must converse; to truly converse is to teach.' I suggested that this is very much on the right track; the policymaker's imperative 'teach efficiently' should give way to the genuinely *educational* imperative, 'teach conversationally'.

In this chapter I want to explore the idea that special educational needs should be understood primarily as *special conversational needs*. The young man with cerebral palsy at Warnock's launch was reeling from the humiliating experience of having been excluded from mainstream schools. No doubt he *was* excluded; it sounded as if no mainstream school in his area would adapt to and accommodate his difficulties. We can imagine how painful this must have been, but we must not lose sight of the fact that the opposite situation can and often does occur, as the mother of an autistic child reminded us. Some children are excluded from the *special schools* they desperately want to attend, and one of the reasons they want this is that subtle or not-so-subtle forms of cruelty from other children bring a pervasive sense of humiliation in the mainstream. They see special schools, rightly in many cases, as settings in which their special conversational needs are likely to be met. Admission into such a school means that, for the first time in an institutional context, they will feel properly heard and understood.

Other children, including the young man with cerebral palsy when he was at school, are desperate to engage in 'mainstream conversations', feeling that special school attendance magnifies and distorts their difficulties. They want to participate in a full range of conversations with those who have no obvious disabilities, and they want others to respect and adapt to their specific conversational needs, appreciating that having a speech defect, like having defective vision or hearing, need present no significant impediments to full social and educational engagement.

The question of how schools can treat disabled children or children with 'difficulties' with proper respect is to the fore at the present time, and this is due, in no small part, to Warnock's 1978 and 2005 interventions. The question should, I am arguing, alert us to a wide range of conversational needs. The needs of a child who cannot see, hear or speak are very different from those of a child with learning difficulties, or the social and emotional difficulties characteristic of what is called autism. Understandably, members of the first group often resist being associated with members of the second group, because such an association may have an *excluding effect* by suggesting that people with visual, auditory or speech defects are compromised as participants in social and educational conversations. For obvious reasons, many find this offensive and hurtful.

We are talking here about *feelings of exclusion*, and of course these can be devastating. They bring a sense of shame, humiliation, injury to one's self-respect, being diminished or demeaned. They can profoundly inhibit a person's moral and emotional development, as can the tendency to ignore or overlook such feelings in another. The launch of Warnock's pamphlet was memorable because a prominent ideological issue (inclusion is after all an *idea* behind which most of us rally) found embodiment in the dramas of human beings whose suffering was naked and raw. The young man with cerebral palsy was not recollecting his childhood experiences 'in tranquillity'. He was painfully reliving them, and his communication to the launch attendees was that the injury to his self-respect was not healed and may never be healed. Special school attendance, he was saying, had scarred him, and he did not know whether he would recover.

The mother of the autistic child had the same basic message. If the young man was saying 'I suffered terribly in a special school', the mother was saying 'My child suffers terribly in the mainstream.' There is a good deal of written testimony to both kinds of suffering. The first kind – enforced exclusion from mainstream institutions – is perhaps easier to understand than the second kind. Charlotte Moore, parent of two autistic boys, writes beautifully in her book *George and Sam* (2005) about the bullying and other trials autistic children often experience in mainstream schools. She says:

> Autists, with their naïveté, their odd mannerisms, their failure to understand social rules, are obvious victims. And when they are bullied, they have no idea of how to deal with the aggressors. At best, they won't notice or care; it will be water off a duck's back. But, more often, they will notice; they will be hurt and frightened. They won't understand the nature of the attacks, whether verbal or physical. They won't know how to alter their behaviour to make themselves more acceptable. (p. 173)

For such children, the environment itself feels alienating:

> Strip lights flicker, radiators hum, the chatter of other children is bewildering and incomprehensible. (p. 177)

This is obviously not the same situation as that of children who feel wrongly excluded from mainstream schools by cerebral palsy or other conditions. But if one is used to focusing on institutional arrangements, as our aversion to segregated education inclines us, this is a confusing situation. I believe the lesson of Warnock's launch was that our commitment to inclusion is inherently confusing. This becomes obvious if we move beyond commitment to the *idea* of inclusion and listen carefully to human beings telling their stories, reliving their dramas, expressing their anguish. Attendees at the launch were exposed to these, and their restlessness when the young man spoke for 15 minutes or so was not (I have suggested) simply about professional impropriety. It was about the discomfort we often experience when we are forced to attend to someone's profound pain, and it was compounded by the fact that identical feelings of exclusion appear to be experienced in ideologically opposed institutions.

Claire Sainsbury describes herself as having Asperger's syndrome. She a attended a mainstream school and was thoroughly miserable, eventually publishing a book about her educational experiences called *Martian in the Playground* (2000). Passages like these aren't easy to read:

> People.... . said things like 'you're weird' and 'there's something wrong with you' – and I agree with them.
>
> I pressed my nose to the window and tried to pretend that I wasn't there, that I wasn't really being teased etc. This kind of withdrawal and semi-disassociation set up a pattern that would continue for years to come. (p. 85)

These passages are heartbreaking, and the point I have been making is that they could as well describe the experience of a child who is excluded from a mainstream school as that of a child who is forced to attend one. In the first case, 'people' might be pupils from the local mainstream school encountered on the street: neighbourhood kids, abusing a child who is 'different', walks differently, talks differently, goes to a different school. The window to which the child's nose is pressed could be that of the bus on which they travel together every day. From fragments of speech, it was clear that the young man at the launch was telling us about bullying by children who repeatedly asserted their superiority over him. This message is heard again and again, from children at different kinds of schools, feeling excluded in different sorts of ways. No wonder the debate at Mary Warnock's launch was fiery and confused.

What is inclusion?

I have identified two layers of difficulty in this area of debate. One is emotional: it can be hard to listen, *really* listen, to a person who is in profound pain. Yet this is sometimes required if we are to do what Joseph Dunne describes as 'truly converse'; you can't converse with someone at a deep emotional level if you aren't really listening to what they are trying to tell you. The second layer of difficulty is intellectual. Recall Avishai Margalit's concept of negative politics, discussed in Chapter 4. 'What hurts us into politics?' he asks. 'On many occasions we recognise what is wrong with something without having a clear idea, or any idea at all, about what is right with it.' I would suggest that many people, if not most, are 'hurt into' special education (or a concern about this field) by the terrible injustice of adding humiliation and disrespect to the difficulties that are already experienced by poor vision, hearing, muscular control etc. In the post-war period the ugly manifestation of this injustice was a segregated educational system. This provides a clear negative target: *not* to reproduce the ills that were endemic to that system. It doesn't follow that we have a 'clear idea' of the alternative, an inclusive educational system, and it is important to confront the fact that, having abolished the segregated system, the agonies of *feeling excluded* may be no less acute than they were for segregated children in the 1960s or 1970s.

That they are a minority of children seems like a cruel aside. No one should feel excluded as Claire Sainsbury felt excluded, and the sad reality is that, irrespective of the inclusive ideology that permeates mainstream schools, many continue to do so. Part of the reason – and it was this that Warnock tried to target in 2005 – is the growth of a curious discourse in which people who rally under the banner of inclusion dig their heels in, refusing to listen to or take seriously the testimony of people like Sainsbury. They offer instead a rather partial explanation for why mainstream schools don't address her difficulties adequately. The explanation is that *special schools continue to exist*, and this makes it harder for mainstream schools to *adapt* to children with a diverse range of needs. Instead of bringing their special expertise and experience into the mainstream, special schools continue to function as a kind of magnet for children with difficulties or disabilities (and particularly their parents), offering a 'special' (rarefied, exclusive) environment that cossets these children without offering what they really need. What they need is preparation for the 'real world' in which they will eventually be expected to make their way, and this is achieved by creating social institutions that pool rather than siphon off expertise. Mainstream education may not make every child happy, but it is a microcosm of society in which diversity is properly represented. The hard lessons of diversity can be taught in no other way.

We see here an analogue of the argument discussed in Chapter 4, that children must be 'equipped for life' through a relevant, twenty-first-century curriculum.

And I want to say about radical inclusion what I said about that argument: it is not without merit but must not be allowed to deflect proper *respect for individuals* who may not fit into this worthy ideological mould. There is no inconsistency in the recognition that we must do at least two things: we must *generally* prepare children for a pluralistic society, and we must listen sensitively to those for whom this idea has little purchase, because they have severe learning difficulties, for example, or no real capacity for social engagement. I was struck by the remark of a radical inclusionist at Warnock's launch when asked how she felt about autistic children who were miserable in inclusive mainstream schools. Her answer was swift: 'They need to get used to it. That's how it is in the real world'.

One of the disturbing things about this debate is that it sometimes introduces a tone of harshness towards children who are obviously struggling. It seems natural to respond to someone who insists that a child she has never met 'needs to get used to it' with a sense of despair and anger. Painful emotions erupt, as they did at the launch, and what lie behind them are thoughts like 'you aren't listening to me', 'you don't understand'. Harsh words tend to elicit passionate, even hysterical ones, and this is a poor basis for well-thought-out policies. Once again we find ourselves in a morass of confusion through which we need to 'find our way'.

Plumbing problems

The confusion arises, in part, from what Mary Midgley calls, using the metaphor of plumbing, 'conceptual malfunction':

> Is philosophy like plumbing? I have made this comparison a number of times, wanting to stress that philosophising is not just grand and elegant and difficult, it is also needed.. . . . About plumbing, everybody accepts this need for trained specialists. About philosophy, many people not only doubt the need, they are often sceptical about whether the underlying system exists at all. It is much more deeply hidden. When the concepts we are living by work badly, they don't usually drip audibly through the ceiling or swamp the kitchen floor. They just quietly distort and obstruct our thinking.
>
> We often don't consciously notice this obscure malfunction, any more than we consciously notice the discomfort of an unvarying bad smell or of a cold that creeps on gradually. We may indeed complain that life is going badly – that our

actions and relationships are not turning out as we intend. But it can be very hard to see why this is happening, or what to do about it. We find it much easier to look for the source of trouble outside ourselves than within. (2000, p. 1)

I am perhaps less inclined than Midgley to locate 'plumbing problems' at the heart of philosophy, but there is no doubt that this passage resonates with Wittgenstein's metaphor of losing our way. The flow of thought is somehow disrupted or blocked. Because of its associations with respect, vulnerability and the possible abuses of children, the field of special education has been debated intensely, conceptualized and re-conceptualized by people with a variety of interests. More than any other area of education, perhaps, it is beset with distortions and obstructions. What resources are available to a philosophical plumber who seeks to rectify matters?

Let's start with this. We say 'inclusion is good, exclusion is bad' without exploring the obvious questions: included *in what*? Excluded *from what*? I suggested that our aversion to exclusion is clearer and more vivid than our positive conception of inclusion. Like 'good' or 'respect' (to both of which 'inclusion' is related), we need to *work towards* a viable and truly ethical conception of inclusion, given (as I have argued) its inherent unclarity. We have historical pictures of what exclusion can mean: pictures of the negative phenomenon by which many people are 'hurt into' this practice or area of enquiry. These are pictures of divided societies in which 'superior people' are admitted to a range of social institutions (cinemas, clubs, swimming pools, rented accommodation etc, not to mention schools) to which 'inferior people' are refused entry. Signs like 'no Negroes, no Irish, no dogs', common in the 1950s, still fill us with horror, and I am suggesting that the same kind of horror – its offspring, as it were – permeates the radical inclusion argument.

Consider this short passage from the website of an organization called Parents for Inclusion (2006), whose policy objective is to get all special schools closed by 2020:

> The 2020 campaign is based on the experience of disabled adults who went to special education schools and colleges. They experienced abuse, isolation and failure that emotionally scarred thousands for life. End this shameful exclusion that ruins lives.

This passage seethes with 1950s horror. It glides over the pertinent distinction between people like the young man with cerebral palsy, who are desperate to attend a mainstream school, and others who are desperate to escape from such a school. This 'gliding' tendency prompts disclaimers like the following, from a young man who describes himself as autistic:

> I do not know of any advocate from within the disability community who believes that inclusion should not be an available option. Disability advocates believe that disabled people should be *able* to go anywhere and do anything in mainstream society.... . However there are concerns within the disability community that inclusion is not always the best option . . . (Sinclair J, cited in Cigman R, 2007, p. xvi)

Gliding is a watery or navigational image; some thoughts are *deflected* in order to make way for others, as water may be deflected in order to make way for water from a different channel. In other words: people speak, and it is sometimes as though they have said nothing at all.

There is something paradoxical about this. The argument is that special school attendance *means* 'shameful exclusion that ruins lives'. It doesn't mean one thing to one child and another thing to another child; it means shame and humiliation for *every* child who attends a special school. This imports a new kind of exclusion, a new kind of disrespect, into the arena, and it is a strange move to make if you are committed to opposing division in favour of harmonious inclusion for all. As I have written elsewhere: 'What is interesting about this position is that it is universalist in aspiration but not in meaning. It aspires towards a society in which all children attend mainstream schools, but it is based on an understanding of what special schools mean which is conspicuously unshared.' (Cigman 2007, p. xviii) This is *conversational* rather than institutional exclusion, and it takes the form 'you may speak, but I shall not hear you'.

The radical position returns a simple answer to the question 'excluded from what?' *Exclusion from mainstream institutions* is the target of their argument, but the question of choice and the background of personal suffering (not to mention dramas of unlearning) are tantalizingly overlooked. A key phrase from Warnock's (2005) pamphlet was 'exclusion within inclusion'. She was talking about the *feelings of exclusion* that afflict many children in mainstream schools, particularly children on the autistic spectrum who are expected to 'fit in with the crowd' though they have little idea of what 'fitting in' means. (Nor, in many cases, do they seem able to learn.) The radical position is that such feelings and limitations *will surely be surmounted* when special schools are closed and mainstream schools garner the expertise of specialists and learn to adapt to diverse needs. I have chosen my words carefully: the idea that feelings and limitations 'will surely be surmounted' captures the idealism, the wishful thinking and ultimately the *unreceptive* tendency of this way of thinking.

This is important not only for special education, a field in which it is hoped by some that we will 'make children better' by arranging things institutionally so that they will become truly respectful towards others. It is important for the philosophy of education in a general sense, by which I mean an exploration of children's learning and development within a strictly ethical frame. In the last chapter I distinguished (following Margalit) between i.e. and e.g. styles of thinking. The e.g. style imports a willingness to *trust our experience* of certain people, events or encounters. The i.e. style distrusts these unless they are stylized or snapshot-like; it draws primarily on arguments, ideas, explications, definitions. I talked about the importance of somehow combining these styles, so our attention to examples doesn't degenerate into anecdote, and our attention to arguments or explications doesn't lose contact with reality. This is essential if our reflections on education are ever to achieve their purpose, which is to influence children's lives (and sometimes those of adults) for the good.

The radical inclusion argument is predominantly i.e. in tenor. Its launch pad is not the experiences of a wide range of children, each considered carefully on his or her own terms. It starts with a definition or explication that could appear in a handbook of educational terminology (*educational exclusion, i.e. education in a non-mainstream institution*), and explains why exclusion understood in this sense is so unacceptable:

> The discrimination inherent in segregated schooling offends the human dignity of the child.... Segregated schooling appeases the human tendency to negatively label and isolate those perceived as different. It gives legal reinforcement and consolidation to a deeply embedded, self-fulfilling, social process of devaluing and distancing others on the basis of appearance and ability in order to consolidate a sense of normality and status. (Parents for Inclusion, cited in Cigman 2007b, p. 777)

The word 'segregated' in this passage announces that the humane evolution represented by the word 'special' is to be pointedly ignored. An aspect of this evolution is, in principle if not in fact, careful attention to individual need and a refusal to send children to non-mainstream schools on the basis of simple classification. Special education has many weaknesses and continues to cause pain to many children. There is escalating demand for statements of special need and many local authorities refuse to provide these for reasons that may be economic or political. But the principles that drive referral to non-mainstream schools are kinder than they normally were in the 1960s or 1970s. By replacing categories of handicap with assessments of individual need – albeit reductively checklist-based in most cases – there has been a valuable shift towards 'people' rather than 'kinds of people'.

The radical inclusionist ignores the growth of a more e.g. style of thinking in this sense. She is concerned quite abstractly with offences to the *dignity of the individual*, and the importance of according unconditional respect to all by eliminating condescension, contempt or bullying. These are fine ideals, and the failure to attend impartially to individuals does not alter this fact, but condescension can be exceedingly hard to gauge in the absence of attention to examples. The devil of condescension is very much, in many cases, in the nuanced perceptual detail, or so I shall argue in Chapter 8. As a thinker in the i.e. style, the radical inclusionist is a kind of Kantian, which is to say a paradigmatic analyst of ideas. It is a Kantian thought that every person without exception should be treated with unconditional respect. It is a Kantian idea that, by virtue of their capacity for rational reflection, human beings are fundamentally and indefeasibly equal. And it is a Kantian principle that we ought never to treat others in ways that we would not, in their position, want to be treated ourselves.

In a world without special schools, radicals believe that these principles would be expressed by welcoming every child, not just some, into truly ethical centres of learning. Good mainstream schools teach these Kantian lessons at a variety of levels: practical, emotional, conversational etc. They *tackle* the bullying that is rampant in our society by treating this as an educational issue of the first importance. They don't pretend that education is one thing and learning to respect diversity is another; they devote all their energies to the creation of an ethos that is inimical to disrespect and shows diversity to be a joyous aspect of our human condition. This, at least, is the intention.

In this world, the labelling of people becomes otiose; or so it is argued. We only refer to children as autistic, dyslexic or even blind because we are unwilling to recognize them as worthy human beings to whom we must adapt as we adapt to everyone else. We pretend that there is a human norm outside which these children fall, instead of thinking of human beings as the subjects of an endless variety of needs, temperaments, strengths and weaknesses. In the post-war era, some children were routinely described as 'stupid' or 'thick'; they were also called 'educationally subnormal', referring to a norm outside of which, and indeed beneath which, such children were to be placed. Inclusively orientated mainstream schools have no need of labels; they see children as the individuals they are, each one different from every other. Labels are basically route markers to a kind of 'special provision' such as 'segregated schools' offer.

This brings us to troubled issue of political correctness. There are said to be respectful and disrespectful ways to speak about people. Not only must we choose our words carefully; we must also observe a kind of grammatical propriety. George and Sam aren't 'autistic children'; they are, at most (and insofar as we cannot avoid such language), 'children with autism'. The offensive label 'autistic' loses some of its sting if we observe the grammar of 'person-first', identifying the person before we identify her difficulties so that her status as a person or human being like any other – her *ethical* status – isn't tarnished by the category or box in which she is thought to fall.

In fact grammar doesn't, and never did, work this way. There is, as we see from other languages, no grammatical hierarchy such that being positioned earlier in the sentence confers status on a word, rather as the Queen leads lesser royals in a procession that culminates in the humblest of attendants. We do not pay homage to words by privileging them grammatically and sending words like 'autistic' to the back of the queue. What we know is that a sense of exclusion and inferiority was built into the old concept of a handicap, along with a labelling free-for-all that was often highly offensive. The 'person-first' ideology aims to restore dignity to those whose human status has (it is believed) been denied or undermined. However, some people with disabilities and difficulties value and seek labels, believing them to provide pathways to dignity and valued provision rather than obstacles. If their dignity is at stake, it isn't (they contend) because of labels; it is because some people continue to embrace negative conceptions of conditions like autism that others have left behind.

Jim Sinclair, quoted earlier, for example:

> I am not a 'person with autism'. I am an autistic person.... Saying 'person with autism' suggests that autism is something bad – so bad that it isn't even consistent with being a person. Nobody objects to using adjectives to refer to characteristics of a person that are considered positive or neutral'. (Sinclair, 1998B)

This suggests that some feel humiliated rather than respected by efforts to redirect the flow of language and thought. Why, they ask, should 'autistic' suggest unworthiness?

What we see here is the tendency to cherry-pick amongst the testimonies of those who are involved in special educational practices. As with the question of mainstream and non-mainstream attendance, so it is with the question of labelling; radicals base their arguments on what they see as a representative few, and flatly ignore others. Sinclair's objection to 'person-first' ideology is a pertinent one: as an avowed 'autistic person', he describes his *discomfort* with the ideology, suggesting that it intensifies rather than alleviates humiliation.

We should be concerned not only with the *ideal* of unconditional respect, but also with *how respect is shown*. For this we need e.g. thinking, thinking by example, which imports a willingness to reflect on the hospitality or non-hospitality of contexts, dramas or encounters to ideas like respect. The Kantian ideals are inspiring and indisputable; in Part Three of the book I shall suggest that the idea of cherishing (unclear as it is, and in need of explication) may be built upon the Kantian ideal of unconditional, universal respect. You cannot cherish a person without respecting her unconditionally, but the attitude of cherishing – including the attitude of *seeing a person as cherishworthy*, as discussed in Chapter 2 – goes deeper. We shall explore this through explication and example.

My concern about the young man with cerebral palsy at Warnock's launch was twofold in this sense. In a general way, of course, it was important to show respect, but a difficult and additional question arose: *how is respect shown to this individual on this occasion?* The importance of respect was not in doubt; the question over which delegates wrangled was *how* it might have been shown to one person without withholding it from everyone else in the hall. As I have indicated, philosophy is not normally well-attuned to the second kind of question.

This person, that person

Words like 'this' and 'that' don't have a natural home in philosophy. Nor do other indexical words like 'here' and 'now'. I have been suggesting in this chapter and the last that references to this child or that adult need to occupy a secure place in our enquiries. I mean that in some sense we need to privilege individuals, though we don't yet understand what this means. Our basic concern, after all, is with guiding people towards better lives. If we don't in some sense ground our reflections in people we know and regularly encounter, the errors of enhancement thinking are likely to remain intact. We shall be more interested in ingredients of people than people themselves. We shall pretend that self-esteem is one thing and happiness or resilience another, and we shall persuade ourselves that virtue is the master-ingredient, as it were, that embraces action, emotion and reason in an irresistible ethical package. We shall disappear into laboratories where we can measure quantities of virtue, and we shall forget Socrates' wise reference to the man of 'true simplicity of character who.... wants "to be and not to seem good"' (Plato 2003, 361 C).

Kristján Kristjánsson disregards Socrates' distinction when he asks how we can know if a friend is a 'character friend', i.e. a truly virtuous person whose judgements about other people's characters can be 'relied upon' as a source of knowledge. 'In order to know if a friend is really a character friend', he writes, 'we need to be able to measure her character' (2015, p. 70). This removes an *ordinary condition* of our lives from the arena of philosophy with a gusto that resembles the meticulous removal of breadcrumbs from orthodox Jewish homes at Passover. Unless we are deeply unfortunate, one of these conditions is our inability to doubt that *some* of our friends and family are fully as good as they seem. We trust them to be and not merely to seem good, and are not tempted to measure their virtues or conduct any other tests.

Trust is a foundational concept for our enquiry. It *involves* emotions but it *is not precisely* an emotion, because it has more to do with the flow of life and the barriers to this flow than articulate belief and experience. Not only is it at the heart of our ministrative relations; it permeates our conceptions of what can and cannot be known, what methodologies we deem adequate and inadequate. It should hardly need saying that the imperative to trust must be accompanied by an imperative not to trust gullibility or naïvely.

Wittgenstein took a giant step for philosophy when he responded to epistemological distrust by introducing the word 'this' into his philosophical enquiries. 'A good ground is one that looks *like this*', he writes (1953, para. 483). He was responding to sceptics like Bertrand Russell who thought it was impossible ever really to know whether chairs exist or other people have minds. You can only entertain such doubts in Wittgenstein's view by attacking the very core of what we call meaning and understanding, which means the very core of ordinary life. 'Just try – in a real case – to doubt someone else's fear or pain' (1953, para. 303). This short sentence cuts scepticism and counter-scepticism down to size by bringing the reality of this person or that person in this or that context into our philosophical reflections. It suggests that to banish 'real cases' is to introduce a kind of artifice into the proceedings, and this artifice is a kind of exclusion: the exclusion of real people.

A good ground for recommending a child's transfer from a mainstream to a non-mainstream school may *look like this*. It may look like the child we have been struggling to absorb into classroom activities: her bewilderment, her evasions, her pain. It may look like the bullies we have confronted and failed to subdue, as well as subtle forms of contempt from kinder children. It may look like the impassioned conversations we have had with the child and her parents, of which our carefully worded reports give hardly a hint.

The philosopher who distrusts examples wants part of the story but not the whole. It is easy, I think, to suppose that this is how philosophy or ethics must be, if it is to be a respectable academic subject. What is noteworthy is that, despite his enormous and justified kudos, Aristotle thought otherwise. He saw ethics as an inescapably practical enquiry, believing that its imperative to influence our lives *for the good* has significant methodological implications. He was both an i.e. and an e.g. philosopher who explicated the concept of virtue while insisting that ethical judgements about who is and is not virtuous 'end in perception'. Like Wittgenstein, then, he believed our language and reflections must be *porous to reality*, and that this imposes significant limits upon meaningful explication.

The following passage, for example, tells us a good deal about virtue, but pointedly leaves it up to us to discover in whom it is embodied:

> virtue is an active condition that makes one apt at choosing, consisting in a mean condition in relation to us, which is determined by a proportion and *the means by which a person with practical judgement would determine it*. (2002a 1107a) (my bold)

There is, for Aristotle, no code for picking out 'people with practical judgement' from a crowd, though a code of sorts may give us some good clues (especially about who isn't such a person). To demand this is to ask too much from language and too little of reality.

The errors of the radical inclusion argument should alert us to some valuable points. Examples are needed if we are to think well ethically: e.g. thinking is non-optional if we are seriously to attempt to 'make people better', rather than merely articulate the principles and ideals (important as they are) by which we are moved. We need to reflect upon a range of testimonies without prejudging their importance, and the 'person-first' ideology, misguided as it is, has something to contribute here. It *rightly* emphasizes the *person as such*, irrespective of her disabilities, difficulties or other attributes. It *rightly* notes the importance of language as a vehicle of respect and disrespect, alerting us to the dangers of converting people into kinds. We must be careful not to oversimplify this situation (as political correctness sometimes requires) or ignore those testimonies that disturb the tenor and flow of our thoughts.

The words 'person' and 'human being' are often used interchangeably, but in the final section of the book our focus will shift decisively towards the latter. We may cherish cats or dogs, trees or statues, but our cherishing of other humans will, in general, occupy a central place in a good human life. Genuine cherishing of human beings is expressed not only in *what* people do, but also *how* they do it; not only in *what* they say, but also *how* they say it. Its domain, in short, is grammatically rich, extending beyond the line up of verbs and adjectives that are typically used to describe the 'kind' of person someone is, the 'kinds' of actions she performs. It extends, one might say, into the domain of the adverb.

Aristotle understood this. His texts are punctuated (particularly around the explication of virtue) with adverbs (beautifully, violently, slackly) and adverbial notions (the 'manner' or 'way' in which people act). 'God loveth adverbs' say the Puritans, meaning that we often need to reach for adverbs and adverbial constructions when we seek to capture a person's true virtue or character. In the domain of disability, we aren't merely concerned with correct actions or admirable attributes. We are concerned with the *manner* in which people with disabilities or difficulties are acknowledged or unacknowledged, respected or disrespected, and we are concerned with this at the deepest level. I return to these matters in Part Three.

Part Three

Cherishing Children

7

Humanness and the Difficulty of Reality

One of the twentieth century's most significant contributions to philosophy.... is a working through of the idea that there can be no viable distinction between the existence of concepts and the lives we live with them. There can be no fundamental divide between thought and life.

Jonathan Lear (2001), p. 8

What is cherishing? In the final part of the book we shall close in on what I take to be a distinctively *human* engagement that belongs at the heart of our ethical lives. No doubt there are semblances of cherishing in other species, and we may (eventually) want to cast our net wide to include the thought that some non-human species cherish rather as we do. But I am doubtful. All animals feel, and no doubt some animals think, but it does not follow that they feel and think as we do.

At any rate, the focus of our enquiry is human cherishing. To understand this better, we need to probe a concept that has been problematized by many philosophers: the idea of the human. Are human beings *valuable as such*? Or is the assumption that this is so a case of species-bias? Should we not build our moral philosophy on a distinctively moral concept, namely the concept of a person? Persons (say some) have particular capacities, notably the capacity to reason and be aware of oneself through time. It is *by virtue of* this capacity that a creature, human or non-human, acquires moral status or importance. Human infants and profoundly or severely cognitively disabled people (disabled by genes, accident or disease) therefore have *less intrinsic worth* than smart non-humans like dolphins or chimpanzees.

To believe this is, among other things, to place parents who cherish their infants or severely cognitively disabled children in an anomalous position. They cherish creatures that have no intrinsic moral worth. They value what is value*less*; indeed, they find limitless importance in this fundamentally worthless being. No amount of forbearance or concession to the evolutionary importance of bonding removes the sense of oddity here, not to mention the implied insult to infants while they are infants, and people with cognitive disabilities (in most cases) forever. Personhood theory is a theory of value, constructed by reason, with implications that are, to most people I believe, repugnant. The concept of cherishing to be forged here will respond to the disfiguring claims of personhood theory, not so much by disputing its claims as by reflecting on its setting in individuals, rather than what I shall call communities of cherishing.

We have two kinds of question to consider. The first: what is cherishing? What does cherishing *mean* in terms of attitudes, feelings, commitments, thoughts, beliefs and aspirations? How does it relate to *reality itself*, an often difficult and tantalizing demand or response from the world with which we struggle to engage? The second: *in what terms* can we speak meaningfully about cherishing? What conceptions of knowledge, emotion and truthfulness, for example, not to mention humanness, are needed to make sense of this idea? From a philosophical perspective, what *style of thinking* is required? What kinds of philosophy create barriers to understanding? How can we bring to light an idea of cherishing that isn't sickly, sentimental or pious?

In the remainder of the book, I shall explore a way of thinking that I believe is essential for this topic. In speaking of Wittgenstein, Aristotle, Iris Murdoch and others, I have been building towards this point. Particularly significant at this juncture is Margalit's conception of the *priority of the negative*, illustrated by the thought that we are 'hurt into' certain professions or practices by something that is clearly hateful and must be opposed. Systematic disrespect and humiliation, for example: many go into politics or careers of protest by their painful awareness of groups who are subjected to these. Others are 'hurt into' primary school teaching or psychotherapy by their awareness of disadvantaged or abused children who are struggling to learn (and in danger of remaining disadvantaged) or suffering from depression. Abuse is obviously hateful, as is parental neglect, as are the repetitive dramas of unlearning with which many teachers must engage. Positive concepts, like flourishing, well-being, cherishing, are less easily understood.

'On many occasions', says Margalit, 'we recognise what is wrong with something without having a clear idea, or any idea at all, about what is right with it' (2002, p. 113). Cherishing is inherently an unclear idea, refined, elusive but powerful. It refers to an intimate attitude, and is bound to intimate human dramas; we know that philosophy has difficulties with knowledge and truth when *this* person or *that* person enters the scene. This is why it is so important to think about styles of thinking, for if we get this wrong, we shall hardly progress beyond a conception of virtue as behaviourally identified and even measured. But it is not identification that matters, and it is certainly not measurement; it is the *meanings* of difficult ethical concepts – particularly positive ethical concepts – that we need to probe and absorb into our lives. As Iris Murdoch said about courage and (following her) I said about happiness and respect, in ethical matters our understanding hopefully deepens over time. (We saw that Jeremy Bentham's understanding of happiness conspicuously failed to do this.) The idea of cherishing is not one simply to analyse or define; it is one to 'complicate, alter and deepen' (as Murdoch puts it) in the dramatic settings of our lives.

'All the world's a stage', says Jacques in Shakespeare's *As You like It*, and I have been focusing on this insight – dramas of everyday life, particularly in the home and classroom – in the book so far. This represents a shift from the perspective of educational policymakers who see classrooms as so-called factories of learning: places in which, if all goes well, learning is enhanced through validated techniques and interventions. The basic insight of happiness agendas and the like is that many children are caught up – to their own serious detriment and that of others – in dramas of unlearning that are emotionally inspired. If children resembled computers that learned what they were programmed to learn, or if their intelligence was genetically enhanced and their personal idiosyncrasies subdued, we might be gratified by, rather than anxious about, their progress. (We might then be worried about matters other than learning!) The frantic flow of imperatives and new 'magic bullets' would become a thing of the past, and we would no longer look sideways at nations where children reliably excel, coveting their prosperity and researching their methods.

Arguing with Shakespeare, Goffman (1956) remarked, 'All the world is not, of course, a stage, but the crucial ways in which it isn't are not easy to specify.' (http://www.sociosite.net/sociologists/texts/goffman_self.php) I'm not sure what he had in mind but for present purposes, Shakespeare will do. This is not because human life should be seen as a series of performances, but because it is passionate, active, endlessly transformative and riven with conflict and meaning. There is, I suppose, no drama when we sleep (it may be there when we dream), but even boredom, imbued with desire and frustration, can be dramatic, giving rise to dramas of unlearning. This is sufficient, I believe, to justify the thought that human life and learning are inherently dramatic. Compelling pictures of *ethical importance* will hopefully emerge as we consider what this means.

The nature of the phenomenon

Cherishing exists, first and foremost, within intimate dyads, like parent/child, teacher/pupil, friend/friend. It can exist within groups – we may cherish our families or pupils *en masse* – but 'group cherishing' does, I think, supervene upon attention to individuals as far as possible: attention that aims to be 'just and loving', in Iris Murdoch's words. I suggested earlier that, hyperbolic as it may sound (even as an ideal) to describe teachers as cherishing every pupil, they must see each one as *cherishworthy*. This suggests a way of taking responsibility for others that is potentially transformative for both people, and it includes what I earlier called 'beliefs in', completing this phrase with something like 'the other person's real good', 'the possibility of real happiness for that person'. Only when things look very bleak for the other person might this be modified to something like 'hoping for' or 'wishing for'.

Much of what I shall say about cherishing can be said about love, but cherishing has a physical and even sensual nature: it takes delight in *details* of how another looks, feels, thinks or speaks in ways that aren't necessarily true about love. We can possibly love a dead person; we can certainly cherish her memory. But we can no longer cherish the person herself, for the conditions do not support cherishing. The soft skin of the infant, the quality of a person's breath, the delicate brushstrokes of the painting, the quiet gestures of kindness: it is on such *specific* qualities, discovered in a person or object, that the person who cherishes dwells. This aspect of cherishing has inspired a great deal of poetry, good and bad, yet cherishing is not (or not simply) a state of delusion, for to cherish is to reject caricatures of the cherished one, and seek to bring the real person, the cherished object, into view.

In education, John Holt provides rich examples of what it is for a teacher to cherish a pupil. The intensity of his interest in *how pupils think and avoid thinking, learn and avoid learning* shows an engagement that is compassionate and irreducibly individual. It is true that he generalizes as well, advancing principles of child-centred theory, but the real value of his work, I believe, is his unremitting vision of the good (the *real* good) for specific, pseudonymous children. He exemplifies what it is to attend 'justly and lovingly' to the realities of individuals, attempting to capture these in ordinary language untethered by theory.

To cherish a person is to hope, not that everyone will do the same, but that people will see her as *properly* cherished and not debase her. This is why personhood theory shocks: it is a *rational denigration theory*, saying that many cherished individuals are not in any real sense worth cherishing, though cherishing may be 'excused' or 'scientifically explained' in parents and a few others. There is nothing more tormenting than to see a cherished person denigrated, and the person who cherishes is sensitive to this. This sensitivity *may* be excessive, but it can also alert us to veiled forms of condescension from those who are ideologically committed to treating everyone as equals. People who denigrate others don't necessarily understand that this is what they are doing, but the person who cherishes is likely to be aware, and she minds.

The feelings and attitudes of cherishing are *essentially* non-condescending; they include a sense not only of the value of the object, but also of the *unsurpassable* value of the object. I cannot cherish you if I feel that you are valuable, but that I am (or she or he is) somehow more so. We cherish our young and, if we permit ourselves to do so, we cherish those who are developmentally young but physically more mature. To cherish is to be acutely conscious of the fragility and vulnerability of the object, and this can apply both to people who are vulnerable by any lights (e.g. because they are newborn or disabled) and to those who are vulnerable simply by virtue of being human. The cherished object *as such* is seen as vulnerable to loss, harm or extinction, and we who cherish them are also vulnerable (terrifyingly at times), for our well-being is experienced as inseparable from theirs.

Cherishing, then, is a truth-seeking, uncompromisingly *equalizing* (or respectful) attitude that is responsive to another in a variety of ways. It is impossible to cherish another from the moral (or any other) high ground, and to say, as I wish to, that every human being *needs* to be cherished – and particularly, to *have been cherished* as an infant – is to say that human beings have from the outset a sense of the regard in which they are held by others (especially, of course, the parents). In Chapter 2 I quoted Alice Miller's remark that every human being needs to be 'noticed, understood, taken seriously, and respected' from the first weeks and months of life (1983, p. 49). To cherish is to be aware of vulnerability – need, desire, pain – but never condescendingly, never in the spirit of: you are a weakling, I am strong. For every human being, need and desire must sometimes remain unfulfilled, and pain must sometimes be endured. Those who cherish are hardened to this difficult truth to varying degrees, and if they are tempted constantly to weigh in with 'helpful' solutions, they try to think again.

I want to explore the way in which our ministrative engagements with others – particularly in Montaigne's 'indivisible domain' that includes education and upbringing – occur on a *difficult interface* between thought, feeling and reality. To cherish a person is not merely to feel passionate and loving towards a creature that one sees as 'extraordinarily important'. It includes a *wish to learn* when one might have misjudged, misunderstood or inadvertently mistreated the other person, as well as a wish to bring about valuable learning. For the person who cherishes takes responsibility for her part in directing the other towards genuinely good transformations, a good human life. She has a sense of how difficult this can be: how much easier it is to go wrong than right. All this is true, I believe, whether one is a good or poor learner about such matters. Autistic people have difficulty learning about other people's emotional lives, but the obstacles to their truly cherishing others are not this; as for all of us, the obstacles are having no desire to learn, no belief in the other's 'good', no sense of responsibility (even in extreme circumstances) in trying to bring this about and no sense of the person's equal and unconditional worth.

In this chapter and the following two chapters, we shall unpack some of these thoughts, focusing on the idea of humanness and the importance of cherishing in human life (this chapter), and the nature of human emotion and its development from infancy (next chapter). I shall suggest that infancy, far from being a condition in which human beings lack intrinsic value, is a period of distinctively human learning and development that we neglect at our peril. With psychoanalytic thinkers like Donald Winnicott and Alice Miller – although they use very different language from mine – I shall suggest that it is by *being cherished as the particular human being one is* that one learns to cherish others, as well as practices and phenomena or domains: the planet, nature, music and so on. I shall also suggest that the capacity to cherish is a foundation for a flourishing or happy life.

None of these suggestions should be considered simple or absolute. We may speak about what human beings typically need (e.g. the capacity to cherish) without talking about 'necessary conditions' or denying another feature of humanity: that on occasion, it dramatically confounds expectations. I see Winnicott, like Holt, first and foremost as an astute and compassionate observer of human beings, whom he studies without theoretical preconceptions in such a way that *discovery* is a permanent possibility. This brings the work of both thinkers into line with Wittgenstein, whose insights permeate this book. 'Don't think, but look!' said Wittgenstein famously (1953, para. 66), and what he meant, of course, is not that we must never think, but that our thinking must be true to what we see and find before us.

The difficulty of reality

One aspect of our topic that provokes bewilderment as well as philosophical argument is that, not only do we not all cherish the same people or creatures; in some cases (as with severely cognitively disabled people) people cherish precisely those whom others find disgusting or repulsive. Philosopher Eva Feder Kittay has a severely cognitively disabled daughter, now adult, and describes the 'maddening' dissonance between her own perception of her daughter and other people's. Most painfully, this occurred between her mother and herself when her mother urged her to put her beloved daughter (when she was a young child) into an institution so that Kittay could get on with her life. 'It made me crazy', says Kittay. 'I could not comprehend it' (1999, p. 152).

She offers another example, from a parent in a similar situation:

I liked [the potential new babysitter] immediately, and his enthusiasm seemed to equal ours – until he met Jody. At that moment his jaw dropped; mumbling something about checking his afternoon schedule, he hastened out of the door.... . I suddenly found myself looking at Jody through adolescent eyes. I saw not the cheerful, handsome seven year old whom I care for every day, but a seriously deviant little boy who drools and makes strange, uninterpretable noises. (Ibid., p. 168)

Kittay's melancholy comment on this passage is: 'I don't want to see Sesha [her daughter] as others see her. I want others to see Sesha as I see her' (Ibid).

Perceptual dissonance is an ordinary feature of life. Perhaps I have no idea what my friend sees in her new partner, why she admires him so. This only becomes a serious problem when the dissonance is extreme; it becomes apparent, for example, that my friend is in a sado-masochistic relationship that she refuses, or is unable, to see as such. It can be agonizing for a parent to discover that her cherished child is perceived by others as 'seriously deviant', strange or abhorrent. This is not, it seems, a rare occurrence for parents of severely cognitively disabled children. These children – largely unverbal as they are – cannot complain or write reports about their mistreatment. Like infants, but for many people, less appealingly so, they are entirely dependent on the ministrative attentions of others.

Cora Diamond discusses what she calls the 'difficulty of reality' that may be experienced when such a situation arises. She doesn't discuss cognitive disability, but her examples resonate with these 'maddening' experiences of parents. I do not have space to explore this topic in detail, but I want to outline what Diamond means by 'difficulty of reality', indicating its relevance to what I call dramas of unlearning. I shall suggest, controversially, that the capacity to find reality 'difficult' in Diamond's sense is not only human, but is also present as a possibility, if not an actuality, from more or less the beginning of human life. (Diamond herself does not suggest this.) This is not *why* we normally value humans over non-humans; I am not attempting to replace personhood theory's capacities for reason and self-consciousness with another set of value-conferring capacities. Nor am I insisting that we are the only species that experiences reality as difficult in Diamond's sense (though I suspect this is so). I am simply offering a perspective that will hopefully help us to understand why the rational denigration of non-rational, non-self-conscious human beings seems profoundly wrong.

'Reality' is a notoriously tricky idea (the ultimate positive concept, perhaps), with a large non-specialist as well as specialist following. Many people who keep themselves aloof from philosophy declare (as though this is an obvious rather than philosophical thought) that there is 'no such thing as reality'; there are only *realities*, yours, hers, mine. Philosophers disagree about access: Is 'true reality' theoretically unknowable (as in Kant's noumenon)? Does it reside in ordinary events, people, objects? Is talk of 'true reality' a sign of confusion about what philosophy can do or mean? Diamond has written about such questions, but what she calls the 'difficulty of reality' lifts the topic out of realms of abstraction. It is a 'working' difficulty in the sense of being a difficulty of feeling, thinking and living.

Diamond illustrates what she means by 'difficulty of reality' through examples. (She is, indeed, a thoroughly e.g. kind of philosopher, and one of the things we need to do in this section of the book is explore more deeply what this means.) I shall discuss two of her examples here, not in order to follow every aspect of her thought, but in order to shed light on dramas of unlearning. Since these are (as suggested) emotionally driven, we need a conception of emotion that includes the powerful and often buried feelings of children in homes and classrooms. I shall suggest that the difficulty of *learning* that some children experience often has a source in the experience of finding *reality* difficult in Diamond's sense.

Her first example: a Ted Hughes poem talks about 'contradictory permanent horrors' in the contrast between a photo of six young men smiling into the camera, and the knowledge that, within six months, they will all be dead (they are soldiers and the year is 1914). These horrors: 'Smile from the single exposure and shoulder out/One's own body from its instant and heat.' (Cavell 2008, p. 44) Here is Diamond's comment:

What interests me there is the experience of the mind's not being able to encompass something which it encounters. It is capable of making one go mad to try, to bring together in thought what cannot be thought: the impossibility of anyone's being more alive than these smiling men, nothing being more dead. (ibid, p. 44)

Diamond describes this, following Hughes, as an experience of 'bodily thrownness', making a point that is rarely considered in philosophy: thinking can be excruciating, and the body may be implicated in its torment. Life within death, death within life; how can we experience the disjunct between these if not, somehow, through the body? How can we read this poem, if not as a vivid vision of life set against a stomach-churning vision of corpses on a battlefield?

One imparts an intimate smile,
One chews a grass, one lowers his eyes, bashful,
One is ridiculous with cocky pride –
Six months after this picture they were all dead.

Part of what I take Diamond to be doing here is, as Murdoch says, 'complicating, altering and deepening' familiar philosophical conceptions of emotion. Most philosophers believe, following Aristotle, that emotions are constituted primarily by judgements or beliefs; if there is sensation (and of course, there often is) this is incidental to the identity or meaning of the emotion. Diamond goes deeper than most philosophers into the emotional lives of human beings, uncovering a kind of torment to which we are prey. What happens when the mind cannot encompass something it encounters? We talk here about 'going mad', being 'shouldered out of one's body' and, perhaps (if it is Hamlet we have in mind), inertia or paralysis.

Diamond's second example differs from the first, and also resembles it. Elizabeth Costello, a character in JM Coetzee's novel of the same name, is an elderly novelist invited to give a lecture to an audience of academics. Something curious happens. Instead of delivering the formal lecture on literature that her hosts expect, she speaks with passion about the horror of what human beings do to animals. This is not simply a surprising change of topic. It is the outpouring of a 'wounded woman' who can hardly bear to live with what she knows; she is haunted, she suffers a terrible 'rawness of nerves'. It is as though *she too* were suffering the degradation and terror that is meted out to non-human animals on the back of human indifference and sophisticated justification. She *knows what this degradation and terror are like*; she feels them in her body.

Part of her agony is that she must speak to people who have an entirely different, *disembodied* sense of what it means to be human. She must speak to academics, philosophers, people with elegant arguments and opinions about the 'issues' surrounding animal rights and non-rights. She appears before them as a wounded woman, knowing that (like her daughter-in-law in the audience, who mutters, 'she is rambling'), they will be impatient and uncomprehending. She wishes she could 'find a way of speaking to fellow human beings that will be cool rather than heated' (1999, p. 22), but she has no idea how to do this.

What happens is that she 'uncovers her wound', anticipating little or no sympathy or understanding but having no alternative options before her. She 'speaks with her body', pointing to an *example* that she knows many will find tasteless, if not abhorrent (and she is right). She speaks of the Nazi death camps:

> The particular horror of the camps, the horror that convinces us that what went on there was a crime against humanity, is not that despite a humanity shared with their victims, the killers treated them like lice. That is too abstract. The horror is that the killers refused to think themselves into the place of their victims, as did everyone else. They said, 'It is they in those cattle cars rattling past.' They did not say, 'How would it be if it were I in that cattle car?' They did not say, 'It is I who am in that cattle car.' They said, 'It must be the dead who are being burned today, making the air stink and falling in ash on my cabbages.' They did not say, 'How would it be if I were burning?' They did not say, 'I am burning, I am falling in ash.' .... In other words, they closed their hearts. (1999, p. 34)

For members of Costello's fictional audience, as for many philosophers, the 'issues at stake' have nothing to do with the poetry of this passage, or the *example* of the wounded woman who is inspired to speak this way. *I am burning, I am falling in ash.* It has nothing to do with the *reality* that is searingly evoked by Coetzee's novel: that of a suffering human animal who stands on no moral or philosophical high ground, but *feels complicit*, feels we are all complicit, as if (like the people in and around the death camps) we are saying 'they' rather than (imaginatively) 'I'. Something is 'making the air stink', and we turn our attention to cabbages, refusing to 'think ourselves into the being of another'. We indulge a collective fantasy about the moral acceptability of non-human suffering, which releases us from the demands of imaginative feeling. 'There are no bounds', says Costello, 'to the sympathetic imagination' (p. 35). (This is one of a few philosophical claims she makes, and it will be discussed in the next chapter.) Nor are there bounds to her need, hopeless as it feels, to impress on others the horrors surrounding the industrial production of meat. She tells her audience about a drive she took in the local area earlier that day:

> I saw no horrors, no drug-testing laboratories, no factory farms, no abattoirs. Yet I am sure they are here..... They are all around us as I speak, only we do not, in a certain sense, know about them. (Ibid., p. 21)

We know and we do not know, says Costello, and through her, Coetzee; this is how things stand with us human beings.

There are many threads to draw out of this rich discussion. One of them is Diamond's exploration of *deliberate or persistent evasion of understanding*, which she describes using Stanley Cavell's concept of deflection. Many philosophers, says Cavell, deflect their awareness of appalling or frightening realities into argumentation. Take philosophical scepticism. It appears to some philosophers to be an interesting question whether *other minds* – minds that are not my own – can ever really be known. After all (they say), your pain is different from my pain; your impression of redness is different from mine. I am, from this vantage point, imprisoned in my own mind, and as Descartes famously argued, even your existence as a thinking, feeling being like myself may be doubted.

To this, there is an anti-sceptical response, which says that scepticism about other minds is confused. It is built on the supposition that language is a private system of meaning, rather than a public system the meanings of which are (as Wittgenstein argued) embedded in common judgements, common 'forms of life'. The sceptical argument doesn't make 'common' sense; it denies something (that I might 'be in your position') that couldn't possibly be asserted. In what sense *might* I 'be in your position'? I would have, somehow, to 'become you', and this is not an intelligible thought.

As a Wittgensteinian, Cavell might be expected to join the anti-sceptic here, but his response is far more radical. He finds a 'truth in scepticism', namely the 'scary' truth of human separateness. He writes:

> The sceptic comes up with his scary conclusion – that we can't know what another person is feeling because we can't have the same feeling, feel his pain, feel it the way he feels it – and we are shocked; we must refute him, he would make it impossible ever to be attended to in the right way. But he doesn't *begin* with a shock. He begins with a full appreciation of the decisively significant facts that I may be suffering when no one else is, and that no one (else) may know (or care?), and that others may be suffering and I not know, which is equally appalling. But then something happens, and instead of pursuing the significance

of these facts, he is enmeshed – so it may seem – in questions of whether we can have the same suffering, one another's suffering. (1969, pp. 246–247)

The real issue for Cavell (and by 'issue' I mean that this is where he redirects the conversation) is that 'the human creature's basis in the world as a whole, its relation to the world as such, is not that of knowing, anyway not what we think of as knowing' (Cavell 1999, p. 241). Our 'basis in the world' is not knowing but *acknowledging*, which means attending to reality in a mode of openness and affirmation, rather than evasion and intellectualization. Bernard Williams once said deprecatingly of moral philosophy that: 'all the important issues are off the page, somewhere, and.... great caution and little imagination have been used in letting tiny corners of them appear' (1993b, p. xviii). In Cavell's terms, the 'important issues' are *unacknowledged and deflected*; they become material for analysis at a safe but shallow level. Except where 'tiny corners' appear, feelings like torment, bewilderment and rawness of nerves are 'off the page'. In a strikingly Wittgensteinian move, Coetzee restores them to our attention.

At the time of writing, the UK is reeling from a devastating fire in West London in which a twenty-four-storey building went up like a torch, trapping many people, men, women, children. Heroic firefighters saved considerable numbers, but they had to make terrible choices. Many people had to be carried, and firefighters had to take some and ask others to wait. The atmosphere amongst these desperate people can hardly be imagined. Everyone knew that waiting was likely to carry a sentence of death.

Personhood theorists conduct thought-experiments in which precisely this kind of emergency is imagined. The burning building thought-experiment poses the question: if only one person can be saved and another (or others) must be left to die, what is the proper basis for a rational decision? May we sacrifice a cognitively disabled child in order to save a cognitively able one? Or a cognitively disabled child in order to save a 'superchimp' whose cognitive capacities exceed those of the child? To save or not to save: *that* is the question, and it is answered (not tentatively but definitively) using the principle of moral personhood. Recoil as we may from rational comparison along these lines, it is, say the personhood theorists, something we *ought* to do. The sense of moral catastrophe, whereby *whatever* one does will be terrible and wrong, is deflected; reason is available as an alternative to the hopelessness of certain moral choices. *The tragedy does not exist.* Or if it exists, it is personally affecting rather than humanly inevitable.

Diamond's contribution to philosophy through the concept of a difficulty of reality is original and important. I believe she is right to note, with Cavell, the tendency of philosophers to deflect their appreciation of such difficulties into knock-down arguments, supposedly. Diamond's discussion promises to 'complicate, alter and deepen' standard conceptions of emotion in exactly the way that is needed to understand the notion of cherishing. It is noteworthy, however, that she speaks exclusively about adults, and in particular about professional philosophers. (One might add here: certain kinds of intellectuals.) She does not speak about the young, and I want to suggest that children as well as adults can find reality difficult in the senses to which Diamond draws our attention. Children can find themselves exposed to horrific, unthinkable situations: the alcoholic transformation of a parent, the terrors of a war zone, the death of a sibling and so on. They can be haunted by irreconcilable conflicts of vision, as when one parent cares deeply about principles or values that the other dismisses as hogwash. Many children struggle at what I called the difficult interface between thought, feeling and reality exactly as adults do, both knowing and fearing to know. We might even say that the capacity to reside at this interface and the propensity to deflect (in effect, to flee) are *human* in a lifelong sense. If certain writers on infancy are to be believed (Winnicott, notably), reality often becomes difficult for human beings at a very early age, and much will depend for them on whether they are able to surmount this difficulty, and how.

Thinking about infancy

Peter Singer writes:

> In thinking about this matter [which creatures have objective moral worth] we should put aside feelings based on the small, helpless, and – sometimes – cute appearance of human infants. To think that the lives of infants are of special value because infants are small and cute is on a par with thinking that the baby seal, with its soft white fur coat and large round eyes, deserves greater protection than a gorilla, who lacks these attributes. (1993, p. 170)

Small, helpless, (sometimes) cute. If you add 'human', 'non-rational' and 'non-self-conscious', you have, for Singer, a baby. To accept this characterization without unease or discomfort is, I suggest, to switch off a *humane* response for which this inventory of attributes seems deflective and deeply cynical. It is to become, in a sense, a caricature of a philosopher, for whom emotions are never (as Sherman says) *bringers of the moral news*; they are barriers to truth and objectivity.

Consider an alternative perspective. In this passage from Marilynne Robinson's *Gilead,* the narrator is an elderly preacher with heart disease:

> now that I am about to leave this world, I realise there is nothing more astonishing than a human face.... It has something to do with incarnation. You feel your obligation to a child when you have seen it and held it. Any human face is a claim on you, because you can't help but understand the singularity of it, the courage and loneliness of it. But this is truest of the face of an infant. (p. 75)

Between Robinson and Singer, there is *descriptive dissonance,* akin to the perceptual dissonance discussed earlier. Robinson finds meaning and dignity in the faces of infants; Singer finds 'cuteness' (reminding us of the modern rage for Facebook 'likes'), akin to that of a baby seal, as well as theoretical attributes of non-reason, non-self-consciousness. This is a difference of vision as extreme as any other, and it points to the real chasm between personhood theorists and their baffled or 'wounded' critics. Human worth is not, for the latter, about the presence or absence of attributes. It is something we find within communities of cherishing: families, schools, neighbourhood and other communities in which people are cherished or seen as cherishworthy. We cherish others, on this view, not as we find or fail to find attributes or capacities, but as they enter our moral worlds, and particularly as they come into intimate moral proximity.

I am committed in this book to exploring the latter view. Cherishing, I suggested, is a truth-seeking attitude, and one of the reasons we may prefer Robinson's vision to that of Singer is that it captures rather than deflects a poetic truth implicit in Cavell's notion of 'appalling reality'. *I may be suffering when no one else is, and no one may know or care; others may be suffering and I not know.* This, Robinson seems to say, is the *claim* that human faces make upon us, and the faces of infants most of all. They are 'singular' and 'lonely' in the sense that, as human beings, they are destined (sometimes, often, always) to suffer alone, without acknowledgement from others when it is urgently needed. In philosophical idiom, this is our *metaphysical predicament,* and far from finding, as Singer does, the likeness of a baby seal in an infant, Robinson finds humanness itself, quintessentially as it were.

This is the point to which an exploration of cherishing leads. I want to express the insights of Robinson, Cavell and Diamond by saying: any human being 'makes a claim' fully to belong to a *community of cherishing,* rather than have its existence denigrated or ignored. If you don't believe this, look at a human face in an attitude of acknowledgement rather than cynicism. I would go further and say that the justice of the claim is a *foundational moral truth*, the point to which all moral thinking ultimately leads. It may be expressed as an imperative: we *cannot, must not,* turn our backs on human beings who are not cherished as members of some community or other; nor must we condescend to them, as if they had lesser worth. This is 'truest of a human infant' in the sense that human infants are helpless, needy and dependent to an extreme.

Most people, I think, affirm this truth vigorously and intuitively. I earlier referred to the claims of personhood theory as 'disfiguring', meaning that they are intended to disrupt deeper layers of thought and feeling that flow from the sense that our 'basis in the world' is acknowledgement rather than knowledge. When philosophers discuss moral objectivity (are moral claims objective or subjective?), the example of finding an abandoned infant on one's doorstep is sometimes cited. You *must not ignore this child on your doorstep.* This is like our moral default, a claim so compelling that it is hard to imagine a perspective from which it can be sanely doubted. We may disagree about many ethical matters, but not this.

Robinson finds courage in the human face, the face of an infant most of all. Is this a metaphor? Can she be serious? The Aristotelian conception of courage, as well as the everyday conception I think, involves the making of choices between alternative courses of action, and sometimes struggling to *feel* less fearfully, less selfishly, more honestly. It involves the wise confrontation of dangers or threats, neither rashly nor as a coward. Moral deliberation is not, obviously, in the infant's gift, but the idea of courage has *poetic* resonance for a creature that is destined to suffer and think. For Robinson, as I understand her, an infant is an incipient thinker, a creature who is *learning* to think more or less from birth, and *will suffer* certain difficulties of reality. The human being in utero has no need of thinking, because she has no need of a conception of reality. This is about to change.

Donald Winnicott has a simple way of referring to reality (1960a, in Winnicott 1985, p. 38). He calls it 'not-me'. This refers, obviously, to the reality of others, rather than oneself. To learn about the difference between me and not-me is, he implies, the fundamental task of a creature that is destined to think. It belongs, he says, 'to extreme sophistication and to the maturity of the individual'; like Iris Murdoch's concept of the good as an inexhaustible and magnetic reality, learning about the difference between me and not-me, and particularly 'deepening, altering and complicating' this learning indefinitely, is our basic maturational call as human beings.

There is another side to this. 'Humankind cannot bear very much reality', said TS Eliot, and we may think in this connection of Elizabeth Costello. *Why* can she not bear the suffering of animals to the extent that she carries this as a wound in her body? Is she *too* attuned to reality? How far can one go down this path and live a decent human life? This is a question we all face – are we attuned too little or too much? – and it is beautifully expressed by the other literary Eliot, George, who says in *Middlemarch*:

> If we had a keen vision and feeling of all ordinary human life, it would be like hearing the grass grow and the squirrel's heartbeat, and we should die of that roar which lies on the other side of silence. As it is, the quickest of us walk about well wadded with stupidity.

How much reality can or should a human being bear? When might one reasonably block reality from view, or encourage another person to do so? These questions go to the heart of what it means to aspire to live well and help others to do the same. To live well is not only to act well; it is also, as Aristotle understood, to *think and feel* well, *think and feel* appropriately, whatever this turns out to mean. I am connecting this idea with Diamond's concept of the difficulty of reality, suggesting that children sometimes need to be helped to bear realities that they perceive as impossible to bear. (Sometimes we must leave them, provisionally perhaps, to their fantasies.) This is part of what it means, in a serious sense, to attempt to educate a person's emotions, or enhance her character. And my Aristotelian view is that rules and formulae play a limited role: if we meet a child who, like Costello, seems *tormented* by reality, we owe her some sensitive, conversational encounters.

'A Tremendous Development'

'By feelings', says Aristotle, 'I mean desire, anger, fear, confidence, envy, joy, affection, hatred, yearning, jealousy, pity, and generally those things which are accompanied by pleasure or pain.' To be virtuous, he says, is:

> [to] bear ourselves well or badly towards the feelings; for example, in relation to being angry, if we are that way violently or slightly, we bear ourselves badly, but if in a measured way, we bear ourselves well, and similarly in relation to other feelings. (2002a, 1105b 26)

In the next chapter, we shall explore a trio of concepts: the concept of emotion as a condition in which we 'bear ourselves badly or well'; the concept of reality as potentially or actually *difficult to behold*; and the concept of virtue as a disposition in which we 'bear ourselves well' by engaging appropriately and even bravely with reality. To nurture *courage in relation to reality* (the courage to persist in the endeavour to see things clearly) is, I believe, a key responsibility for those who cherish the young. It is not simple, however, for reasons we have been discussing. For some human beings, in relation to some realities, what George Eliot calls 'keenness of vision and feeling' is too much to bear; there is a risk of 'dying of the roar which lies on the other side of silence', in other words, suffering serious and enduring trauma. This is especially so with human beings who are highly vulnerable or immature. It is a theme with which Winnicott's work deals illuminatingly.

The topic of educating emotions is familiar amongst philosophers; it is a crucial aspect of Aristotelian moral education. I have been unable, however, to find a philosophical text that explores emotional development in a way that is intimately tied to *metaphysical* development. By this I mean the development of a mature conception of 'true not-me' from the point at which we had no notion of a distinction between me and not-me. This is moral development of a kind that not everyone achieves; some people, sadly, persist throughout their lives in seeing others as characters in their own dramas (and therefore bound to admire them or comply with their will). Implicit in this notion of development is the thought that some human beings experience 'rawness of nerves' in their efforts to engage with reality, and are tempted to avoid or deflect these. Examples might be the death of a parent or the birth of a sibling: experiences that can produce a sense of 'dissonant reality' by confounding the child's fundamental assumptions about what is real and important.

Such difficulties can produce lasting misery, repetitive patterns, strategies of evasion, dramas of unlearning. In the next chapter, we shall discuss a child called Emily who appears in John Holt's *How Children Fail* (1990). Her 'difficulty of reality' is represented by the thought that she *must* be right; she can't 'bear to be wrong, or even to imagine that she might be wrong'. Her solution to the reality of educational assessment, tantalizing to her teachers, is to employ some intriguing, and relatively transparent, strategies of evasion. We do not cross a red line between education and therapy by reflecting on the possible infantile or early-childhood sources of such difficulties. My aim in this chapter has been to explore the idea of the human in an ethical rather than scientific sense, and the point is not to speculate (or recommend that teachers speculate) about the early causation of dramas of unlearning; least of all is it to 'blame the parents'. We are concerned with human development, not (as for many psychologists) in terms of chronological stages, but in terms of what Iris Murdoch calls the 'progressing life of a person'. This is partly an empirical matter, and partly an exploration of meaning. In short, Diamond *and* Winnicott.

I agree with Martha Nussbaum when she argues:

> that the childhood history of emotions shapes adult emotional life: that the emotions of adult life originate in infancy, and that this infantile history shapes their adult structure in powerful ways. (2001, p. 230)

It is puzzling that so few philosophers have explored the infantile origins of human emotion, and in the next chapter I shall speculate about why this is so. To discuss emotional development without reflecting on its source, or consulting astute observers like Donald Winnicott, seems deflective in a worrying sense. Emotions may derail in all sorts of ways, and it is hardly speculative to suggest that *early* emotional derailment, at a point where reality is minimally conceived but also maximally threatening, can have deep and lasting effects.

Winnicott discusses what I call metaphysical development quite simply in this passage:

> Mothers with babies are dealing with a developing, changing situation; the baby starts off not knowing about the world, and by the time they have finished their jobs the baby is growing up into someone who knows about the world and can find a way to live in it, and even to take part in the way it behaves. What a tremendous development!
>
> But you will know people who have difficulties in their relation to the things that we call real.... For some people their personal imaginative world is so much more real to them than what we call the real world that they cannot make a good job of living in the world at all. (1969, p. 69)

How can such people be helped to make a *better* job of living in the world? Writing in the 1950s, it was natural for Winnicott to refer this problem exclusively to the mother, where nowadays we would refer to parents, close friends, other family members. His answer was: we need to have had a mother who was 'able to introduce the world to us in small doses'. In the next chapter, I shall paint a picture of emotional development and education that bears the imprint of this thought alongside thoughts of Aristotle. We help others to make a 'better job of living in the world' by presenting it to them 'in small doses': doses that, like the wise doctor's medicine, are finely judged and neither toxic nor inert. This is how, in Aristotle's terms, we inculcate good emotional habits in the young, though he didn't take infancy seriously enough to explore what this means in the earliest stages. It is also how we may modify or transform the not-so-good emotional habits of older people who were neglected or mistreated during childhood.

Humankind cannot bear very much reality, but for each of us, there is a 'well-judged dose' that is ministered in 'friendship' (*philia*) in Aristotle's sense: ministered by the good-enough parent, teacher or friend (in a conventional sense), who wants 'good things' for another for his or her sake. One of the challenges of school education is that a 'well-judged dose' for one child or several children may bring torment and 'rawness of nerves' to others. An ethic of cherishing, as elaborated in the final chapter, will hopefully shed light on this situation.

8

Aristotle and the Transformation of Emotion

> *What Aristotle doesn't fully appreciate is that emotions can change and develop through continuing clarification of the stories that inform them.*
>
> Nancy Sherman (1995)

In John Holt's *How Children Fail* (1990), we meet a child called Emily. We do not know her age, but she is old enough to be expected to spell (or to make a decent stab at spelling) the word 'microscope'. The word appears in a spelling test, and Emily writes 'MINCOPERT'.

Her teacher, John Holt, says:

> She obviously made a wild grab at the answer, and having written it down, never looked at it, never checked to see if it looked right. I see a lot of this one-way, don't-look-back-it's-too-awful strategy among students. (pp. 19–20)

Don't-look-back-it's-too-awful is one of a repertoire of evasive strategies meticulously described by Holt. Another is *mumble*, which in the context of a French lesson looks like this:

> Just make some mumbled, garbled, hideously un-French answer, and the teacher, with a shudder, will give the correct answer in elegant French. The student will have to repeat it after him, but by that time he is out of the worst danger. (p. 23)

Other strategies are *take-a-wild-guess-and-see-what-happens* and *get-the-teacher-to-answer-his-own-questions*. Emily has mastered these brilliantly, and she needed to do so because, as Holt tells us, she *must be right*.

> She cannot bear to be wrong, or even to imagine that she might be wrong. When she is wrong, as she often is, the only thing to do is to forget it as quickly as possible. Naturally she will not tell herself that she is wrong; it is bad enough when others tell her. When she is told to do something, she does it quickly and

fearfully, hands it to some higher authority, and awaits the magic word *right* or *wrong*. If the word is *right*, she does not have to think about that problem any more; if the word is wrong, she does not want to, cannot bring herself to think about it. (pp. 21–22)

This is a child who acts 'quickly and fearfully' in ways that are inimical to learning. Even when she succeeds – when her teacher utters the magic word 'right' – she is unable to enjoy her achievement, let alone develop or refine it. She must move on, like a cat on a hot tin roof. Sadly, says Holt, she is often wrong, but she fails in intriguing and paradoxical ways:

She feels safe waving her hand in the air, as if she were bursting to tell the answer, whether she really knows it or not. This is her safe way of telling me that she, at least, knows all about whatever is going on in class. When someone else answers correctly, she nods her head in emphatic agreement. Sometimes she even adds a comment, though her expression and tone of voice show that she feels this is risky. It is also interesting to note that she does not raise her hand unless there are at least half a dozen other hands up. (p. 22)

Emily seems to have made a risk assessment with a view to replacing the official objective of learning with her personal objective of *appearing* to learn. She wants to deflect the awful thought that she is 'guilty' of making an error; if anyone is 'guilty', it had better not be her. Her solution to the problem represented by the imperative to learn – her grand strategy, as it were – is to muddle her mind, confusing herself and others, planting doubts about where the 'guilt' really lies. Is it with Emily or with those who misunderstand her? For now, at least, the stigma of failure is allayed.

Holt describes a task in which the class was trying to judge where a weight should be placed in order to balance a beam. The beam could be locked in a balanced position by using a peg, and the children then had to judge which weight, placed at which point, would make the beam balance when the peg was removed:

One day it was Emily's turn to place the weight. After much thought, she placed it wrongly. One by one, the members of the group said that they thought it would not balance. As each one spoke, she had less and less confidence in her choice. Finally, when they had all spoken and she had to unlock the beam, she looked around and said brightly, 'I don't think it's going to balance either, personally.' Written words cannot convey the tone of her voice: she had completely dissociated herself from that foolish person (whoever it was) who had placed the weight on such a ridiculous spot. (p. 24)

Emily doesn't have a learning difficulty in the usual sense of that phrase. Her problem is emotional; she *dissociates* herself from herself, becoming both a bright, receptive member of the group and a 'fool' who makes silly errors. When her confidence plummets in response to the scepticism of the class, she is unable to rethink her answer; indeed, serious thinking and learning seem beyond her much of the time. She is not only 'fearful', as Holt says; she seems so ashamed of who she is and what she is capable of that her expectation of failure becomes self-fulfilling. Questions and answers, other people and herself, become scrambled, and Holt sums up her thought (or what he takes to be her thought): 'These teachers want me to do something. I haven't got the faintest idea what it is, or why in the world they want me to do it. But I'll do *something*, and then maybe they'll let me alone' (p. 25).

This kind of child presents acute challenges in the classroom. Emily lacks the *confidence to fail*, needed by every learner (see Cigman 2001). She is what Holt calls a *producer*, 'only interested in getting right answers', as opposed to the *thinker*, who tries to 'think about the meaning, the reality, of whatever it was [they were] working on' (pp. 11–12). This difference will resonate with many teachers, but it doesn't go far enough, as Holt himself is aware. Some students are neither producers nor thinkers; they are, at some level, more interested in getting *wrong* than right answers. They lack the confidence to *succeed*, and when success is within reach, they backtrack or feel anxious.

Holt discusses two examples:

> I can't get Nell out of my mind. When she talked with me about fractions today, it was as if her mind rejected understanding. Isn't this unusual? Kids often resist understanding, make no effort to understand; but they don't often grasp an idea and then throw it away. Do they? But this seemed to be what Nell was doing. Several times she would make a real effort to follow my words, and did follow them, through a number of steps. Then, just as it seemed she was on the point of getting the idea, she would shake her head and say, 'I don't get it.' Can a child have a vested interest in failure? (p. 11)

Trudy is more willing than Nell to succeed. A poor speller initially, she makes good progress, until one day she does well on a spelling test. Astonishingly, reports Holt, when he told her the result, Trudy looked 'not pleased or satisfied, but anxious'. He continues:

> I thought, 'Becoming a better speller presents risks to this child. What on earth can they be?' And then I saw why for some children the strategy of weakness, of incompetence, of impotence, may be a good one. For, after all, if *they* (meaning

we) know that you can't do anything, *they* won't expect you to do anything, and *they* won't blame you or punish you for not being able to do what you have been told to do. I could almost hear the girl saying plaintively to herself, 'I suppose he's going to expect me to spell right all the time now, and he'll probably give me heck when I don't.' (p. 109)

How Children Fail is Holt's affectionate, depressing and illuminating account of anomalies like these. They can be sources of great frustration to teachers who suppose that ordinary kindness, interesting tasks, praise and good humour will encourage children to work hard, enjoy learning and be proud of their successes. It is not always so, and it seems natural, when confronted by children like Emily, Nell or Trudy, to look for *causes* of their resistance to learning and achieving. They have too little self-esteem, they are too unhappy, frightened, ashamed; they have insufficient resilience or perseverance. *Therefore,* schools must inculcate greater or lesser 'quantities' of these educationally consequential 'qualities'.

This is reminiscent of the person who tunes a piano or violin: a little higher, not too much, that's too high, now a fraction lower. Of course, no one really believes that children's emotions can be tuned to the 'right pitch', but the suggestion of uniformity (as every instrument in the orchestra is tuned to the piano's A), combined with the objective of enhancing collective achievement, should (I have argued) concern us. Dramas of learning often form patterns; as Holt says, evasive strategies like *mumble, don't-look-now-it's-too-awful* and so on, are not rare but common. But they are also the dramas of particular children who fear failure or success in particular ways.

Some teachers may be tempted to send children like Emily, Nell and Trudy to a psychologist or therapist, where their resistances to learning may be 'fixed'. This can be useful in some cases, especially if the problems seem intractable; but I think Holt is right to suggest that it is very much the business of teachers, as of parents, to attempt to engage with children's difficulties thoughtfully (as time allows) before passing them on to mental health professionals. It is *appropriate* for a teacher to raise questions like 'does this child have a vested interest in failure?' and 'what worries this child about becoming a better speller?' The problem with scientific approaches to education is that they often seek to deter teachers and parents from the essential work of *feeling puzzled* and giving time to such questions.

In this chapter, we shall discuss a virtue that informs sensitive conversational responsiveness between parents and infants: the virtue that Aristotle calls *phronesis*, translated as practical judgement, practical rationality or wisdom. *Phronesis* is needed for wise cherishing, where we are frequently called upon to make good judgements – often difficult, consequential ones – on behalf of another. Wivestad describes Aristotle's conception of *phronesis* well when he says it is 'an active condition for inexact practical wisdom, enabling a person in changing circumstances to see and calculate and do what is good for oneself and conducive to the good life in general'. Such a condition is obviously hard to acquire, but how much harder it is when one aims to 'see and calculate and do' what is good for a person whose importance in some ways exceeds one's own.

Difficulties of reality?

Emily, Nell or Trudy could turn up in any classroom of children around (what I take to be) 9 or 10 years old. Do they struggle with difficulties of reality in Diamond's sense, as discussed in the last chapter? Is it helpful or misleading to draw comparisons with Elizabeth Costello?

Our answers to these questions depend on several things. First, it is clear that, for all her uncertainty about how to speak to an academic audience, Costello is a highly articulate sufferer from the difficulty of reality. She knows where she stands. She needs to 'raise awareness', not in a clichéd political sense, but in a sense that flows agonizingly from a personal need. She stands on no moral high ground. There are holes in her argument – she refuses to eat meat but not to wear leather – and in the end she says (somewhat dejectedly) she is only trying to 'save her soul'. She knows her arguments are philosophically unsustainable and her imagery (arguably) tasteless; but she is able to do something we call 'communicating about herself' to those who are willing to listen.

The children discussed by Holt are not like this; they enact and betray rather than articulate their difficulties. Like most young people, they do not set out to explain to adults the precise nature of their struggles, and in all probability, they could not say much about what scares them about school. A difficulty is no less difficult, however, because it is unrecognized or a mute. There are signs that children like Emily experience something that has a real kinship with Costello's difficulty of reality.

In Chapter 7, I explored Diamond's idea of a difficulty of reality, as she does, primarily through examples. She also *characterizes* the idea (using language 'at full stretch') in this passage:

> That is a phrase of John Updike's, which I want to pick up for the phenomena with which I am concerned, experiences in which we take something in reality

to be resistant to our thinking it, or possibly to be painful in its inexplicability, difficult in that way, or perhaps awesome and astonishing in its inexplicability. *We take things so.* And the things we take so may simply not, to others, present the kind of difficulty, of being hard or impossible or agonising to get one's mind around. (2008, pp. 45–46)

Hard, impossible, agonizing to get one's mind around.... . This is a response to 'something' or 'someone' that is tantalizingly (awesomely, astonishingly) beyond, separate, outside. It is akin to what philosophers call an intentional object, an object of thought, except that there is neither a clear object nor a clear thought. It is hard to describe, hard to pin down, and Diamond's simplest formulation appears when she speaks of instances of rare goodness or beauty: 'they can give us the sense that *this* should not be .... yet it is'. The phenomenon that concerns Diamond thus includes *wonder*, an astonished attraction to what is beautiful or good. This suggests a corollary, a flipside, to the idea of difficulty of reality. Instead of dissonance, there may be harmony; instead of the impulse to deflect, there may be an extraordinary and seductive allure. It should not surprise us that reality can strike us in such opposing ways. The allure of reality, like its difficulty, is obviously implicated in learning.

We are speaking, then, about modes of attention to reality, bringing emotions that seem quite out of sync with the list-forming everyday-ness that belongs to the Aristotelian treatment of emotions. In the previous chapter, I quoted this:

by feelings I mean desire, anger, fear, confidence, envy, joy, affection, hatred, yearning, jealousy, pity, and generally those things which are accompanied by pleasure or pain. (2002a 1105 b 22)

Yes, one might say, but what sort of anger? What sort of hatred or fear? Not every experience of anger, hatred or fear is *unthinkable*, as Diamond describes. (I hate swimming in cold water, but there is nothing here to 'get my mind around'.) I suggested in the last chapter that Diamond's concerns apply not especially to philosophers, intellectuals or academics, but quite generally to human beings. If we turn our attention to infancy, drawing (non-cynically) on our own experiences with infants, as well as those of novelists like Marilynne Robinson and specialist observers like Donald Winnicott, we see the difficulty of reality as a *human predicament* that is more keenly felt by some than others, susceptible to deflection and bound up with learning and unlearning.

What is the reality that Emily finds resistant to thinking? Holt suggests an answer to this question when he describes a meeting with a professor at the MIT graduate school, who says that his students use exactly the strategies that Holt discusses: *mumble, take-a-wild-guess-and-see-what-happens, get-the-teacher-to-answer-his-own-questions*, etc. Holt continues: 'I later realised, these are the games that all humans play when others are sitting in judgement on them' (p. 29). The reality that Emily can't get her mind around is the institution of school, constructed much of the time around scrutiny and judgement from authority figures. Holt is right to suggest that many human beings (not only children) cannot deal with this, and resort to evasive strategies as a desperate solution. It seems hyperbolic to suggest that 'all humans' do so. Some people tolerate judgement well, and even invite it, choosing stage careers or taking up pressured jobs that put them constantly in the public eye. (Think of those who work on live television.) If they have nerves, they subdue or conceal them, proceeding as though they had none. They *learn well*, knowing that their performances are scrutinized, possibly by millions; in many cases, they go from strength to strength. Emily is not like this, and nor are many others. *Being judged* presents unthinkable difficulties for some.

There is something here that it makes no sense to *exclude* from education. At a basic level, learning is a form of attention to reality, and we are concerned in this chapter with the deep, intense and conflicted emotions that such attention may bring. Not mild anxiety but paralysing fear; not fleeting embarrassment but agonizing shame. On the other side, and in ways that may be celebrated rather than deplored: not a willingness to learn but a *need* to learn, as though the sense that '*this* should not be ... . yet it is' demands attention and investigation *by me*. This may bring fulfilment, a gradual growth of insight and understanding. Or it may become compulsive, a barrier to relationships that the person wants and needs.

If we are to capture the depth and intensity suggested here, we need a conception of emotion as *vertical* rather than *horizontal*. Or perhaps we should say that emotions are *dimensioned*, since they weave a dramatic course through time, as well as exhibiting depth. We do not merely experience a succession of emotions, one emotion replacing another in response to events and happenings around us. Some emotions go *down* into the body, *down* into the memory and into the past, *down* into the depths of one's being. To think this way is to move beyond the Aristotelian worldview that accommodates emotion in a serious but limited way. Reading Aristotle, one is aware of both the importance of our emotional histories and the inappropriateness of too great a preoccupation with these for 'manly' individuals like himself. Friends are important, but mainly because they provide opportunities to enhance our well-being by sharing pleasures and doing favours for others. As far as possible, we protect our friends from our painful emotions, and emotional excesses like 'too much fear' or 'too much anger' are assigned to the domain of non-reason in which women but not men are destined to reside. Also condemned to this domain are those who have had a 'poor upbringing': unlike the well-born and the well-bred, these people are pretty much beyond help, living at the mercy of their feelings and unreceptive to rational arguments or guidance.

In these ideas, there is a mixture of emotional truth and elitist condescension. There is truth in the thought that the kinds of people we are, the kinds of people children will become, bear the marks of early emotional tendencies. Elitism arises from a deterministic sense that those who were *not* 'beautifully brought up by means of habits' (but rather, one might say, 'vulgarly') will never fulfil their potential as human beings. I believe that Aristotle shows a serious (albeit understandable) lack of imagination here. At one level, he resembles the people Elizabeth Costello describes when she says that the real horror of the concentration camps is the refusal of the killers to 'think themselves into the place of their victims'. Aristotle does not ask: *how would it be if I were a slave? Suppose historical events had favoured others over myself.* He believes (without a hint of supporting evidence) that 'the deliberative faculty in the soul is not present at all in a slave; in a female it is present but ineffective' (*The Politics* I.xiii 1260 a 11). An aristocratic man who never questions these assumptions must work hard to suppress his imagination when he interacts with slaves or women. He must develop a *habit* of moral and visual dullness towards some human beings.

The following passage suggests that this suppression is incomplete, as one would expect from a thinker like Aristotle:

> Mothers delight in loving, for some of them give up their own children to be brought up, and feel love just in knowing them, not seeking to be loved in return if both are not possible; it seems to be sufficient for them if they see their children doing well, and they love them even if the children, in their ignorance, give back nothing of what is due to a mother. (2002 1159 a 28)

Though Aristotle doesn't say as much, this passage describes virtue in its finest sense. Through practical reason – understanding what is best for their children, judging that they are in certain circumstances better off without them and loving them all the same – women may *accept* the crushing loss of giving up their own children. This may be metaphorical rather than literal, involving the acceptance of another person's questionable claim on one's child: that of the child's father, for example, in a situation of acrimonious divorce, where a certain amount of 'letting go', though painful, is judged best for the child. This is cherishing, and it surpasses Aristotle's virtue of friendship or *philia*, at the heart of which, he says, is 'wishing for good things for a friend for his own sake' (2002 1155 b 32). To cherish is not simply to wish for good things for the other; it is to struggle to see things justly and lovingly, to feel and act as reality demands, even if that means losses to oneself. Aristotle offers a glimpse of motherhood as he sees it, and moves on; he can make nothing, it seems, of this *quiet* form of heroism, which lacks the public honour of heroism on a battlefield.

We must think more imaginatively than Aristotle was able to. How much 'difficulty of reality' is suggested by this story of mothers who are satisfied if they see their children doing well, despite giving 'nothing of what is due to a mother'? What must it take to *reach* this point of satisfaction, and how much torment, bodily thrownness, rawness of nerves must have been endured? Aristotle isn't interested, of course, in the painful nuances of mothering (or fathering for that matter), but I see his moral framework as the place to start because it is built on a non-rational foundation that allows us to think vertically about emotions. As Aristotle scholar Myles Burnyeat says: '[Aristotle] reacted [against Socrates' intellectualism] by emphasising the importance of beginnings and the gradual development of good habits of feeling. What is exemplary in Aristotle is his grasp of the truth that a morality comes in a sequence of stages with both cognitive and emotional dimensions' (1980, p. 70). He is right, and this truth is not to be taken for granted. Aristotle allows us to glimpse the infant in the child, the child in the adult and, indeed, the infant in the adult. He is the philosopher we need to advance this conversation, as well as the philosopher we need to leave behind.

Aristotle on beginnings

Aristotle makes the point several times: 'It makes no small difference, then, to be habituated in this way or in that straight from childhood, but an enormous difference, or rather all the difference' (2002 1103b 20). Human beings need to develop habits of feeling and acting well, and they need to do this young. By the time they are citizens of the world, these habits are to a great extent irreversible. The 'right education' involves habituating a child to 'take delight and feel pain in those things in which one ought' (2002 1104b 11). Habituation in this sense is rather like nature itself. If you let go of a stone, it naturally falls down rather than up, and in a similar way, the 'right education' inculcates impulses that become 'second nature'. No more than a stone understands why it goes down rather than up do young children understand *why* it is good and feels good to share one's toys, be affectionate rather than aggressive, generous rather than mean. That will come later, when the person is 'experienced in the actions of life', no longer 'apt to follow their [untutored] impulses' (2002 1095a 4–6). By then, she understands *what* is required by the moral life, and *that* it feels better to live morally than immorally.

So Aristotle tells us: 'one who is going to listen adequately to discourse about things that are beautiful and just [e.g. his own *Nicomachean Ethics*], and generally about things that pertain to political matters, needs to have been beautifully brought up by means of habits' (2002 1095b 5). Such a person is apt to make good choices in all spheres of life, and 'this has grown up with us all from infancy, and for this reason it is difficult to scrub away this feeling, since it is ingrained in our life' (2002 1105 a 8). I am quoting (as usual, unless otherwise stated) Joe Sachs' translation, but it is interesting also to look here at the translation of Broadie and Rowe (2011): 'pleasure is something we have all grown up with since infancy; the result is that it is hard to rub us clean of this impulse, dyed as it is into our lives'. So our tendencies to experience pleasure and pain in certain ways and at certain times are 'dyed into our lives' – and indeed, our souls – from the beginning.

It is an evocative image. If a white fabric is dyed indigo, it will become resistant to bleach and other chemicals, impossible to restore to its former whiteness. In moral psychological terms, this is like saying that if a young child develops habits of distrusting people who wish her well, or feeling constantly frightened, ashamed or enraged, she is likely to remain that way, though she may learn to hide such feelings much of the time. Early emotional tendencies are *intransigent* or *stubborn*; but a great deal hangs on what we understand by this. What does it mean in terms of adults *giving up on* children, choosing harsh methods of controlling or subduing them, excluding them from schools or classrooms in the belief that they are emotionally ineducable? What *follows* from the thought that emotional tendencies are 'dyed' into young souls? What do we believe about the possibilities of character transformation? And how do such questions interact with our political proclivities: to preserve or challenge the status quo? To promote or impede social mobility?

Our project, it will be recalled, is to explore what it means to minister to the good, the real good, of another person. The natural focus for this question is engagements between adults and children in practices (upbringing, education) that I call ministrative; but of course adults often minister to the good of other (especially vulnerable) adults, and wise *children* sometimes minister to the good of vulnerable or disorientated adults. We have explored ideas around the concept of enhancement: that we minister to another person's good by enhancing her happiness, self-esteem, self-respect, character and so on. My emphasis throughout has been on shifting the focus from agendas – evidence-based policy interventions that may help some, but allow others to fall through the net – to the settings in which these questions have their original home, namely intimate human engagements.

To understand these engagements, we need to think about emotional transformation, and at one level, the answer to the question 'how stubborn are difficult emotional tendencies formed at an early age?' is the answer given by Coetzee, through Costello. *There are no limits to the imagination.* This means that we think unjustly if we insist that it is *impossible* for a disturbed or abused child to achieve emotional growth as required to live a decent life. We think unjustly if we think that, just because we can't *imagine* such a transformation, it cannot happen. We think unjustly, finally, if we fail to say to ourselves (as discussed in the last chapter) 'I' rather than 'she' or 'he' when we consider the predicament of the child. These limitations of our imaginations may inhibit our conversational responsiveness, our capacity to see clearly and respond aptly.

Emotional transformation is not the same as emotional correction or manipulation, in which Aristotle certainly believed. (*The Rhetoric*, sometimes described as a manual for the courtroom, analyses the cognitive content of different emotions and shows how they can be modified, revised or defused by altering the beliefs on which they are based.) If a child with 'ugly' emotional habits is to develop into a child with 'beautiful' emotional habits, someone needs to engage deeply with her emotions; it isn't simply a matter of cognitive revision. That there are no limits to the imagination means that this child may grow emotionally, in part, by imaginatively enlarging her world, learning to see it differently; but it is a rare and exceptional human being who does this alone. Here is a place (not the only place) for the concept of cherishing: engaging deeply with another who may be emotionally 'ugly', full of hatred and anger, without returning these emotions. I repeat what I said above: it is appropriate for teachers to accept *some* of this difficult work that is conventionally assigned to parents and therapists. I'm thinking especially of teachers of very young children, who wear their pain transparently; but the same is true, I believe, of teachers of all ages.

The concept of a difficulty of reality takes us, as I said in the last chapter, to a difficult interface between feeling, thought and reality. In Aristotle's concept of *phronesis*, we find an ancient working of this idea, alongside a reluctance to plumb the depths of human torment in the belief that such emotions are in most cases irrational and 'unmanly'. The next section will be the most technical part of the book, but I hope to make its 'real life' significance clear.

Phronesis and its temptations

Aristotle's theory of moral education underwent a renaissance in the last few decades, largely as a consequence of Elizabeth Anscombe's groundbreaking article 'Modern Moral Philosophy' (1957). This article should be read by non-philosophers who associate moral philosophy (disapprovingly) with absolutist notions of right and wrong action, and moral education (even more disapprovingly) with the coercive inculcation of this knowledge into children. Donald Winnicott, who died three years before the article was published, would have found it an eye-opener. His own work on moral education was directed against people like the headmaster who said to a child: 'You will believe in the Holy Ghost by 5 o'clock this afternoon or I will beat you till you do.' Anscombe rejected philosophies based on concepts like *duty* and *obligation*, suggesting that they are residues of divine modes of thinking, and senseless in the absence of these. It is not 'profitable', she said, to do moral philosophy until we have an 'adequate philosophy of psychology, in which we are conspicuously lacking'. She directed her readers towards Aristotle's *Nicomachean Ethics*, and I have suggested that Aristotle's moral psychology (his philosophy of psychology) is complemented and enriched by the work of Winnicott and others who have paid close attention to infancy. In the following, I shall explore some moral psychological matters concerning emotional growth and transformation.

Chronologically and psychologically, as we have seen, Aristotle starts in the right place, with the wise cultivation of early, non-rational impulses or feelings. Moral development depends on living with others from the start of life in a good, caring environment. Becoming virtuous, for Aristotle as for Plato, means that these impulses become 'suffused with', 'obedient to', practical reason. What is practical reason? This is the formal virtue of making good judgements, whatever they may be. If, as a parent, you have several children, you need the virtue of justice, so that you do not give unfair advantages to some over others. More generally, if food and alcohol are plentiful, not to mention soft sofas to recline in and TVs to watch, you need the virtue of temperance so that you do not spend all your time eating, drinking, lazing about. If you ask: *how* should I balance the needs of my children? or: *how much* may I eat and drink? you will receive gestural or indicative answers. You must act and feel as practical reason dictates.

Of course, this is expanded, but only in general terms; we do not learn from Aristotle precisely what the virtuous person does and feels. His *general* answer is that virtuous people have 'beautiful habits' of acting and feeling; that these habits develop from infancy through the ministrations of wise adults; that they are gradually 'suffused with reason' and freely chosen according to the principle Aristotle called the mean. What this means (again, in general terms) is avoiding irrational extremes, like feeling too angry or not angry enough, too frightened or not frightened enough, acting too rashly or timidly for the circumstances in which they occur. The basic principle of virtue (*arete,* or excellence) is that it involves feeling, acting and judging well, and enjoying doing so. It is not only better for others if we become virtuous human beings, but also for us, for our capacity to lead a 'happy' or flourishing life.

About the precise constituency of virtue – how it manifests in daily life – Aristotle gives, as I said, formal or indeterminate answers. We are given the contours of virtue, without being told how to distinguish in every case between a virtuous person and a non-virtuous person, or even how to recognize a virtuous action or emotional response in a particular situation. We have some useful pointers, but they will not always provide answers to such questions for, as Aristotle says repeatedly, 'the judgement is in the perceiving' (2002 1109b 24). There *are* ways in which we should act and feel; Aristotle is no relativist about morality, and he believes that actions can be right or wrong, feelings can be appropriate or inappropriate, for the circumstances in which they occur. But if you ask for further clarification, you will receive an evasive answer.

Here's what he says about how we ought to feel:

> it is possible to be afraid or to be confident or to desire or be angry or feel pity, or in general to feel pleasure or feel pain both more and less, and on both sides not in the right way; but to feel them when one ought, and in the cases in which, and toward the people whom, and for the reasons for the sake of which, and in the manner one ought is both a mean and a best thing, which is what belongs to virtue. (2002 1106b 19)

In this tortuous passage, Aristotle resists the kind of specification that many demand. We should act in the 'best way', avoiding 'bad extremes', and the same is true of feelings. Don't feel too much (e.g. hysterically) or too little (e.g. dully), and much of the time you are unlikely to go far wrong. But of course, there are circumstances in which intense feelings are demanded (on the battlefield, in the company of a dying friend), as well as circumstances in which dullness of feeling (or even deflection) may be appropriate, so that you can get on with the job. The 'mean' is not a fixed point; it is judged by those with good practical judgement, and every one of us needs to develop such judgement in preference to living our lives by a handbook.

This picture of *phronesis*, practical reason or judgement, can be tantalizing. And indeed, I associate it with Diamond's difficulty of reality, as I remarked, for the discovery that moral principles are at best, as I put it, 'gestural' leaves us with no alternative but to engage with life in the raw. We must grapple with conflict, and sometimes suffer its wounds, rather than trying to resolve it according to a ready-made set of moral instructions. We act justly or temperately when we act 'in the way that just and temperate people do' (2002 1105 b 8–9), and we 'bear ourselves well [virtuously] .... towards the feelings' when 'for example, in relation to being angry we are that way.... in a measured way [rather than violently or slackly]' (2002 1105 b 25–27). So virtue is the tendency to act and feel, not 'violently', not 'slackly', not 'too much' or 'too little', but as a virtuous people act and feel.

This says nothing to those who are looking for a moral code, but it says a great deal to those who are enquiring more broadly *and more psychologically* into the nature of the moral life. It speaks to those who want their philosophical reflections to be 'populated', informed by examples of 'real' human beings, rather than snapshots or cartoons as discussed in Chapter 5. It points towards disciplined and open-ended responsiveness to reality (people, dramas, encounters) as basic modes of ethical thinking. It reinforces Murdoch's idea about deepening understanding based on the effort to *see clearly*, rather than scientific modes of enquiry. It implies that we must *find out* whom to trust, who is worth listening to, from whom we may learn about the serious matters of life. Instead of authority figures to whom we owe compliance, the moral world contains *phronimoi*, people who are 'worth listening to', taking seriously and learning from. But like *phronesis* (which the *phronimos* exemplifies consistently), this is a perceptual matter; our moral judgements (as Aristotle repeatedly insists) *end in perception*, and our judgements about who is and is not 'worth listening to' must do the same.

This, I submit, is sound psychology, especially for older children and young adults, for whom Aristotelian *phronesis* – the requirement *not* to live by rules or submit to authority – might be seen as a gift. When children are very young, they are usually receptive to adult instruction and guidance, so that Aristotle's principle of habituation – we become virtuous by acting virtuously, rather as people become 'housebuilders by building houses or harpists by playing the harp' – has a ring of psychological truth. ('We become just [he says] by doing things that are just, temperate by doing things that are temperate, and courageous by doing things that are courageous' (2002 1103 a 34–1103 b 2).) Parents and teachers are able to direct and improve children's behaviour, not by getting them to repeat exactly the same acts, but by getting them to do what the student harpist does: repeat certain actions with gradually increasing self-awareness, self-criticism, emotional discernment. In *The Fabric of Character: Aristotle's Theory of Virtue*, Nancy Sherman helpfully unpacks this process, calling Aristotle's 'we become just by doing things that are just' (and so on with the other virtues) an 'abbreviation'. We need to *practice* virtue in order to become fully virtuous, but this doesn't mean mindless repetition any more than it does for the harpist; it means *critical habituation under wise guidance*, the refinement of moral thought and feeling.

What is learned relatively simply in the early years becomes more complex as *phronesis* is introduced. We learn about justice by acting justly, but not, says Myles Burnyeat, 'without regard for the spirit of justice and the ways in which circumstances alter cases. What Aristotle is pointing to is our ability to internalize from a scattered range of particular cases a general evaluative attitude which is not reducible to rules or precepts'. How do we acquire this extraordinary ability? The short answer is: slowly, with difficulty, with many stumbles and wrong turns. We learn about moral matters, in part, from those we deem wise enough to teach us (help us, guide us) about moral matters. Beyond the early years, we must *judge who is suitable to teach us about judgement*; and this circularity (I am suggesting) is a tough psychological reality at the heart of our moral lives.

Summarizing Kant's theory of maturity, Susan Neiman talks about the 'wisdom to find a path between mindlessly accepting everything you're told and mindlessly rejecting it' (Neiman 2014, p. 4). This captures the difficult moral psychology surrounding the *phronimos*; we tend to move, developmentally, from acquiescence to rebellion, with particular individuals (teachers, parents and others) featuring as know-alls and know-nothings in our lives. We must 'find a path' between these extremes if we are to mature, and the most difficult parent is the one who tries to block these efforts, insisting she is right about everything, knows everything and her children are duty-bound to conform. I am not forgetting the 'naughty child' here: the obstinate or unlearning child who is obviously germane to my concerns in this book. The child who 'mindlessly rejects' everything she is told from a very early age has difficulties that our moral psychology must address.

The issue here is moral and intellectual *trust*, and Aristotle's doctrine of the mean directs us, rather as Kant does, against trusting too little or trusting too much. Unfortunately, Aristotle had a social philosophy that was deeply conservative, dedicated in some respects to blind rather than reflective trust. This presents dangers for Aristotelians in the sphere of moral education, as we shall see.

A Dystopian vision

In Book 1 of *Nicomachean Ethics*, we are told that the soul has two parts, rational and non-rational. The latter is also divided into two. One part is 'vegetative', involving nutrition, growth and so on; it is animal-like and cannot 'listen to' reason. The other part is 'desiderative'; it involves desire and emotion, and is capable in a specifically human way of 'listening to' reason. A reasonable person, or the reasonable part of myself, may observe that I am too angry or unrealistically hopeful, and should temper my anger or hope. I may 'listen to the case' and modify my feelings accordingly; or I may ignore this person, or my own better judgement, and remain irrational.

In the final section of the book, Aristotle rounds off his important discussion about what it means to be practically rational, drawing on Homer for a dystopian vision of what humans (or quasi-humans like the one-eyed Cyclops) may become if they fail or refuse to 'listen to' reason in this way. To describe this, I shall turn directly to Homer, and quote him at greater length than Aristotle does.

The Cyclops, says Homer in *The Odyssey* (2003), were a 'fierce, lawless people'. They:

> have no assemblies for the making of laws, nor any established legal codes, but live in hollow caverns in the mountain heights, where each man is lawgiver to his own children and women, and nobody has the slightest interest in what his neighbours decide. (p. 113)

The luckless Odysseus and his crew were washed up on the Cyclops' island, finding themselves at their mercy. When Odysseus reminds their host of his 'duty to the gods' ('Zeus is the champion of suppliants and guests'), the Cyclops replies:

> 'We Cyclops care nothing for Zeus and his aegis, nor for the rest of the blessed gods, since we are much stronger than they are. I would never spare you or your men for fear of incurring Zeus' enmity, unless I felt like it... .' [Shortly afterwards] he jumped up and reaching out towards my men, seized a couple and dashed their heads against the floor as though they had been puppies. Their brains ran out on the ground and soaked the earth. Limb by limb he

tore them to pieces to make his meal, which he devoured like a mountain lion, leaving nothing, neither entrails nor flesh, marrow nor bones, while we, weeping, lifted up our hands to Zeus in horror at the ghastly sight. We felt completely helpless. (p. 117)

This is what can happen amongst people who 'care nothing' for their neighbours, reason, law, the gods! But they provide a wonderful foil for those who are tempted to question Aristotle's social philosophy. For this is based on a picture of rational harmony, in which reason and non-reason are properly balanced, the non-rational members of societies and households 'listening to' the rational members with due attention and respect. In Aristotle's world, virtuous men preside over a household that is harmonious in exactly the sense in which their souls are harmonious. The non-rational members of the household, like the non-rational parts of the soul, are suffused with, obedient to, the rational members/parts. Slaves can't deliberate, but they may *listen to* authority figures, exhibiting the virtues of the ruled as opposed to the virtues of the ruler (1981, I, xiii). The same is true of women and children.

The Cyclops story reminds us that the penalties are dire if things get out of balance. We risk becoming diseased, mad or bestial, and who can doubt that people like this are likely not only to be at war with their neighbours, but also with their children, their wives and generally among themselves? (Imagine the problems of disaffection among their young.) There is no question of *judgement* here. The Cyclops are out of balance in an absolute sense, and the aristocratic Athenian household is precisely the opposite. Slaves are naturally non-rational; females are naturally *ineffectively* rational (at best); and boys but not girls are naturally educable. But with a rational male as their head, harmony prevails, and boys are educated for the role currently occupied by their fathers.

This arrangement would hardly work if the head of the household had a vivid imagination, akin to that of Elizabeth Costello. What would happen if he *identified with* rather than *governed* slaves and women? Worst of all would be a man with the kind of imagination George Eliot describes as having a 'keen vision and feeling of all ordinary life'. What self-respecting aristocrat wants to hear the grass grow or the squirrel's heartbeat? Why should *he* die of the roar which lies on the other side of silence? There is no space in Aristotle's worldview, except at the fringes of sanity, for a Costello-like or Eliot-like imagination. To say with Costello, '*I* am the cow or lamb that is being led to slaughter' would be for Aristotle pure madness. Here is an *excess of compassion*, fashioned around a thought that this is not so much poetic as unhinged.

I said that Aristotle is unable to accommodate emotional depth: bodily thrownness, rawness of nerves and so on. He relegates persistent emotional excesses to the domains of bestiality, immaturity or femininity. Aristotle's picture of an Athenian aristocratic household includes a person whose *assured* virtue stands in unimaginative contrast to the assured *non*-virtue of the slaves, women and children in the household. Aristotle seems to have forgotten that *phronesis* is a purely formal concept, a judgement that 'ends in perception'. He has installed his own kind – the educated, wealthy male – in the role of *phronimos*, closing down pathways for judgement and perception.

This is an unresolved tension in Aristotle's concept of *phronesis*. He makes it theoretically impossible to discover a female *phronimos* for whom reason is *not* ineffective, or an enslaved *phronimos* on whose behalf we need to mount a protest. This is not simply the familiar and just complaint about Aristotle's sexism and elitism. It is a concern about Aristotle's conservatism and the dangers of following him if we are inclined to deflect the difficulties of reality inherent in the meaning of *phronesis*. The *moral psychology* of *phronesis* is anything but conservative; it is open to what I called life in the raw and the growth of personal judgement rather than unimaginative compliance to authority. In *Nicomachean Ethics*, Aristotle leaves us in no doubt that *phronesis* – the intellectual, judging aspect of virtue – is difficult to acquire and difficult to theorize, these difficulties combining in a phenomenon that is exceedingly difficult to teach. There is a fine line between showing children what we believe to be good and right, and acknowledging our human limitations so that, decent as we hope we are, we do not set ourselves up as *phronimoi*, embodiments of reason in an absolute sense.

I have spoken often of difficulty: 'difficulties of reality' that can be acutely (and even physically) painful; the difficulty of making good judgements and resisting the temptation to deflect this difficulty by codifying morality; and now the difficulty of guiding the young and earning (or deserving) their trust, without presenting ourselves as better than we are. Many philosophers would like to resolve all these difficulties through evidence and sound methodologies, in order to help children to become higher achievers and better human beings. I applaud their efforts up to a point, but I have emphasized frequently that the focus of my concern is not *children in general*, many of whom are well on the way to becoming decent, mature human beings, with or without enhancement interventions. My focus is children who are in one way or another stuck, engaging in repetitive dramas that inhibit their learning in the arenas of subject disciplines and morality. (We saw in Chapter 2 that these are not necessarily distinct; virtues are developed and expressed through the learning of disciplines.) These children, I have suggested, are likely to fall through the net; as the minority, they stand outside statistical generalizations about young people today, and if we are unwilling to accept the difficulties of reality attendant on *phronesis* in a formal sense, they may simply become invisible.

The unresolved tension in Aristotle's concept of *phronesis* is an aspect of the tension I described in Chapter 5 as existing between populated and unpopulated philosophy. Aristotle's social philosophy is unpopulated; it is inhabited by 'snapshots'. There is a head of household to whom most of us must defer, because he is 'educated', 'virtuous', 'practically rational'. Other members of the household partake of these properties to varying degrees, but are absolutely not capable, like the head, of achieving moral excellence. Aristotle *idealized* the aristocratic Athenian household, and this includes relationships between parents and children. 'There is friendship in children for their parents,' he says, 'as in human beings for gods, for something good and superior, since parents have done the greatest good for them'. (2002 1162 a 4–6). Not only trust, then, but also love and gratitude form the basis of moral learning.

This is not so much wrong as incomplete, as we discover if we return to *populated* philosophy inhabited by real, complex human beings. To neglect this is also to neglect our distinctively human powers of judgement (*phronesis* in the formal sense) through which we become aware of, concerned about and hopefully sensitive towards those for whom life and learning present the greatest difficulties. If we cling to the unpopulated world of 'studies show', we may be reassured by surveys establishing (for example) that *most young people* see their parents or religious leaders as their primary role models, rather than celebrities, criminals or drug addicts. But these are the lucky ones, assuming their parents are 'good-enough', and what we need is the formal conception of *phronesis* that brings us into contact with *perceived* individuals, some of whom have difficulties precisely because they are in awe of those who represent antisocial values. We need to be sensitive to their facial expressions, their gestures, their physical realities through which we learn about their difficulties and reflect on how we may help them.

Engaging with reality this way, we may affirm with Aristotle that children love their parents, without denying that they sometimes hate them too. We may observe how they see their parents as role models, as well as stuffy, embarrassing, uncool. They trust their parents and also distrust them. On some occasions, they believe that their parents have done the 'greatest good for them'; on others, they believe they have done them the greatest harm. Many children navigate these contradictions successfully, emerging as adults with the happy conviction that their parents were 'good-enough'. Others are not so lucky, but my point is that, good or not-so-good, all parents are hated by their children *at times*, finding themselves demoted from their pedestals. Teachers suffer the fall-out, more from some children, obviously, than from others. This tortuous and ambivalent reality forms the setting for moral exploration and hopefully maturation.

Nancy Sherman elaborates Aristotle's idealistic picture in this passage:

> The stable attachment between parents and child facilitates the parents' role as educator in several ways. The preeminence of parents in the child's life makes them ready to hand models for emulation, as well as attentive judges of the child's specific needs and requirements. The child's acknowledgement of the parents' love and trust engenders a willingness to learn from them and a readiness to comply. (1989, p. 152)

The stable attachment between *which* parents, *which* children and at which stages in their lives? Sherman follows Aristotle in her assumption that children develop their characters, and develop them well, through love, trust and a readiness to comply. Indeed, on the face of it this assumption seems innocent and true, but I would suggest that, even in the best-case scenario, there is another aspect to parent–child relations. Children develop their characters through love and trust as well as through *conflicts* between hatred and love, distrust and trust. They are sometimes distressed and bewildered by the discovery that the person they love is denying them precisely what they believe they need. As Diamond says about the Ted Hughes poem (see Chapter 7), there is 'the sense of a difficulty that pushes us beyond what we can think. To attempt to think it is to feel one's thinking come unhinged' (2008, pp. 57–58). How many children never experience this? How many never throw tantrums when their parents refuse to succumb to their wishes?

One of the things we learn from psychoanalysis is that there can be emotional *violence* in these conflicts, as well as potential maturation as we overcome our tendency to idealize others, and learn that *all* human beings have weaknesses as well as strengths, are 'bad' as well as 'good', and are decisively, but not necessarily threateningly, not-me. When Aristotle says without qualification that children see their parents as 'gods', he exposes a limitation in his moral psychology. Again, this seems to discourage us from *judging* how particular children feel about their particular parents. We are not to notice how, despite appearances to the contrary, some children struggle with the perception of their parents as 'gods', because they want to believe this but know that in reality, they are anything but.

'Children see their parents as gods' belongs to the domain of what I have called the snapshot: a domain that fails to reveal the ways in which reality (especially for some) is far more complex than this. We know that Aristotle generalizes absurdly about men, women and children, and we must take care not to follow him in an effort to avoid emotional depth as (I believe) he does. In *Middlemarch*, George Eliot explores this tendency to *skim perceptual surfaces*, in order not to see clearly or feel what others feel. The following passage appears immediately before the passage quoted in the previous chapter, where Eliot suggests that 'vision and feeling' can be *too keen*. We miss something, however, if we go to the other extreme, in which ordinary life is permitted to bring no surprises. Dorothea Casaubon (beautiful, intelligent, young) has recently discovered to her horror that the man she married for his wisdom and maturity is emotionally and intellectually crippled. We find her 'sobbing bitterly', and the following passage *dramatizes* the tendency to deflect difficulties of reality:

> Nor can I suppose that when Mrs Casaubon is discovered in a fit of weeping six weeks after her wedding, the situation will be regarded as tragic. Some discouragement, some faintness of heart at the new real future which replaces the imaginary, is not unusual, *and we do not expect people to be deeply moved by what is not unusual.* That element of tragedy which lies in the very fact of frequency, has not yet wrought itself into the coarse emotion of mankind; and perhaps our frames could hardly bear much of it. If we had a keen vision and feeling of all ordinary human life, it would be like hearing the grass grow and the squirrel's heartbeat, and we should die of that roar which lies on the other side of silence. As it is, the quickest of us walk about well wadded with stupidity. (My emphasis) (p. 194)

It is obviously important that parents don't fuss unduly about trivial miseries that children will soon put behind them, but sometimes what *appears* to be 'usual' is not in fact so. A child might be experiencing anguish of a kind that she is unable to overcome, and this may become 'dyed into her soul' if there is no sensitive adult response.

In this passage from *Culture and Value*, Wittgenstein steps outside what we think of as his normal sphere of concern with a remark that illuminates the foregoing discussion:

> Anyone who listens to a child crying and understands what he hears will know that it harbours dormant psychic forces, terrible forces different from anything commonly assumed. Profound rage, pain and lust for destruction. (1929, 2e)

This is not in fact outside Wittgenstein's sphere of concern, for the emphasis on listening (*really* listening) is consonant with his repeated emphasis on looking (*really* looking) in order to avoid idle thinking. Today, empirical psychologists and psychoanalysts tend to unite in affirmation of the thoughts Wittgenstein expresses here. When Aristotle refuses to codify morality, insisting on a circular conception of judgement that embraces reality as perceived by the seeing, hearing *phronimos*, we know that his moral psychology contains the possibility of engaging truthfully with human beings as Wittgenstein and Eliot suggest. Unfortunately, as I tried to show, Aristotle's social philosophy points in another direction.

Conversational responsiveness revisited

In *The Rhetoric*, Aristotle teaches his readers how to manipulate people's emotions by altering the judgements or beliefs on which they are based. Lawson-Tancred, translator of the Penguin edition (1991), introduces the book this way:

> Can there be a science of persuasion? It would be hard to deny that the ability to persuade, convince, cajole or win round is one of the most useful skills in human life. It is a capacity that shows its importance equally easily in the market, the court, the council chamber and the bedroom. (p. 1)

This shows the purpose for which emotional transformation is sought by Aristotle in *The Rhetoric*. The book is a manual for thoughtful people, explaining that anger can be defused by demonstrating that a perceived insult was not an insult at all; fear can be defused by helping someone to see that the feared object or person is not, as they believed, dangerous or threatening. And so on.

It is surprising, given this obvious manipulative purpose, that *The Rhetoric* is thought to provide a useful basis for transforming the emotions of the young. Yet this is what many Aristotle-inspired educationists believe. In 'The Moral Perspective and the Psychoanalytic Quest' (1995), Nancy Sherman points out the weakness of this view. She observes that 'the mental content of emotions isn't always evidentially warranted beliefs. What we have good reason to believe often doesn't dislodge the more tenacious thoughts that inform our emotions' (p. 233). Aristotle understood this but, as Sherman continues:

> What Aristotle doesn't fully appreciate is that emotions can change and develop through continuing clarification of the stories that inform them. Although he is the first to lead us explicitly to the notion that emotions have intentional (or ideational) [i.e. cognitive] content, he doesn't fully grasp the implication of that view, namely that our tendencies to feel anger or fear or shame can shift as we *make more explicit to ourselves just what the beliefs are that rationalise those*

emotions.... . He does not see the possibilities of dynamic emotional growth implicit in his own theory (ibid, my emphasis). (p. 234)

This important passage paves the way for a psychoanalytic approach to children's difficulties, but there is a great deal more to it than that. It hugely enriches the concept of conversational responsiveness that, following Joseph Dunne, I located at the heart of education, upbringing, efforts in a general way to minister to other people's goods. We are not interested, like the orator, in swaying the emotions of crowds, or even individuals, by correcting the beliefs at their cores. We are concerned about repetitive and destructive patterns, and we know that these can become entrenched, not because the evidence supporting the beliefs in question is overwhelming, but because we are creatures who *feel historically*, telling ourselves stories about ourselves that bear reflection, modification, alteration and so on. To cherish wisely is to understand this, and to want to help the person who *suffers* from her stories to make them explicit and responsive to fresh understandings.

Cherishing is an ethical concept, with genuine and counterfeit forms. Crises of cherishing (e.g. neglect, at home or in school) must be one of the primary sources of the kind of drama we have been considering. (In Chapter 2, we discussed Nathan, whose habitual aggression appears to have been related to teacher neglect.) Contemporary theories of character education tend to place great emphasis on the importance of role-modelling for the young, but role-modelling is *not* an ethical concept, and it often operates at a shallow level of meaning, whereby a person models in her behaviour desirable moral standards without reference to what Wittgenstein calls 'imponderable evidence'. In Chapter 2, I discussed Wittgenstein's remarks about the genuineness of expressions of feeling. There are, he says, 'those whose judgement is "better" and those whose judgement is "worse"', and one of the things we want for those we cherish is that they should *trust wisely* by *judging well*. We want them to become good judges of character, sensitive to nuances of gesture and expression that constitute 'imponderable evidence' of a person's sincerity or insincerity. In this respect, we must put Aristotle's social philosophy behind us, for the inhibition of *phronesis* in favour of elitist or other preconceptions has no place in an ethic of cherishing.

If some teachers believe that they must *model* goodness for children, they are wrong. They should aim to be, not merely appear, good. Or perhaps, as I would prefer to say, they should aim to be good-enough, for the *reality* of being good-enough is worth a great deal. They should, in other words, be thoroughly decent human beings, and it is my view that the ideal of moral excellence should be treated with caution; it is not something that (except perhaps in the rarest cases) we are likely to point to with the words *for example*. An athlete may exemplify the perfect human body, as a violin-maker or knife-maker may produce a perfect violin or knife, but the most admirable human beings are likely to fall short. In the next chapter, the meaning of 'good-enough' and its significance for cherishing will be explored.

9

An Ethic of Cherishing

Hence what I have called morality's maxim: act as though you loved.

André Comte-Sponville (2003)

The concept of good-enough is *good enough* to occupy a place at the heart of an ethic of cherishing. This is what I suggested at the end of the last chapter. Let me explain.

I have been discussing a moral stance between two human beings, one of whom depends on the other for learning, maturation, protection and so on. At the heart of this stance, if all goes well, is a *genuine desire* for *genuine good things* for the other, as well as a commitment to learning (as far as possible) what 'genuine good things' means in this case; and a desire to express this wish practically and emotionally, to the best of one's ability. This desire is devoid of condescension, and it is normally accompanied by 'belief in' the possibility of a good, happy life for the other: a life towards which one hopes to make a contribution as appropriate or required. The concepts of goodness and happiness in this context are inherently unclear in Margalit's sense, and require deepening in Murdoch's sense. They are of course positive concepts, and they play a critical role in our moral lives. I believe the same is true of the concept of cherishing.

I want to discuss Winnicott's contribution to this discussion. I shall use language that he does not use, such as *cherishing, difficulty of reality, virtue, habituation, phronesis*. In speaking this way, I hope to reinforce links between Winnicott, Aristotle, Murdoch, Wittgenstein, Diamond and others. The term *cherishing* is my own contribution, and I offer it in the belief that it captures aspects of Winnicott's work that are needed for an adequate moral psychology. When Winnicott said, famously (1960a, in Winnicott 1985, p. 39): 'There is no such thing as an infant', he meant, in his words, that 'whenever one finds an infant one finds maternal care, and without maternal care there would be no infant'. At the very least, one finds an adult who is attuned to the child, listening out for a cry, thinking about the next feed. Much of the time, this adult is holding the child, providing comfort and care. In truth, this adult may be attuned or mis-attuned to the infant's world, but if there was no attunement at all – the adult simply walked away – there would be little chance for the infant.

I want to start with a philosophical account of the moral origins of a human being, not from Aristotle himself, but from philosopher Nicholas Dent, who both presents and helpfully amplifies the Aristotelian view. From this point, it will be possible to show where and why, in my view, Winnicott is needed. Dent writes:

> I would like to put forward the notion that the acquisition of virtues involves the refinement of attachments... In the great majority of instances, virtues are rooted in emotions... Our emotions disclose our concern with, are tied to, something we feel to be good, important or significant to us. Fear discloses our concern to avoid pain and injury as evils; pity, our concern to ease another's suffering... Even early in life there are different patterns in people's reactivity. One child may be affectionate, open, trusting and loving – in general, vividly responsive to the joy of other people – while another may be imperious, short-tempered, volatile, passionate and deeply preoccupied with the force of his presence and the power of his will.
>
> This is all quite familiar. My purpose is to suggest that virtues develop out of such material, with its first small, shifting, fragmentary growths of a sense of value and disvalue, of what urgently matters and what is indifferent... This will involve the consolidation, extension, harmonisation, sifting and integration of all these various registerings of value and importance, which is achieved principally through the regulation and re-direction of our emotions and the attachments they incorporate. A growing conscious awareness of what it signifies to have these patterns of emotional reactivity, in terms of what one finds important, will be a substantial part of this development. This growing consciousness does not merely incorporate reflection on how things stand with one, as if one was an object of curiosity. Rather, it involves seeking out possibilities of greater significance, more enduring meaning and worth; seeking to lay hold on life in abundance. (1999, pp. 28–29)

This passage captures the Aristotelian view that there is a maturational path from our earliest beginnings to our capacity to find meaning and enjoyment in life, 'a life [says Dent] we shall be glad we have lived'. We shall be glad, not only because we have had pleasurable experiences, but also because we have virtuously shared this life with others, and enjoyed doing so. We have also enjoyed the friendship and companionship that, barring tragedy, such a life brings. The passage points to a gulf between moral theories that 'begin at the beginning' and trace the emotional and moral development of human beings, and theories that ignore moral psychology in favour of principles of action. Kant's theory, for example, is based on the imperative to act impartially, in such a way that you could will everyone in similar circumstances to do the same. We must *submit* to this imperative, says Kant, sweeping aside our emotional proclivities even if they are (for example) 'affectionate, open, trusting and loving'. For Kant, our temperaments or emotional tendencies have nothing to do with morality, which has its source in our faculty of reason.

Dent comments perceptively: 'But how extraordinary it is to think that the central postures of moral acceptance are those of submissive obedience' (p. 24). Aristotle's theory, by contrast, builds on 'patterns of reactivity', and requires personal attention and refinement precisely because these are so varied. Dent doesn't mention parents or teachers in this passage, but he clearly believes with Aristotle that the young depend on loving guidance for the cultivation of what Aristotle calls 'beautiful habits'.

What neither Dent nor Aristotle appear to understand is that there is a very good reason why people who lacked a good early upbringing have a disadvantage that they may never overcome. The reason is that, contrary to what Dent says in this passage, the early 'sense of value and disvalue' is not 'small' but 'huge'. An infant is helpless; she cannot think, talk or act. All she can do is *feel*, responding to what the Greeks called the *apeiron*, the boundless reality within which we all move. In the case of the infant, not only is reality boundless, but there is also a potentially terrifying absence of knowledge about the difference between me and not-me, what is coming in the next few minutes or hours, object-stability and so on. She can't distinguish initially between the temporary and permanent disappearance of those on whom she depends, and the 'sense of disvalue' attendant on her helplessness can be overwhelming.

Daniel Stern uses the imagery of the storm to describe the violence of infantile feelings when there is hunger, discomfort or fear. Martha Nussbaum quotes a passage from Lucretius that uses similar imagery. The newborn child, says Lucretius:

> ... like a sailor cast forth from the fierce waves, lies naked on the ground, without speech, in need of every sort of life-sustaining help, when first nature casts it forth with birth contractions from its mother's womb into the shores of light. And it fills the whole place with mournful weeping, as is right for someone to whom such troubles remain in life. (2003, p. 182)

It is a beautiful passage, and it is supported by developmental neuroscience, which shows that there may be neural impairments for infants who are left to 'weep mournfully' without the comfort they desperately need (Schore, 2001).

'For the little child', says Winnicott, 'and how much more for the infant, life is just a series of terrifically intense experiences' (1969, p. 70). Wittgenstein makes a similar point when he talks about the crying child who harbours 'terrible forces different from anything assumed'. It is a serious but understandable error to suppose that because infants are small, their emotions are small. To be fair to Dent, he also talks about the sense of 'what urgently matters and what is indifferent', but I am suggesting that the description of early emotions as 'small, shifting, fragmentary growths of a sense of value and disvalue' is misleading. What I have suggested, on the contrary, is that infants can experience *difficulties of reality* as acutely as adults do. They *cannot think*, or they only do so incipiently, and it is one of the marks of Diamond's concept of the difficulty of reality that it 'pushes us beyond what we can think' (2008, p. 58), and *this* is what we find tormenting. While the brain is still forming, and thinking is primitive or absent, it should be no surprise that powerful and persistent feelings of helplessness may become (to return to Aristotle's quaint image) 'dyed into the soul'.

The good-enough parent is extraordinary because she guides the child through the storms of infantile helplessness in such a way that a non-threatening reality, a sense of me and not-me, may begin to emerge. To understand this is to think about *knowledge* and *ethics* in ways that are essential for our topic.

The good-enough parent as moral exemplar

As a person who cherishes, we hope to be *good-enough* for the other. Winnicott uses this phrase with great portent (1960b in Winnicott 1985, p. 145). We know that we shall never be perfect and that the idea that we might achieve perfection is not only silly, but also deluded. We know too that we shall never make the other person into a perfect human being. There is a problem with Aristotle's thinking here, for the term 'arete', meaning excellence, is applied to inanimate objects and members of non-human species, which sometimes *do* achieve perfection, as well as human beings, which (I think it is safe to say) do not. At the Chelsea Flower Show, you may see some perfect roses and lilies. Not so in the theatre of human life.

The idea of the good relates to the idea of perfection, but only as an ideal, something to which we may aim. As Murdoch says, 'Moral tasks are characteristically endless... To speak here of an inevitable imperfection, or of an ideal limit of love or knowledge which always recedes, may be taken as a reference to our "fallen" human condition' (p. 28). We are not perfect, and we do not act or feel perfectly; it is important to recognize our 'inevitable imperfection'. Doret de Ruyter has emphasized the importance of ideals for the young (2003), and Wivestad says that ideals are like 'stars that help us to navigate in life' (2008, p. 308). They are things to which we personally aspire, and I am deeply mistaken if I see myself as an ideal human being or you, the person I cherish, as following in my ideal footsteps.

What I may reasonably hope for is to be good-enough, and we must take care with this phrase, for it may be used defensively by unloving parents, when their children are old enough to understand that their love was defective. *I never claimed to be perfect, but I was good enough…* In fact, good-enough parents in Winnicott's sense are deeply loving, and they are both ordinary and extraordinary. Winnicott studied thousands of mothers and babies, and as a paediatrician, he was able to observe them in a 'good condition' or *euexia*, as Socrates said of the healthy soul (1960, p. 18). Unlike many psychoanalysts (which Winnicott eventually became), he met many mothers who were good-enough, and many infants who were doing well apart from an allergy or other medical problem.

What is a good-enough mother? Winnicott's answers are surprising, and there is much to learn from these. Especially while her child is still young, the good-enough mother *does* achieve what we might describe as an ideal. She achieves this, in part, by *failing* in specific but valuable ways. What does this mean? We can't answer this question without taking a step back to the work of Melanie Klein, by which Winnicott was strongly influenced.

Klein was concerned with personal maturation as an evolving engagement with fantasies of goodness and badness. For infants, says Klein, these belong to distinct categories. To put it simply, the mother who provides food, warmth and comfort is a 'good mother', whereas the very same person who fails to provide these things, leaving the child hungry or alone for a while, is a 'bad mother'. There is, according to Klein, an important task for every human being, namely to understand that the 'good mother' and the 'bad mother' are in fact one and the same imperfect person. The task is to understand this deeply, rather than notionally.

What is important is not whether the theory is right or wrong in all its details. It is that it has explanatory power, and much of this is recounted in Klein's clinical case histories. Most of us know individuals who cannot bear to be thwarted. I don't mean individuals who are upset or angry when thwarted (which is sometimes fair enough); I mean ones who *generally* find the experience of being thwarted impossible to bear. Most unbearable of all is the thwarting of one's wishes by a person one loves or depends on. (Think of Lear, who disowned his favourite daughter when she refused to comply with his insane demand that she should love him before all others.) Then this good, loved person magically transforms in one's mind into a malevolent, hateful one. The problem here is that the good, loved person is not (at a deep level) a real person at all, for real people sometimes assist us and sometimes thwart us. They are sometimes dedicated to fulfilling our wishes and sometimes have other things on their minds (including the precedence of their own wishes over ours). That is what real people are like, including decent people who care for us a great deal.

Obviously, I have only sketched Klein's ideas here. I have offered a simple account of a complex phenomenon that according to psychoanalytic theory (this aspect of Kleinian theory is widely accepted) dominates the lives of individuals who love and hate, hate and love, to the point where relationships become unsustainable. They engage in what Klein calls *splitting*, imagining that people are *either* good *or* bad, where 'bad' essentially means thwarting one's own wishes. The point about such individuals is that they have no real conception of what Winnicott was later to call not-me. To understand that another is truly independent of myself is to understand that some thwarting, some failure, some alternative sources of interest, are inevitable.

At the beginning of life, human beings cannot understand this. They depend on *cherishing adults* to 'bring about learning' about the mixtures of 'goodness and badness' (sources of satisfaction and dissatisfaction) that are human beings. I earlier quoted Winnicott's words: 'the recognition of a true "not-me" ... belongs to extreme sophistication and to the maturity of the individual' (1960a in Winnicott 1985, p. 38). We don't expect to find such maturity in schoolchildren, but many are on the way; they can, for example, tolerate disappointment by seeing another person's point of view. Others have no conception of, no capacity to imagine, a perspective that is not their own. The mild disappointment of their classmates becomes frenzied rage. This might produce a tendency (as we saw with Nathan in Chapter 2) to smash things up in a way that prompts the fear that *people* will also be attacked.

Winnicott writes:

> I am often thought to be talking about mother, actual people with babies, as if they were perfect or as if they were corresponding to 'the good mother' which is part of Kleinian jargon. Actually I always talk about 'the good-enough mother' or 'the not good-enough mother' because in point of fact we are talking about

the actual woman, we know that the best she can do is to be good enough, and the word 'enough' gradually (in favourable circumstances) widens in scope according to the infant's growing ability to deal with failure by understanding, tolerance of frustration, etc. (cited in Abram, 2007, p. 221)

Klein talks about good/bad mothers as 'internal objects', i.e. *fantasies* about the good or ill will of the person who *feels* like two different people. Winnicott talks about good-enough mothers because he wants to anchor our understanding of human development in real, flesh-and-blood human beings. He wants to describe the process whereby an infant matures and develops a moral sense, becoming a decent human being instead of a deluded one who splits good and bad in the manner described by Klein.

In order to understand this, suggests Winnicott, we must trace our moral concepts, good and bad, to their emotional, developmental source. Philosophers have noted the connections between emotion and what we see (as Dent puts it) as 'good, important or significant to us'. Martha Nussbaum expresses this in terms of well-being: '... emotions involve judgements about the salience for our well-being of uncontrolled external objects' (2001, p. 2). What is omitted here, as by philosophers generally, is the aspect of feeling that I call vertical; the fact that the sense of importance or significance goes *deep into the body*, where we do not so much *judge* as *experience* agitation, menace, a sense of threat or, conversely, a sense of safety, tranquillity, bliss. For the child who is roughly handled, there may be a sense of falling, and for the child who screams long and hard for sustenance, there may be a sense of terror and void. These are the *meanings* of helplessness for an infant, experienced not as testable propositions or corrigible knowledge, but pre-verbally, as a 'series of terrifically intense experiences'.

All this, suggests Winnicott, is universal. What is not universal (though it is present, he believes, in most cases) is a good-enough adult who is finely attuned to the helplessness of the infant. Like a *phronimos*, this person judges what is needed to protect the child from fears and anxieties that are too much to bear. She presents the world to the child in what I called 'well-judged doses': not so small that the child learns nothing, not so large that the child experiences difficulties of reality that may be impossible to resolve.

I spoke in Chapter 7 about 'metaphysical development', thinking both about Winnicott's account of maturation in terms of the discovery of not-me and Murdoch's account of the 'progressing life of a person', understood ethically rather than scientifically. At the start of life, we are primitive solipsists, without conceptions of me or not-me. Good-enough parents 'bring about learning' about moral metaphysics, in which there is no crash course. There is only the patient work of ministrative engagement, for which the vocabulary of virtue (generosity, kindness and so on) sounds rather lame. As Comte-Sponville (2003) says:

> The mother who gives her child everything she possesses is not being generous and does not need to be generous in order to do so: she loves her child more than her own self. The mother who would die for the sake of her child is not being courageous, or rather her courage is, as it were, supplementary: she loves her child more than life. The mother who is prepared to forgive her child for anything at all and accepts him unconditionally as he is, regardless of what he has done or might do, is not merciful; she loves her child more than justice or the good. (pp. 266–267)

There is something extraordinary about this ordinary human being – the loving parent – engaged in a task that is normally taken for granted. It goes on in the shadows, the intimate bond between parents and children that is neither introverted nor extroverted but somewhere in between. This is especially so at the beginning, the all-important beginning that Aristotle recognized as such, but did not explore. It will not last, or not in this form; the good-enough parent adapts to the child's growing independence, that very independence that she has been striving to bring about. Winnicott writes:

> The mother will grow up out of this state of easy devotion, and soon she will be back to the office desk, or to writing novels, or to a social life along with her husband, but for the time being she is in it up to the neck. (1963a in Winnicott 1985, p. 88)

The child may protest, but this is fine if she is starting to learn *both* that her mother is not-me (not under her control) *and* that she is no less cherished than she was when her mother was 'in it up to the neck'.

Winnicott offers an account of metaphysical development that relies on good-enough parenting, or what he sometimes calls ordinary devotion. For a helpless being, reality presents (as Nussbaum says) 'uncontrolled external objects' that strengthen or undermine our sense of well-being, and the inability to control these or predict their appearances and transformations is the *difficulty of reality* that all human beings initially encounter. It is appeased by good-enough parents, intent on bringing about emotional learning, and something similar occurs with good-enough teachers of children who suffer from reality in this way. The point is not that such children *must* have been neglected or abused as infants;

it is that they *suffer from their stories* and their dramas include feelings of being hopelessly out of control.

It should come as no surprise that the basic message of this book is that children develop – become 'better' and more mature – primarily through love. Comte-Sponville makes a similar point (ibid., p. 266) when he describes 'morality's maxim' as: *Act as though you loved.* To cherish another is to have no immediate need of morality; it is to be virtuous not for the sake of virtue but for the sake of the other. But there is a *secondary* need that may arise when the cherished person is condescended to, abused or harmed. We may call this the need to assuage, or find a place for, hatred in our hearts.

How much reality can we bear?

Marilynne Robinson is an award-winning writer whom I have quoted a couple of times. As with Winnicott, I would say that the idea of cherishing is at the heart of her work, though it isn't flagged up as such. In Chapter 3, I discussed a passage from *Home*, in which Glory observed her brother (the 'prodigal son' and ex-jailbird who has done terrible things and is about to do another) throwing an apple onto a roof, catching it and throwing it again, as he did when he was a boy. This, Glory reflects, 'might have been happiness', and I suggested that this signals a robust (albeit subjunctive) meaning for the term 'happiness', as for the idea of cherishing. In her manner of observing Jack in this scene, it is clear that Glory cherishes him.

In Chapter 7, I quoted a passage from *Gilead*, the first book in the trilogy that proceeds to *Home* and culminates in *Lila*. *Gilead* is a letter from an elderly preacher, John Ames, to his young son who will grow up without a father because Ames is dying. Without going as far as Martha Nussbaum when she writes about Henry James' *The Golden Bowl* ('I presuppose the quotation of the entire novel' (1992, p. 149)), I believe there is much to learn from Robinson's books about the meaning of cherishing, and some of this is captured by quotations. Consider this passage from Ames' letter:

> Sometimes now when you crawl into my lap and settle against me and I feel that light, quick strength of your body and the weightiness of your head, when you're cold from playing in the sprinkler or warm from your bath at night, and you lie in my arms and fiddle with my beard and tell me what you've been thinking about, that is perfectly pleasant. (p. 189)

Or this:

> There's a shimmer on a child's hair, in the sunlight. There are rainbow colours in
> it, tiny, soft beams of just the same colours you can see in the dew sometimes.
> They're in the petals of flowers, and they're on a child's skin. (p. 60)

Here are the sensual details of which I have spoken; good-enough parents
experience the beauty and wonder of their own children in rather these ways,
and this seems to be as true of parents of plain or disabled children as of the
parents of conventionally attractive children. In Chapter 7, I discussed Jody,
a disabled child whose parent was shocked by the stranger who saw him as
'seriously deviant' (drooling, making strange noises and so on), rather than
'cheerful and handsome'.

Ames is a decent human being, and though a preacher, never doctrinaire.
I think most parents would be happy for their children to emulate this man,
though he is by no means perfect. For the very Jack Boughton whom Glory
cherishes, John Ames regards with envy and suspicion. This is a problem, not
least because Jack's father is Ames' closest friend. Jack is in his forties and
becoming increasingly friendly with Ames' young wife and son. This provokes
an agonizing process of self-interrogation around the question that Ames poses
in this way: 'How should I deal with these fears I have, that Jack Boughton will
do you and your mother harm, just because he can, just for the sly, unanswerable
meanness of it?' He continues:

> Harm to you is not harm to me in the strict sense, and that is a great part of the
> problem. He could knock me down the stairs and I would have worked out the
> theology for forgiving him before I reached the bottom. But if he harmed you
> in the slightest way, I'm afraid theology would fail me. (Robinson 2004, p. 217)

This is fear in its most troubling sense. For theology to fail this pious man is to
allow fantasies of vengeance and even violence to take hold. It is to recognize his
own imperfect humanity, for as a human being he falls foul of what appears to
him now as the miserable truth of cherishing. We are unable to direct this good
feeling – the hopes, wishes and fears it imports – equally and indiscriminately.
We cannot bear the *reality of suffering* for the cherished person when we are (in
prospect) absent or dead, though we bear it (with relish perhaps) for the person
who harms him. We may struggle to forgive, or struggle to help others to forgive
when they suffer from their stories. But in some cases, we shall fail.

In *Elizabeth Costello*, Coetzee exposes us to the *texture of horror* for a person
who cannot accept or forgive. Ames' horror is also exposed when Robinson takes

us into the dialogue he conducts with himself under the designation 'Moriturus' ('the dying one'):

Question: What is it you fear most, Moriturus?

Answer: I, Moriturus, fear leaving my wife and child unknowingly in the sway of a man of extremely questionable character.

Question: What makes you think his contact with them or his influence upon them will be considerable enough to be damaging to them?

Now, that is really an excellent question, and one I would not have thought to put to myself... The truth is, as I stood there in the pulpit, looking down on the three of you, you looked to me like a handsome young family, and my evil old heart rose within me, the old covetise I have mentioned elsewhere came over me, and I felt the way I used to feel when the beauty of other lives was a misery and an offence to me. And I felt as if I were looking back from the grave.

Well, thank God I thought that through. (p. 160)

It isn't easy to engage in conversational responsiveness with oneself, and the weaving of first and second person, involving ironic self-congratulation ('that is really an excellent question, and one I would not have thought to put to myself') and self-appreciation (at the end he seems not only to be thanking God, but also himself), provides a telling glimpse into how imperfect beings like ourselves may minister to our own goods, as well as those of others. An adequate ethic of cherishing must embrace this cherishing of ourselves.

It is sometimes said that good characters make uninteresting dramas. In the hands of a writer like Robinson, who understands how difficult it is to be good and never confuses goodness with perfection, nothing could be further from the truth. Ames suffers acutely from his 'evil old heart', and it is no coincidence that his physical 'old heart' is soon to expire. Both the moral and physical hearts are dense with stories: the first includes 'covetise' and other unpleasant emotions, while the second includes the imminence of death and the retrospective meaning of one man's life viewed from this vantage point. There is failure at both levels, as this self-communing dialogue makes clear. He has not led a perfect life, and is by no means liberated from imperfect emotions. To amplify this point would require, as Martha Nussbaum says, 'quotation of the entire novel', but I have suggested that, imperfect as he is, John Ames is a person we should greatly admire. He aspires towards a perfection he will never achieve, and he suffers from the painful gap between what is and what might be.

Aristotelian ethics paves the way for moral ranking, as violinists might rank violins until they find (if they are lucky) the perfect specimen. We have seen that this way of thinking lends itself well to empirical surveys into 'how well' the nation's children are doing. I am not concerned here about the nation's children; I am concerned (more modestly, but more saliently I think) about those who engage in dramas of unlearning, appearing destined to remain this way. To cherish such children, or see them as cherishworthy, is to hope to cherish rather than squander their potentialities, which may be no easy task. In different ways, this is what good-enough teachers and parents seek, without the illusion that they will fulfil the task to perfection, or bring about the perfect realization of potentialities of the young.

One of the things we see from Robinson's example is that cherishing is not simply, as it may sound, a soft, sensual or nurturing virtue. It is a *fierce* one that in many cases cannot or will not forgive those who harm the people we cherish. It contains seeds of violence as well as tenderness, and it brings us into contact with realities of human nature that undercut some of our (cherished) ideals. The cliché says that those who have been seriously wronged will 'move on' if they are able to 'let go' of their rage, replacing it with forgiveness. And indeed, some people appear to achieve this, even if they sometimes seem sentimental rather than truthful, with a quality of what Fred Alford calls 'cut-rate forgiveness' (2013, p. 125). Aristotle understood that certain actions and events may 'strain human nature too far, and no one could endure them' (2002 1109 a 26). This has a bearing on the complex meaning of cherishing, which has aspects both of transcendent love and of possible hatred or vengeance. To reflect on this is to remember (as discussed in Chapter 7) that *there are limits* to what human beings can bear, even if we don't know in advance what they are. Conversational responsiveness is needed so that well-meaning reassurance ('You *can* forgive her if you put your mind to it') is reality-checked by just and loving attention to the other.

Vicar Julie Nicholson lost her daughter in the London bombings on 7 July 2005. Fred Alford tells her story in *Trauma and Forgiveness: Consequences and Communities*, and there are similarities between Nicholson's struggle and that of the fictional John Ames. Oppressed by her sense of unworthiness as a priest, Nicholson quit her job. Asked by a parishioner whether she felt she had a *duty* to forgive, Nicholson thought, 'No, actually I don't'. She continues:

> It doesn't matter to me whether people feel that according to the tenets of the Christian faith I have a duty to forgive. Maybe so. But the reality is I don't. (2013, p. 139)

Alford discusses this case in connection with Winnicott's concept of transitional experience: experience that takes place in what he calls the transitional space between me and not-me. Both Ames and Nicholson exemplify what I have called the *difficulty of learning* that is consequent upon the *difficulty of reality*. We have discussed the torment, rawness of nerves, sense of woundedness that the latter may bring. Quite simply, for Costello, the ugly phenomenon of 'what we do to animals' presents an obstacle to living; she appears to talk and think of little else. The question is whether this is something one may *learn* to overcome, and if so, what might be gathered about the difficulty of learning for some people.

Can we *learn to live with* 'unthinkably' difficult realities, including realities that will stay with one forever, like the murder of one's child? Can we accept them? Should we do so? There are cases where such a thing seems obscene; think of the parents of Ian Brady's victims, children who were not only murdered but also sadistically tortured. But if it is impossible to live with certain difficult realities, is it sometimes impossible to do what is right? Do we have a duty at least to attempt to forgive those who have wronged us, and if so, is this a duty to oneself or to the other?

These questions may remind us of Dent's comment, quoted earlier in the chapter: 'But how extraordinary it is to think that the central postures of moral acceptance are those of submissive obedience.' Rather than speaking about a duty to forgive, to which we must submit, we should speak developmentally, progressively, as I have attempted to do in this book, about *learning (and sometimes failing) to live with* difficult realities, through forgiveness or in some other way. The meaning of forgiveness has been much discussed by philosophers and theologians, but it is normally seen as a question about duty rather than about moral learning and its limits. Can we *learn* to forgive? If so, how? What other options might there be?

Unforgiveness is the dark side of cherishing, and one thing is clear: to live in bitterness and rage, with obsessions of vengeance, is not only painful; it reduces reality at large to a story of injustice or wrong-doing that in many cases (though not all) involves a handful of people, a tiny corner of reality. Unforgiveness can be a form of blindness in which injury to oneself or another is the only thing that penetrates the smokescreen. This is not, however, the only way to see it. When Julie Nicholson rejected the 'duty to forgive', she was, I think, confronting the conflict between the imperative to cherish the *memory of her daughter* and the imperative to live without unremitting bitterness or obsession. Her inability or refusal to forgive belonged to a long meditation on what her daughter's death meant or might mean. Alford reports that, in a 'disturbing interview', 'she seems as lost and unsure about forgiveness as any parishioner' (p. 131). She needed, in Wittgenstein's metaphor, to *find her way* between what appeared to be impossible options. Forgiving too easily can feel like a form of betrayal or abandonment. To lose one's daughter in a terror attack ('my daughter had been blown to pieces') must *never* become acceptable; but nor must the rejection of life.

It was in the medial space between impossible options that Julie Nicholson eventually found a 'way to accommodate' her daughter's death. She did this, not through forgiveness, not through acceptance, but through a kind of hope. There was hope in the continuity of life: 'the world keeps turning, the sun keeps shining'. There was hope in the fact that her daughter was not only dead, but also a 'presence' in Nicholson's life and community, which was clearly what I call a community of cherishing. Her daughter came to exist, says Alford, 'somewhere between inside and outside', suggesting that Nicholson learned to live with the appalling reality of her daughter's murder by shaping its meaning with others. As I understand this, the murder became more than 'what Jenny's death means to me', less than the cold reality of a blown-to-bits human body. Within her close-knit community, it became 'what Jenny's death means to us', a cherished memory and tragic loss that does not, however, destroy life itself. This is reminiscent not only of Winnicott's 'transitional space', but also of Wittgenstein's conception of meaning as common understanding bound to common forms of life.

Good-enough schools are communities of cherishing. They are communities in which individuals are cherished or seen as cherishworthy; but not only this. Much educational debate revolves around what I called (with Philip Jackson) the transmission and transformation models. Should we (as John White believes) educate children for well-being, introducing the best literature, history, science etc. *only* insofar as this is likely to enrich them personally, enhance their personal well-being? Or should we (as traditionalists believe) decide what children *ought to know*, and set about transmitting it?

The problem with these questions is that our ministrative engagements with the young are guided by (at least) two principles, not one. On the one hand, we cherish them as human beings and aim to bring about good transformations, good moral and intellectual development, by attending (as Joseph Dunne says) to their 'needs, aptitudes, and difficulties'. On the other, we cherish *impersonal* things, and part of what it means to cherish a person is to want her to cherish impersonal things too. We cherish ideals, memories, principles, for example. These come to the fore in different contexts, but especially when we are hurt by their infringement or neglect. (We saw that Margalit sees this kind of hurt as an impetus to engage with the unclear idea of the good.) We also cherish things idiosyncratically, the Scottish Highlands, the music of Bob Dylan, the paintings of El Greco. In many cases, such cherishing is lifelong, representing who we feel we are. We may be hurt into education by the sense that these wonders are insufficiently cherished today; we want to transmit knowledge *and* transform others through our own infectious passion.

This ought to be possible; it doesn't have to involve pressure or imposition. Some children urgently need personal cherishing, while others will benefit from the passions of teachers who cherish the traditional elements of a good education, Roman history, Renaissance poetry or whatever. The concept of cherishing must be put to work in both these ways. Children who suffer from their stories may be helped by sensitive teachers who offer a kind of friendship, a lingering conversation. Others are ready and eager to learn; they feel the allure of reality, of not-me. They are on the way to discovering, under the guidance of teachers or parents, their own domains of cherishing.

In Chapter 1, I talked about Philip Pullman's description of a government-rubberstamped task for children as one of 'stupefying worthlessness and futility'. Education, he said, should observe the principle that the things we ask children to do in school should be 'intrinsically worth doing'. I would like to express this slightly differently. The things we ask children to do in school should be seen less as *tasks* with successful or unsuccessful outcomes (though of course they are that in part), more as acts of discovering and creating meaning 'somewhere between inside and outside'. Pullman illustrates this beautifully by going into the mind of a person (who could be a child or a published writer) struggling to write a story. It feels like 'fishing in a boat at night'. You are 'calm and relaxed and attentive: truly aware, truly absorbed'. You are also alert for a response, a tug on the line, a cunning fish, a monster that could 'swallow hook, and line, and lamp, and boat, and you'. In other words, you are alert to not-me, and the more 'truly' you are 'aware and absorbed', the more you are likely to see. This may seem like a solitary experience, but meaning is never solitary, as Wittgenstein showed. In the end, you will return with food for the fire, a meal for the family, or you will return with nothing at all.

Reflections on method

If difficult learning is a difficult transaction with meaning, our model for educational debate and reflection should look rather like this:

> F. R. Leavis said that the form of a critical judgement of a poem or novel is, 'It is so, isn't it?' and that the form of response to it is, 'Yes, but...'. It is a fine way of characterising the essentially conversational nature of judgements in the realm

of meaning, their objectivity as well as their necessary incompleteness... It is no different in life. We cannot tell in advance what is possible in the realms of meaning, because we cannot say what vital responsiveness, disciplined by and disciplining a language 'used at full stretch', will reveal to us. (p. 180)

This book may be seen as an extended question: 'It is so, isn't it?' The passage is by Raimond Gaita (2002), who understands the resistance many philosophers have to thinking this way. He continues: 'The fineness of the web irritates some people. Its fragility unnerves them' (p. 181). What irritates and unnerves is a way of *thinking about thinking* that has human beings and puzzlement at its heart. But this is precisely the subject matter we set out to address: children who inhibit or disrupt learning, adults who are puzzled about what to do, how to respond. Our philosophical reflections must be continuous with these troubling scenarios.

The conversational judgements described by Gaita involve people in an everyday sense. One person proposes, another demurs. Then the second person may propose and the first demur, and on it goes. In the case of literary criticism, Gaita says, 'always, it is assumed, the text would be before the conversationalists' (p. 180). In this book, I have spoken repeatedly of children behaving destructively or evasively, and the question throughout has been: how can we engage in populated philosophy, philosophy in the e.g. style, keeping *people* 'before the conversationalists'?

In exactly the way that snapshot of a person is not a person, a conversation may fail (by ignoring its own subject matter) to be a meaningful conversation. It may fail to be a genuine *transaction of meaning*, as in Wittgenstein's example about the right hand giving the left hand money:

Why can't my right hand give my left hand money? – – My right hand can put it into my left hand. My right hand can write a deed of gift and my left hand a receipt. – – But the further practical consequences would not be those of a gift. When the left hand has taken the money from the right, etc, we shall ask: 'Well, and what of it?' (1953, para 268)

Much philosophy takes this form. Exchanges are riddled with assumptions that then become the topic of conversation, rather than the text, the person, the puzzlement of the teacher, which provided the original impetus to converse. Part of the difficulty is that philosophical temperaments differ, and this takes the form of a willingness or unwillingness to think vertically about deeper layers of meaning and emotion. Something like this is evident in philosopher Ian Hacking's response to Diamond's concept of the difficulty of reality. The following is a reduction (a truthful one, I hope) of their conversation.

> Diamond: I want to note how much that coming apart of thought and
> reality belongs to flesh and blood.
> Hacking: I still have not properly taken that in.

Hacking is a philosopher of science in the analytic tradition, not known for his
poetic or mystical sensibilities. Yet he responds to Diamond as though she were
a poet, requiring a contemplative, reticent and above all *feeling* response. A few
pages later, as though fed up with all this, his mood changes and he says in an
almost scolding tone:

> Hacking: Don't knock deflection. Deflecting is one of the things that we do
> quite well. Deflecting blows and deflecting anger is a good thing.

It is as though Diamond had said: 'We humans are not very good at deflecting,
which is just as well because deflecting is always a bad thing to do.' But she has
not said this. On the contrary, she clearly thinks we are rather good at deflecting
(as Freud thought we are good at resisting painful truths), especially when we
fall into certain philosophical habits. Nor I think is she saying it's always a bad
thing to do, though it is true that the idea of deflection as ethical failure is present
in her writings.

The coming apart of thought and reality belongs to flesh and blood. This kind of
thought 'irritates and unnerves' some philosophers, who like Hacking attempt to
treat it as 'poetry' before throwing up their hands and returning to the i.e. style
of thinking that is dedicated to clarity and explication. *This* is home ground,
and from this perspective, the coming together or coming apart of thought and
reality – the endeavour to engage with not-me, and the often painful failure to
do so – is not on the agenda. There is no need for what Gaita aptly calls 'vital
responsiveness, disciplined by and disciplining a language "used at full stretch"'.
There is no need for life-like examples, for examples are essentially ornaments
to a well-constructed argument. Nor is there any need to consult our own lived
experience.

How can we talk about people?

What is a person? What do we *owe* human beings, particularly when they are
young or vulnerable? I suggested that these shouldn't be seen as questions about
duty, but as questions about what it is to *live well* with others, to which cherishing
is part of the answer. I distinguished between real and counterfeit cherishing,
and this resembles the distinction between real people and snapshots of people.

Real people, I suggested, can be flesh-and-blood or fictional; if the latter, what makes them 'real' is that they are described 'poetically' or 'at full stretch' in a way that acquires *dramatic* reality, stimulating a sense of personal recognition, sympathy, fear, terror and so on, just like flesh-and-blood people we know. These descriptions don't merely refer to *attributes* of people, telling us how clever, brave or mean they are. They *characterize* individuals, enabling us to imagine them, showing us what they are *like*, what it is like to be in their presence, converse with them and so on.

As so often, Iris Murdoch sheds light on what this means:

> When we apprehend and assess other people we do not consider only their solutions to specifiable practical problems, we consider something more elusive which may be called their total vision of life, as shown in their mode of speech or silence, their choice of words, their assessments of others, their conception of their own lives, what they think attractive or praiseworthy, what they think funny: in short, the configurations of their thought which show continually in their reactions and conversations. These things, which may be overtly and comprehensively displayed or inwardly elaborated and guessed at, constitute what, making different points in the two metaphors, one may call the texture of a man's being or the nature of his personal vision. (1956, p. 39)

It may sound portentous to talk about the texture of a young child's being, or the nature of her personal vision. The latter is obviously something that develops over time, but 'texture of being' sounds like the kind of thing Dent has in mind when he mentions children who, from an early age, are 'vividly responsive to the joy of other people'. The texture of a person is hard to capture in words, but if we are aware of its importance, we will be dissatisfied by a picture of human beings as (essentially) propensities to act and feel.

Murdoch is right to suggest that we need a deeper view. To think ethically about human beings is to go beyond an inventory of their personal attributes or tendencies. This is understood by the philosophers I have highlighted in the book – Wittgenstein, Cora Diamond and Raimond Gaita, in particular – and the latter tells a story about a personal encounter he had in his youth, that illustrates this well. Aged 17, Gaita was working as a ward-assistant in a psychiatric hospital. The ward was occupied by men whose debasement Gaita captures in a phrase from Simone Weil; they seem to have been 'struck the kind of blow which leaves a being struggling on the ground like a half crushed worm'. One day a nun entered the ward. When she spoke to the patients, Gaita was struck by a contrast between her demeanour and that of the psychiatrists. Gaita admired the psychiatrists, who treated the patients 'well' and spoke movingly of their inalienable dignity. At one point he even describes them as 'noble'; but when the nun appeared, words like dignity, nobility and non-condescension acquired a new meaning:

> Everything in her demeanour towards them – the way she spoke to them, her facial expressions, the infections of her body – contrasted with and showed up the behaviour of those noble psychiatrists. She showed that they were, despite their best efforts, condescending, as I too had been. (2002, p. 18)

The difference is behavioural, but it is so subtle (Gaita implies) that many or most people wouldn't have been struck by it as he was. He was astonished, and moved to reflect; the psychiatrists were oblivious. This is not, in short, the *kind* of difference that one would expect an inspector or auditor to record. Gaita says nothing specific about the acts that were performed, the facial expressions etc. Instead, he speaks about non-condescension and the 'full humanity' of the patients that was revealed by the demeanour of nun:

> [The nun] revealed that even such patients were, as the psychiatrists and I had sincerely and generously professed, the equals of those who wanted to help them; but she also revealed that in our hearts we did not believe this. (ibid., pp. 18–19)

In our hearts we did not believe this... This is a way of speaking vertically about emotion, contrasting professed with suppressed, superficial with deep feeling and being struck by the difference. In my language, the nun exhibited genuine cherishing, unlike the counterfeit (partial, inadequate) cherishing that Gaita and the psychiatrists exhibited towards the patients. Of course, these were decent human beings, trying to treat the patients well, but sometimes we must go further in our efforts to minister to other people's goods. Not mere kindness or generosity but a certain 'texture of being' is required.

Condescension and non-condescension may be matters of texture in this sense, rather than action or behaviour as they are normally understood by philosophers and psychologists. Most people 'talk the talk' of equality these days, but their behaviour, considered at a deeper level, may show that they don't fully subscribe to this. To condescend to a person, albeit subtly, because she is vulnerable, dependent or immature, may be a hard-to-detect failure. Many people, on the receiving end of condescending attitudes and behaviour, are no doubt oblivious of this fact, but others feel it acutely, especially from people to whom they are close. It is a hallowed principle of psychoanalysis – especially as conceptualized by Winnicott – that infants can be profoundly affected by adults who merely *act the part*, 'perhaps acting it quite well at times, and perhaps acting it well because of having learned how to care for infants from books or in a class. But this acting is not good enough.' (1963a in Winnicott 1985, p. 88). A parent may *enact* respect but *betray* condescension, creating a lasting tendency to self-deprecation that in turn may produce dramas of unlearning.

The *enactment* of respect is not good-enough in intimate relationships. True respect is at the heart of cherishing, and cherishing (as I suggest in this book) is something every human being needs. Thinking vertically about emotion allows us to explore emotional truths that may be undetected or denied, and we must be wary of the style of philosophizing that regards 'knowing what the other feels like' in this vertical sense as *necessarily* antiquated intuitionism or folk psychology. Winnicott finds such knowledge in two directions: from good-enough parent to infant and from infant to parent (good-enough or otherwise). It plays a crucial role in the *disciplined responsiveness* to another that I call cherishing, and I believe it is often exemplified by good-enough teachers towards children, and vice versa.

I have written elsewhere (Cigman 2014, p. 806):

> [Gaita's] story *marks a distinction* that is conceptually and ethically crucial, though the reality in which the story is based is (we are given to believe) extremely subtle. Fine discriminations can expose divergent ethical universes.

This recalls Wittgenstein, as discussed in Chapter 2. Discussing the difference between genuine and simulated expressions of feeling, he says: 'Can one learn this knowledge? Yes; some can. Not, however, by taking a course in it but through "experience".... What is most difficult here is to put this indefiniteness, correctly and unfalsified, into words.' I hope that I have by now explored this difficulty without undue falsification.

A note about language

Should we encourage children to cherish every human being (and possibly some non-human ones) unconditionally? Should we promote the virtue of universal love that the Greeks called *agape*, and Christians call *caritas* (usually, but misleadingly, translated as charity)? The term *caritas* is the source of our word 'cherishing', and philosopher of education Stein Wivestad (2008) argues that *phronesis* and *agape* are proper ideals for the young. I agree about *phronesis*, as I argued in the previous chapter, but *agape* is more complex. As a religious concept, it is normally accompanied by the thought that there is a duty to forgive wrong-doers, subject to their sincere repentance. Relationships that were damaged by the wrong-doing must be restored by this route; *caritas* may be resumed. This imports a quasi-divine ethic into the lives of non-believers as well as believers, contra Anscombe's argument that the concept of duty is incoherent in the absence of a commanding deity. It also ignores the *fact* noted by Aristotle, that certain actions and events may 'strain human nature too far'. Making every allowance for the idea of reality as sometimes impossibly *difficult*, certain injustices or abuses – particularly if they have lasting effects – may be impossible to forgive.

I haven't explored the Greek concepts of *philia* (friendship) and *agape* (unconditional love) in this book, and I don't intend to do so in detail. It is a large topic, and though the language of love is obviously germane to my theme, this is not primarily a scholarly book. There are vexed questions about translation that could lead in directions far from the purposes of this book. Consider, for example, the following very different translations of a passage from Aristotle's *Politics*:

> There are two impulses which more than all others cause human beings to cherish and feel affection for each other: 'this is my own', and 'this is a delight' (Aristotle 1992, 1262b 22–3, trans. T. A. Sinclair).

> There are two things above all that make persons love and care: they are a sense that something is one's very own or proper to oneself and a sense that one must be content with it'. (Sherman 1989, p. 146)

The meaning of 'this is my own' or 'something is one's very own' (*to idion*) is straightforward enough. Aristotle is responding (wisely, most would agree) to Plato's proposal in the *Republic* that families should be abolished, so that adults may relate impartially to their biological children, and society may flourish without the hazards of personal attachment. As in the failed twentieth-century experiment of the kibbutz (but much more extreme), *all* children in the community become one's 'sons and daughters'. One of Aristotle's purposes in exploring the idea of *philia*, which he did in detail, was to show how Plato 'waters down' – and thereby misrepresents – the human tendency to love or bond with particular individuals. We *form preferences*, and indeed, indestructible ties. In Wittgenstein's terms, Aristotle was reminding readers of something that belongs to the natural history of human beings. (1953 para 415)

The second difference in the passage quoted above shows how hard it is to get inside the language of cherishing. The Greek verb *to agapeton* is not, I think, satisfactorily translated, 'it is a delight' or 'a sense that one must be content with it'. These phrases attempt to capture (as Aristotle did) the thought that 'love and care' (Sherman), 'cherishing and affection' (Sinclair), respond to something *out there*. We aren't merely *partial* towards our friends and family; we find 'delightful' qualities that others may not, and we are 'content' with what we find in the sense that we hopefully accept these people unconditionally, infuriating though they may sometimes be.

André Comte-Sponville translates *agapan* in classical Greek as 'to welcome in friendship, to love, and to cherish' (ibid, p. 270). The term 'cherish' seems natural and right for a word that will later acquire an aura of divinity, referring to a love that transcends the 'natural history of human life' by (almost impossibly) loving one's neighbour as oneself. Aristotle did not know such a love, and I think he would have regarded the idea of trying to love a treacherous or malicious person (for example) as crazy (rather as he would have seen Elizabeth Costello's anguished compassion for animals as crazy). Nonetheless, I agree with Nancy Sherman (1995) that Aristotle's conception of *philia* contained possibilities of deepening and transformation that he didn't explore. It lends itself to the formation of an ideal.

It seems reasonable to translate Aristotle's *to agapeton* as the *sense of cherishworthiness*, regarding this as an expansion or deepening of *philia* that refers to an ideal connection with reality, though not necessarily a Christian one. We cherish unreasonably much of the time, but I have suggested that there is something more. There is a rational dimension to cherishing, if to be rational is sometimes to reflect with difficulty beyond the aegis (and tyranny) of the ego. In this sense, rationality is a truth-seeking virtue associated with the discovery of the good. We don't 'find cherishworthiness' staring us in the face; this was the point of Raimond Gaita's story about the nun. But we can keep in view the thought that it is there to be found. When adults struggle to cherish children they find obnoxious or troublesome, it is this that they need to keep in mind.

We can no more cherish every human being than we can forgive every injurious act or malicious wrong-doer; absorbing the idea of cherishing in our lives, we cannot but accept the possibility of hatred towards those who violate people we cherish. But we can take this further by attempting to see every human being as worthy of cherishing by someone, if not ourselves. Aristotle, as I said, wouldn't have agreed; but we are post-Kantian thinkers who possess a sense of unconditional moral worth: the equal and irreducible dignity of every human being. (Raimond Gaita calls this inalienable dignity or unconditional preciousness.) *This* residue of divine thinking is something I believe we should retain, for in the domains of education and upbringing, it is needed as a rein on our sometimes unreasonable partialities. Hence the distinction between cherishing others and finding them cherishworthy.

Cherishing is a virtue of intimacy, as well as revelation, and these two dimensions bring possibilities of overcoming hatred and resuming living. One of the most thought-provoking aspects of Gaita's discussion of the nun is the metaphysical lesson he draws from the story. He says: 'the quality of her love proved that [the patients] are rightly the objects of our non-condescending treatment... For me, the purity of the love proved the reality of what it revealed' (ibid., p. 21). Not only was the nun's attitude of non-condescension extraordinary, directed as it was towards patients who seem like 'half crushed worms'. Gaita speaks about *rightness* and *proof*, gesturing towards the *truth* that was revealed to him by the nun. He continues: 'I have to say "for me", because one must speak personally about such matters. That after all is the nature of witness.' The truth invoked here is, then, both objective and personally revealed.

This is an experience of *secular revelation*, for Gaita invokes no deity. He recognizes that many philosophical readers will reject the conception of knowledge this implies. Some further remarks, however, render his thoughts more accessible. Children, says Gaita, 'come to love their brothers and sisters because they see them in the light of their parents' love' (ibid., p. 24). In other words, people can appear lovable by being loved, as well as by having attributes we admire. The same can happen with teachers; though we are not to forget the dramatic potential of this situation. The child who hates another may hate *more* rather than *less* strongly if she discovers that the parent or teacher loves her enemy. This is an ordinary drama of human jealousy, but we must also allow for Gaita's insight, which I would express in the language of cherishing. The cherishworthiness of a person we experience as distinctly *uncherishworthy* may be revealed in personal intimacy, through the cherishing of another. Like Pullman's fisherman who feels a tug on the line, one may experience a tug towards the hated person by *closing in* on her under the loving influence of another. Like a microscope on the skin, proximity may reveal unseen blemishes, but set against the ideal of cherishing, this *closing in* may reveal an individual whose imperfections one can accept without corrosive hatred, because one glimpses the source from which they came.

We understand how they became that way. We learn more about their vulnerability. Literature is important for ethical thinkers because, at best, it brings us into sympathetic proximity to human imperfection, forming a partnership with populated philosophy. Modifying Bernard Williams' words, this aspect of moral exploration and endeavour enables us to keep the important issues *on* the page.

Epilogue

The vulnerability of precious things is beautiful because vulnerability is a mark of existence.

Simone Weil (2005)

We began with a sense of moral crisis: the murder of a headmaster by one of his pupils, insolence, bullying, educational achievement, poor mental health among the young, and so on. Everyone can supply examples like these, and many people share the anxiety, at least from time to time.

We began with a crisis, but where have we ended up? The book is structured by a distinction between *styles* of response, and this may seem somewhat artificial. I have discussed enhancement agendas, intended to 'make children better' in a sense that is meaningful to politicians, meaningful for national statistics, suitable for successful delivery in schools. My own experience with primary schools suggests that, top-down as these agendas are, their delivery by extraordinary teachers – people who are endlessly kind, generous and discerning – means that they sometimes bring great benefits to the young. When this is the case, there is a happy partnership between policy-making and the dispositions of cherishing. Within communities of cherishing, policy agendas may be delivered wisely.

At times, it is true, my tone has been sceptical. It is time to say, however, that for all I know, these agendas play a significant role in raising the graph of decency and achievement among the young. If I have been sceptical, it is because I resist the tone of crusading, back-stage confidence that often overlooks the efforts and achievements of practitioners. This recalls Popham, quoted in Chapter 1, to whom it seemed obvious (back in 1969) that *now* we are on the brink of a new era. The question is whether we are willing to learn from past failures and acknowledge the extraordinary people – the good-enough teachers and parents – in our midst. I have suggested that these exemplary individuals are also, in a sense, quite ordinary.

It is this attempt to acknowledge certain people, dispositions and styles of encounter that has preoccupied us during the final part of the book. Policymakers naturally use a broad brush. Their alliance with teachers and parents is in some ways a curious one, for it seems blindingly obvious that *individuals* constitute a powerful focus of interest for this second group. Good teachers are alert not only to the progress and achievements of a class, but also to the child in the back row who seems keen to remain inconspicuous, the child who keeps skipping school for reasons that are never quite clear, or the compliant child who behaves not well but impeccably, as though she is terrified of disapproval.

This seems obvious, as I say, yet the task of *thinking lucidly* about individuals seems marginal to the concerns of many policymakers and educationists. This brings us to Wittgenstein, whom I have often quoted. The following two passages have been seminal for this book:

> What we are supplying are really remarks on the natural history of human beings; we are not contributing curiosities however, but observations which no one has doubted, but which have *escaped remark only because they are always before our eyes* (para. 415).

> The work of the philosopher consists in *assembling reminders for a particular purpose* (para. 127).
>
> (Ludwig Wittgenstein, 1953, my emphasis)

Proponents of enhancement agendas *usefully* remind us that there is more to education than exam success and the drive for national prosperity. Certain things, however, continue to 'escape remark' because they are 'always before our eyes'. Recognizing this, I have explored a conceptual framework that brings human dramas – particularly dramas of unlearning – to the fore. I have tried to set out some terms in which we think about these, including reality and its difficulties, the concept of the good, emotions that go *down* into the body and the past. I spoke about the possibilities of emotional transformation and pointed to the significant but neglected phenomenon of unreason in education and upbringing. The idea of cherishing (I said) points towards intimate, unreasonable layers of the ethical life, as well as the deepening of wisdom and human connection. This seems like part of the work it is meant to do. It reminds us who we are and who we want to be.

At the heart of the cherishing disposition is the desire to minister to other people's genuine goods. I want to close with a few words about this perplexing concept, the concept of the good, and its connections with the perplexing domain we call ethics.

A child asks: 'Why should I be good? Why should I be kind? Why should I tell the truth if I can tell lies and get away with it?' This isn't just the musing of a provocative and curious child. 'Why should I be good?' is an ancient philosophical question, and with the erosion of traditions, it is one that every one of us is likely to ask from time to time.

The Greeks offered a rich and qualified answer. It is, in a general way, in everyone's *interests* to be good. We will live better, be happier, lead more fulfilled or flourishing lives if we become virtuous individuals, people with 'moral excellences', difficult or painful though these may be to acquire and sustain. Many contemporary philosophers, however, attuned to the scepticism of our age, take issue with this. Bernard Williams, for example, paints a picture of a 'horrible person' (with a 'bright eye and gleaming coat') who is nonetheless 'dangerously flourishing' (1993, p.46).

I am with the Greeks rather than with Williams here. 'Dangerously flourishing' is, I believe, a phrase we should approach with caution. My suspicion is that Williams's horrible person doesn't flourish at all, because he doesn't really know the satisfactions of cherishing. In our cherishing (I have suggested) lies the elusive truth of what we call happiness: a satisfying but vulnerable condition that binds us to the fortunes or proximity of our cherished objects. A life of cherishing is a life well lived. This includes the cherishing of personally significant objects, places and practices, as well as the cherishing of people. Given a reasonable modicum of luck, a life of cherishing is also a good and flourishing life.

I have attempted throughout the book to elaborate these thoughts, but the elaboration hasn't been straightforward. There are no simple pathways of discovery. I *suspect* that horrible people don't really flourish, but what should we make of this suspicion? Is it a gut feeling? Can it be analytically confirmed, so that it becomes knowledge rather than suspicion? Is empirical enquiry the way to go, so that a suspicion becomes a hypothesis, subject to verification?

These questions reflect the difficulty we have finding our feet in the domain we call 'ethics'. At its heart is puzzlement about the concept of the good, and this puzzlement makes it hard to advance collectively – without murky suspicions – on the question of a good human life. Philosophers' blueprints provoke dissent and unease. As Iris Murdoch says, in the spirit of Wittgenstein, we misunderstand 'the place where the concept of good lives'. Does it lie in high standards? Dutiful behaviour? Happiness or well-being?

I have indicated Murdoch's own answer:

> I have spoken of efforts of attention directed upon individuals and of obedience to reality as an exercise of love, and have suggested that 'reality' and 'individual' present themselves to us in moral contexts as ideal end-points or Ideas of Reason. This surely is the place where the concept of good lives.
>
> (1970, p.42)

This is a vision of human beings permanently engaged in a task. 'The good' finds a place, not in an obscure, independent realm, but as a focus of sincere effort in which it is possible *really* to get it wrong. Misunderstanding the place where the concept of good lives means thwarting such effort, redirecting it into science, checklists or narcissistic projects. In the scheme of this book, the good resides primarily in our engagements with others, for whom we want life to go well in an irreducibly singular sense.

My concept of cherishing is a place-marker, elaborating Murdoch's vision. In this place, we find condescension that looks like respect, but isn't, children who look confident, but aren't. We *look and reflect*, attempting to discriminate wisely between genuine and counterfeit goods, and ease people's paths towards the former. Cherishing can be hard, and the disposition to cherish is, I believe, a kind of master-virtue, comprising truthfulness, resourcefulness, patience, courage. It may not make us happy in a simple sense, but I suggested that happiness in a simple sense is a misfit in our ethical lives. By cherishing other human beings and domains to which we are personally drawn, we will (given propitious opportunities) become decent human beings and committed workers, enriched by realities beyond ourselves.

Bibliography

Abram, Jan (2007), *The Language of Winnicott: A Dictionary of Winnicott's Use of Words*, London: Karnac Books.

Ahmed, Sara (2010), *The Promise of Happiness*, Durham: Duke University Press.

Alford, Fred (2013), *Trauma and Forgiveness: Consequences and Communities*, Cambridge: Cambridge University Press.

Anscombe, Elizabeth (1958), 'Modern Moral Philosophy', *Philosophy*, 33 (124), pp. 1–19.

Aristotle (1981), *The Politics*, trans. Thomas Sinclair, London: Penguin Books.

Aristotle (1991), *The Rhetoric*, trans. Hugh Lawson-Tancred, London: Penguin Books.

Aristotle (2002), *Nichomachean Ethics*, trans. Joe Sachs, Newburyport: Focus Publishing.

Aristotle (2011), *Nichomachean Ethics*, trans. Sarah Broadie and Christopher Rowe, Oxford: Oxford University Press.

Baumeister, Roy, Jennifer D. Campbell, Joachim I. Krueger, and Kathleen D. Vohs (2003), 'Does High Self-Esteem Cause Better Performance, Interpersonal Success, Happiness, or Healthier Lifestyles?', *Psychological Science in the Public Interest: A Journal of the American Psychological Society*, 4(1), 1–44.

Benn, Melissa (2011), *School Wars: The Battle for Britain's Education*, London: Verso Books. https://www.theguardian.com/commentisfree/2011/oct/24/student-fees-vocational-apprentiships

Bentham, Jeremy (1962), 'An Introduction to the Principles of Morals and Legislation', in M. Warnock (ed.), *Utilitarianism (and other essays) by John Stuart Mill*, London and Glasgow: Collins, pp. 33–77.

Bruckner, Pascal (2011), *Perpetual Euphoria: On the Duty to Be Happy*, Princeton: Princeton University Press.

Buber, Martin (2002), 'Education', in *Between Man and Man*, trans. Gregor-Smith Ronald, New York: Routledge, pp. 98–122.

Burnyeat, Myles (1980), 'Aristotle on Learning to Be Good', in A. Rorty (ed.), *Essays on Aristotle's Ethics*, Berkeley: University of California Press, pp. 69–92.

Cavell, Stanley (1969), 'Knowing and Acknowledging', in *Must We Mean What We Say?*, New York: Scribner, pp. 238–266.

Cavell, Stanley (1999), *The Claim of Reason*, Oxford: Oxford University Press

Cigman, Ruth (2001), 'Self-Esteem and the Confidence to Fail', *Journal of Philosophical Education*, 35(4), 561–576.

Cigman, Ruth (2004), 'Situated Self-Esteem', *Journal of Philosophical Education*, 38(2), 91–106.

Cigman, Ruth (2007a), *Included or Excluded?: The Challenge of the Mainstream for Some SEN Children*, London: Routledge.

Cigman, Ruth (2007b), 'A Question of Universality: Inclusive Education and the
    Principle of Respect', *Journal of Philosophy of Education*, 41(4), 775–793.

Cigman, Ruth (2014), 'Education Without Condescension: Philosophy, Personhood and
    Cognitive Disability', in Lani Florian (ed.), *The SAGE Handbook of Special Education*,
    Thousand Oaks: SAGE Publications, pp. 803–818.

Claxton, Guy (2008), *What's the Point of School?: Rediscovering the Heart of Education*,
    London: Oneworld Publications.

Coetzee, J. M. (1999), *The Lives of Animals*, Princeton: Princeton University Press.

Coetzee, J. M. (2003), *Elizabeth Costello*, London: Harvill Secker.

Comte-Sponville, Andre (2003), *A Short Treatise on the Great Virtues: The Uses of
    Philosophy in Everyday Life*, London: Penguin Books.

Cooper, Paul (2007), 'Are Some Children Unteachable? An Approach to Social,
    Emotional and Behavioural Difficulties', in R. Cigman (ed.), *Included or Excluded?
    The Challenge of the Mainstream for Some SEN Children*, London: Routledge.

De Ruyter, Doret (2003), 'The Importance of Ideals in Education' *Journal of Philosophy
    of Education*, 37(3), 467–482.

Dent, Nicholas (1999), 'Virtue, *Eudaimonia* and Teleological Ethics', in David Carr
    and Jan Steutel (eds), *Virtue Ethics and Moral Education*, Abingdon: Routledge,
    pp. 21–34.

Diamond, Cora (1995), 'Having a Rough Story about What Moral Philosophy Is', in
    The Realistic Spirit: Wittgenstein, Philosophy and the Mind, Cambridge: MIT Press,
    pp. 367–382.

Diamond, Cora (2008), 'The Difficulty of Reality and the Difficulty of Philosophy', in
    Stanley Cavell , Cora Diamond, John McDowell, Ian Hacking and Cary Wolfe (eds),
    Philosophy & Animal Life, New York: Columbia University Press, pp. 43–90.

Dickens, Charles, *Hard Times*, many editions.

Dunne, Joseph (1993), *Back to the Rough Ground: Practical Judgement and the Lure of
    Technique*, Notre Dame: University of Notre Dame Press.

Dunne, Joseph (2005), 'What's the Good of Education?' in W. Carr (ed.), *The
    RoutledgeFalmer Reader in Philosophy of Education*, London: Routledge.

Dunne, Joseph (2006), 'An intricate fabric: understanding the rationality of practice'
    Pedagogy, Culture & Society, 13(3), 367–390.

Eliot, George, *Middlemarch*, many editions.

Emler, Nick (2001), 'Self-Esteem: The Costs and Causes of Low Self-Worth', York:
    Joseph Rowntree Foundation.

Gaita, Raimond (2002), *A Common Humanity: Thinking About Love and Truth and
    Justice*, London: Routledge.

Gaita, Raimond (2004), *The Philosopher's Dog*, Abingdon: Routledge.

Galton, M., Simon, B. and Croll, P. (1980), *Inside the Primary Classroom*, London:
    Routledge and Kegan Paul.

Goffman, Erving (1956), *The Presentation of Self in Everyday Life*, http://www.sociosite.
    net/sociologists/texts/goffman_self.php.

Gove, Michael (2009), 'What Is Education for?' *Speech to the Royal Society of Arts*. https://www.thersa.org/globalassets/pdfs/blogs/gove-speech-to-rsa.pdf.

Gove, Michael (2011), *Speech to Twyford Church of England High School*. https://www.gov.uk/government/speeches/michael-gove-to-twyford-church-of-england-high-school.

Hacking, Ian (2008), 'Deflections', in S. Cavell et al. (eds), *Philosophy & Animal Life*, New York: Columbia University Press, pp.139–172.

Harre, Rom (1998), *The Singular Self: An Introduction to the Psychology of Personhood*, Thousand Oaks: SAGE Publications.

Harris, John (2010), *Enhancing Evolution: The Ethical Case for Making Better People*, Princeton: Princeton University Press.

Herodotus (2002), *The Histories*, trans. de Selincourt A, London: Penguin Books.

Holt, John (1990), *How Children Fail*, London: Penguin Books.

Homer (2003), *The Odyssey*, trans. E. Rieu, London: Penguin Books.

Ibsen, Henrik, *A Doll's House*, many editions.

Jackson, Philip (2007), 'Real Teaching', in R. Curren (ed,), *Philosophy of Education: An Anthology*, Oxford: Blackwell.

James, William (1971), *The Varieties of Religious Experience*, New York: Fount Paperbacks.

Kenny, Anthony (1973), *The Anatomy of the Soul: Historical Essays in the Philosophy of Mind*, Oxford: Blackwell.

Kittay, Eva (1999), *Love's Labor: Essays on Women, Equality, and Dependency*, London: Routledge.

Kristjánsson, Kristján (2015), *Aristotelian Character Education*, London: Routledge.

Layard, Richard (2006), *Happiness: Lessons from a New Science*, London: Penguin Books.

Lear, Jonathan (2001), *Happiness, Death, and the Remainder of Life*, Cambridge: Harvard University Press.

Margalit, Avishai (2002), *The Ethics of Memory*, Cambridge: Harvard University Press.

Midgley, Mary (2000), *Utopias, Dolphins and Computers: Problems of Philosophical Plumbing*, London: Routledge.

Mill, John Stuart (1960), *Autobiography*, New York: Columbia University Press.

Mill, John Stuart (1962), 'Bentham', in M. Warnock (ed.), *Utilitarianism (and other essays) by John Stuart Mill*, London and Glasgow: Collins.

Miller, Alice (1983), *The Drama of the Gifted Child*, trans. R. Ward, London: Faber and Faber.

Montaigne, Michel de (2003), 'On Educating Children', in M. A. Screech (ed.), *The Complete Essays*, London: Penguin.

Moore, Charlotte (2005), *George and Sam*, London: Penguin.

Mulgan, Geoff (2009), Preface to Roberts Y, *Grit: the Skills for Success and How They Are Grown*, Young Foundation.

Murdoch, Iris (1956), 'Vision and Choice in Morality', *Proceedings of the Aristotelian Society, Supplementary Volumes*, 30, 14–58.

Murdoch, Iris (1970), *The Sovereignty of Good*, London: Routledge and Kegan Paul.

Neiman, Susan (2014), *Why Grow Up?: Philosophy in Transit*, London: Penguin Books.

Noddings, Nel (2003), *Happiness and Education*, Cambridge: Cambridge University Press.

Nussbaum, Martha (1992), *Love's Knowledge: Essays on Philosophy and Literature*, Oxford: Oxford University Press.

Nussbaum, Martha (2001), *Upheavals of Thought: The Intelligence of Emotions*, Cambridge: Cambridge University Press.

Peters, Richard (1966), *Ethics and Education*, Glenview: Scott Foresman & Co.

Peters, Richard (1970), *Authority, Responsibility and Education*, London: Allen & Unwin.

Phillips, Adam (2011), *On Balance*, London: Penguin Books.

Plato (2003), *The Republic*, trans. L. Desmond, London: Penguin Books.

Plowden Report (1967), Central Advisory Council for Education (1967), *The Plowden Report: Children and Their Primary Schools*, London: Her Majesty's Stationery office.

Pomeroy, E. (2000), *Experiencing Exclusion*, Stoke-On-Trent: Trentham Books.

Pullman, Philip (2003), 'All around you is silence', retrieved from https://www.theguardian.com/education/2003/jun/05/schools.news

Roberts, Peter (2016) *Happiness, Hope, and Despair: Rethinking the Role of Education*, New York: Peter Lang.

Roberts, Yvonne (2009), *Grit: The Skills for Success and How They Are Grown*, Young Foundation.

Robinson, Marilynne (2012), *Home*, London: Virago.

Robinson, Marilynne (2013), *Gilead*, London: Virago.

Rosen, Michael (2016), 'Dear Ms Morgan: Sats tests are putting young children through hell', retrieved from https://www.theguardian.com/education/2016/may/03/morgan-sats-test-children-primary-school-pupils.

Sainsbury, Claire (2000), *Martian in the Playground*, Thousand Oaks: SAGE Publications.

Seligman, Martin (2008), *Authentic Happiness*, London: Brealey.

Sherman, Nancy (1989), *The Fabric of Character: Aristotle's Theory of Virtue*, Oxford: Clarendon.

Sherman, Nancy (1995) 'The Moral Perspective and the Psychoanalytic Quest', *The Journal of the American Academy of Psychoanalysis*, 25, 223–241.

Sherman, Nancy (1999), 'Character Development and Aristotelian Virtue', in D. Carr and J. Steutel (eds), *Virtue Ethics and Moral Education*, Abingdon: Routledge.

Schore, Allan (2001), 'The Effects of Early Relational Trauma on Right Brain Development, Affect Regulation, & Infant Mental Health', *Infant Mental Health Journal*, 22, 201–269.

Sinclair, J. (1998), http://jisincla.mysite.syr.edu/

Singer, Peter (1993), *Practical Ethics*, Cambridge: Cambridge University Press.

Smith, Richard (2005), 'Paths of Judgement: The Revival of Practical Wisdom',
 in W. Carr (ed.), *The RoutledgeFalmer Reader in Philosophy of Education*,
 London: Routledge.

Stern, Daniel (2004), *The First Relationship: Infant and Mother*, Cambridge: Harvard
 University Press.

Tarp, R. G. and R. Gallimore (1988), *Rousing Minds to Life*, Cambridge: Cambridge
 University Press, p. 111.

Taylor, Charles (1996), 'Iris Murdoch and Moral Philosophy', in M. Antonaccio
 and W. Schweiker (eds), *Iris Murdoch and the Search for Human Goodness*,
 Chicago: University of Chicago Press.

Tolstoy, Leo, *War and Peace*, many editions.

Walker, Peter (2017), 'Schools to trial happiness lessons for eight-year-olds',
 https://www.theguardian.com/society/2017/mar/12/schools-to-trial-happiness-
 lessons-for-eight-year-olds.

Warnock, Mary (1992), 'The Good of the Child', in *The Uses of Philosophy*, Oxford:
 Blackwell.

Warnock, Mary (2005), *Special Education Needs: A New Look*, London: Philosophy of
 Education Society of Great Britain.

Weil, Simone (2005), *An Anthology*, ed. S. Miles. London: Penguin Books.

White, John (2011), *Exploring Well-Being in Schools*, London: Routledge.

Whitehead, Albert North (1967), *The Aims of Education*, New York: Free Press.

Williams, Bernard (1993a), *Ethics and the Limits of Philosophy*, London: Fontana Press.

Williams, Bernard (1993b), *Morality*, Cambridge: Cambridge University Press.

Winnicott, Donald (1960a), 'The Theory of the Parent-Infant Relationship' in
 Winnicott, D. (1985), *The Maturational Process and the Facilitating Environment:
 Studies in the Theory of Emotional Development*, London: Hogarth Press,
 pp. 37–55.

Winnicott, Donald (1960b), 'Ego Distortion in Terms of True and False Self' in
 Winnicott, D. (1985), *The Maturational Process and the Facilitating Environment:
 Studies in the Theory of Emotional Development*, London: Hogarth Press, pp. 140–152.

Winnicott, Donald (1960c), 'Counter-Transference' in Winnicott, D. (1985), *The
 Maturational Process and the Facilitating Environment: Studies in the Theory of
 Emotional Development*, London: Hogarth Press, pp. 158–165.

Winnicott, Donald (1963a), 'From Dependence to Independence in the Development of
 the Individual' in Winnicott, D. (1985), *The Maturational Process and the Facilitating
 Environment: Studies in the Theory of Emotional Development*, London: Hogarth
 Press, pp. 83–92.

Winnicott, Donald (1963b), 'Morals and Education' in Winnicott, D. (1985), *The
 Maturational Process and the Facilitating Environment: Studies in the Theory of
 Emotional Development*, London: Hogarth Press, pp. 93–108.

Winnicott, Donald (1969), *The Child, the Family, and the Outside World*, London:
 Penguin Books.

Wittgenstein, Ludwig (1953), *Philosophical Investigations*, trans. G. Anscombe, Oxford: Basil Blackwell.

Wittgenstein, Ludwig (1961), *Notebooks 1914–1916*, trans. G. Anscombe, Oxford: Basil Blackwell.

Wittgenstein, Ludwig (1980), *Culture and Value*, trans. P. Winch, Oxford: Basil Blackwell.

Wivestad, Stein (2008), 'The Educational Challenges of Agape and Phronesis', *Journal of Philosophy of Education*, 42(2), 307–324.

Index